you're
not
special

you're not special

a (sort-of) memoir

meghan rienks

gallery books

new york   london   toronto   sydney   new delhi

Note to reader: Certain names and other personal details have been changed.

Gallery Books
An Imprint of Simon & Schuster, Inc.
1230 Avenue of the Americas
New York, NY 10020

Copyright © 2020 by Meghan Rienks

All rights reserved, including the right to reproduce this book
or portions thereof in any form whatsoever. For information,
address Gallery Books Subsidiary Rights Department,
1230 Avenue of the Americas, New York, NY 10020.

First Gallery Books hardcover edition May 2020

GALLERY BOOKS and colophon are registered
trademarks of Simon & Schuster, Inc.

For information about special discounts for bulk purchases,
please contact Simon & Schuster Special Sales at 1-866-506-1949
or business@simonandschuster.com.

The Simon & Schuster Speakers Bureau can bring authors
to your live event. For more information or to book an event,
contact the Simon & Schuster Speakers Bureau at 1-866-248-3049
or visit our website at www.simonspeakers.com.

Interior design by Michelle Marchese

Manufactured in the United States of America

10 9 8 7 6 5 4 3 2 1

Library of Congress Control Number: 2020934868

ISBN 978-1-9821-1010-9
ISBN 978-1-9821-1012-3 (ebook)

To my younger self,
you always wanted a reason for the shit you dealt with.
This was it (I think).

contents

growing up(ward)

finding love and being happy

you're
not
special

the story of
me, myself, and i

I was born on August 4, 1993, at 8:32 p.m. in a suburb outside San Francisco. Which means I'm a Leo sun, Pisces moon, and Aquarius rising. Not that you asked. I grew up as an only child in a town of fewer than eight thousand people without a Starbucks in sight. (Cue the gasps of quirky relatable tweens everywhere.) I was raised by two hippie parents who deprived me of refined sugar and showered me with way too much information about STDs and safe sex. I'll be blunt: I had a weird childhood. I grew up at protests and Grateful Dead concerts wearing tie-dyed T-shirts and Bob Marley beanies. I was basically a stoner baby.

Most only children will tell you that they weren't spoiled, that they're great at sharing, and that their adolescent years were not comparable to *Eloise at the Plaza*. Most of them are lying. I mean, maybe not about the Eloise thing, 'cause I don't think kids really grow up in hotels, unless your life is sweet and your name is Zack or Cody. Don't get me wrong: not having to fight over the last hot dog and being able to watch whatever cartoon you want on TV was an awesome perk of having no siblings, but ultimately it was really, really, really lonely. In order to stay entertained, I'd talk to myself. My options for social interaction were limited to adults (yawn) or the cast of characters I had created in my head. I chose the latter. I'd like to say that it's a common trait among only children, but I don't know that. Maybe it was just me and my flair for the dramatic. Which was pretty much cemented when I wasn't even three years old and my mother caught me practicing crying in front of the mirror. In that moment she decided that her toddler was expressive, not emotionally unstable. From there she made the pivotal choice to enroll me in theater instead of exorcising me. This begins the era that I like to call "Meghan Has No Concept of Failure and *Lizzie McGuire* Changed My Life."

For as long as I can remember, I wanted to grow up to be a "super-star." I'm pretty sure I got this term from the iconic feature film *Life-Size*, starring Tyra Banks. Like Eve, I would be a model, actress, singer, dancer, and any other form of performance where I was the center of attention. By the time I was in elementary school, I was enrolled in singing classes, where I belted Christina Aguilera songs in crop tops that showed off my belly rolls. I was in various dance classes, all displaying some form of cultural appropriation—as I was a plump blonde sporting a bhindi and a sari. (My white parents really fucked up on that one.) Finally, I did theater, where—despite that I longed for the lead role in every production—I also had crippling stage fright. The entire week of dress rehearsals, I would sleepwalk to my parents' room every night until they woke up to see their chubby-cheeked ten-year-old daughter looming over their bed, mumbling something about a "three-legged cat named Frampton." Through school plays, community theater shows, countless dance recitals, talent shows, and an unimaginable number of singing showcases—where I refused to perform anything but Avril Lavigne and Evanescence—I found that the arts were my calling. Sur-prisingly, my parents were behind me 110 percent when I told them I wanted to pursue a career in acting in college. You might think it stemmed from their unwavering love and support, but the truth of the matter is that my only above-average SAT score was in English. My other option was to be a poet, which is just as lucrative as acting.

Now, don't get the wrong idea about my parents. Despite their love of polenta, homeopathic medicine, and their political affiliation with the Green Party (Go, Ralph Nader!), they're academic folk. My mother has her PhD in social psychology, and my father works with juvenile delinquents across California (which directly hurt my teen dating life). I was the child of two save-the-world bookworms who cheated her way through high school and whose biggest ambition was to be on Disney Channel. I know that it sounds like I'm calling myself dumb, and while I favor self-deprecating humor, I'm also aware that I'm not stupid. But I'd be lying if I said I didn't struggle with school more than my peers did. This was largely due to my battle with ADHD and my parents' ignoring a middle school teacher's concerns and desire that I get fully tested for it. I think my mother chalked it up to my *need* for attention rather than my inability to *pay* attention. Some of her friends' kids were socially inept, homeschooled, or shoplifting from Mervyn's, so I think she just wanted to keep up the illusion that I was "better" than them.

While I didn't inherit my parents' natural passion for education, Marin County as a whole was pumping out Ivy League kids left and right. The standard of academic excellence was set pretty high. All my friends had private tutors, and their extracurriculars seldom had anything to do with genuine interests but rather how they'd look on a college application. I, on the other hand, had a tutor because my parents refused to treat my ADHD with anything other than a "Just focus more" and a (superhot) twenty-two-year-old college grad. He basically just did my math homework for me while I entertained him with stories of the drunken debauchery I had gotten up to the previous weekend.

In Marin, the summer before your senior year of high school is typically spent in a precollege program at a university you hope to attend the following fall. Ideally it specializes in the major you're planning to pursue. Has there been a more white-privilege sentence? Throw on an organic hemp sweat suit, a BPA-free thermos full of fair trade coffee with almond milk, and finish it off with a pair of Birkenstocks, and you've got a pretty good picture of the Marin-ites. We did VSCO girl before iPhones. Despite my lack of interest in school, forgoing college was not only not an option, it wasn't a conversation or even a thought I thought I was allowed to think. Plus, I couldn't ignore the fact that the TV show *Greek* and other various depictions of college parties had me thinking that the social scene would hold my interest for a minute. Let me just get it out in the open and say that at no point ever in my life did I plan on graduating from college. If I closed my eyes, I just couldn't see my-self in a cap and gown, shaking some old dude's hand and posing with a diploma, and hundreds of thousands of dollars in debt. I had no idea why I couldn't envision that. It's not like I had this grand scheme of how I'd get discovered and drop out of school; I was seventeen and blissfully ignorant of the logistics. I just took it one step at a time. College was my only ticket out of my parents' house; what I would do when I got there was a whole different battle. I was aware that my grades were nothing remarkable and that my parents had no desire or means to pay for an expensive education. My options boiled down to going to an in-state school or discovering some hefty scholarships that I would miraculously qualify for despite my lifetime of mediocrity. Nonetheless, there was still a part of me that wanted to at least attempt the normalcy of my peers and their college ambitions. So, to prepare for a "rigorous" (lol) BA program at a "top" university (lol), I began to apply for the scholarships I'd need to attend a precollege theater program at Northwestern University.

As my junior year came to an end and the summer parties began, I came down with a cold. Naturally, I ignored my sore throat and instead self-medicated with vodka. What? It's disinfecting. Stop judging me. I kept that up for about two weeks, until my tonsils grew to the size and color of tennis balls. They possessed a porous, spongelike texture and exuded a creamy-looking pus as well as these foul-smelling granules. (You're welcome for that image.) Assuming that I had a nasty case of strep throat, my pediatrician put me on a round of antibiotics, but my throat only got worse. Now, this is the part in the Kate Hudson movie version of my life where "June 12, 2010" would float up on the screen in some ironic Helvetica font. The man who does the deep, ominous voice-overs for movie trailers would say, "And then one day, her life changed forever." (I really hope you read that in the movie guy's voice.) This marks the day that I was diagnosed with mononucleosis.

If you don't know what "mono" is, you probably think I either contracted one of those rare bird flus that were crazy trendy in the late 2000s, or that I made a typo when talking about the cream that cured my life-changing yeast infection. (Is it too soon into the book to make vagina jokes?) Both of these are wrong, by the way. Anyway, let's get Urban Dictionary to define this one for you. Personally, I think one lovely contributor with the username of Schovie said it best in '06, defining "mono" as "an STD for people who have only gotten to first base"—although, if we're going to be nitpicky (always), at that point in my life I had already hit a few home runs. Which is to say, I had had sex. But all jokes and innuendos aside, mono is better described as the worst and longest flu you've ever had. Now, you're probably rolling your eyes at my first-world "illness," but to a party-crazed sixteen-year-old, doctor's orders of complete bed rest for the summer was earth-shattering. It meant no acting program at Northwestern (mostly because I didn't get in), but it also meant no fallback plan. The community theater production of *Seussical* would have to go on without me. Those three months that were supposed to "shape me as an actor" and prepare me for college would instead be spent watching *Hannah Montana* reruns with my skinny, scarf-wearing boyfriend. I was devastated, to say the least. While vomiting uncontrollably, sleeping a minimum of eighteen hours a day, and not being able to get up a flight of stairs in under ten minutes weren't exactly what I'd call "summertime fun," I was also bored out of my fucking mind.

If I even mutter the phrase "I'm bored" under my breath, my mother's preschool teacher senses start tingling, and in under sixty seconds flat she's rattling off a list of all the chores and things I could be doing around the house. After sixteen years I knew this pretty well, and I had found a way around the lecture if I just asked for a list of chores I could do for $10 so I could "go out to dinner with friends." This actually translated to "I need $10, and then Sydney's mom is gonna give us a ride to the mall so I can wear my boyfriend's beanie and watch him do ollies on his skateboard while I drink something off the Jamba Juice secret menu and apply the Juicy Tubes lip gloss my godfather got me for Christmas until Syd's mom picks us up at seven p.m., because I'm actually going to eat dinner at their house, because their family is normal, and also I spent the money on thongs at Victoria's Secret." I had learned that honesty was my enemy when it came to my mom. The less she knew, the less she'd yell. With all my friends away at various Jewish summer camps, internships, and lifeguarding jobs, the only social interactions I had were with my pediatrician.

I'm usually pretty good at entertaining myself and finding things to do to keep me busy and out of the house. If it were any other summer under different (healthy) conditions, I would have signed up for some obscure art class (I once dabbled in Ukrainian Easter egg blowing) or a lyrical meets modern meets electronic meets our-teacher-just-went-to-Burning-Man-and-has-been-on-a-comedown-ever-since dance class. But with strict orders of bed rest, my choice of activities was limited. I was more than surprised when my mother suggested I make a YouTube channel "to get comfortable in front of the camera" (you know, for my future porn star career) and "to talk to somebody other than yourself," she added. My mother—the woman who built a compost bin in our backyard, refuses to use anything but Tom's of Maine deodorant, and considers Walmart one of the seven deadly sins—suggested that I, her one and only child, sell my soul to the internet when she still didn't fully trust the microwave.

So I opened up my 2009 MacBook, used the webcam for something other than a bad Andy Warhol–style photo booth session, and recorded my first YouTube video. And then I uploaded it. And then nothing spectacular happened. My life did not drastically change. Usher didn't discover me and turn me into the next Justin Bieber; a big-time Hollywood director didn't see my videos and pluck me out of my small-town obscurity and turn me into an overnight sensation. Everything was the same. I just happened to spend that entire summer doing exactly what my mom said to do, talking to people other than myself.

In three months I had gained about 1,000 subscribers, which was bigger than my high school. It wasn't like *Hannah Montana*, where I led this hidden glamorous life of fame and then walked the school hallways incognito Monday morning. I'd describe it like being on the swim team, just without swimming. Some kids played lacrosse; others joined the debate team; I happened to record videos of myself in my little blue bedroom and post them on the internet for everyone to see. This indulged my false perception that people cared about everything I had to say about anything ever, another beautifully self-focused side effect of only-childism.

In the spring of my senior year of high school, I auditioned for acting programs at nineteen different universities across the country. I was waitlisted at three and rejected by the rest. Chapman said they'd accept me if I proved that I took the "summer chemistry course" that was on my transcript. That would be impossible, since I never finished it. Syracuse and DePaul were out because my poor circulation couldn't handle real seasons. That left only the schools I had applied to on grades and SATs alone. Let's just say, if any of my other classmates were left with my options, they'd probably pass on college, just travel, take ayahuasca, and "find themselves." But like I said, college wasn't at the top of my must-do list, so I didn't get down on myself about the stack of skinny envelopes. I shrugged off the USC, UCLA, and NYU rejection letters like I was too good for them—like University of California, Riverside, was where I was truly destined to be. (Gag me.)

I'm not sure if I blame Netflix for having the entire series of *Greek* streaming or my friends' cooler older siblings for setting my expectations so high for college; regardless, to say they weren't the best four years of my life would be an understatement. Mostly because I didn't even make it two years. I did everything by the book. I joined a sorority, made friends, dated frat boys, attended formals in sparkly dresses, and spent Thursday to Sunday with some form of animal ears on my head. To the untrained Facebook stalker, it looked like I had it all. And my freshman year, I really felt like I did. My biggest worry going into college was that I'd have no friends. But weeks before freshman year even started I Facebook-messaged with another blonde who planned on rushing too. We met at orientation and quickly bonded. We rushed together and pledged together, and there we met our "sister" and third blonde to this story. I only bring up our hair color so much because it coined the nickname our classmates gave us: "the Barbies." We were inseparable. Suddenly the idea of spending four years there wasn't so daunting and scary; it was comforting and kind of exciting. I spent the summer before my sophomore year back in Marin, where my hometown friends and I traded stories of our newfound freedom and just how much cooler college had made us. In September, I moved into my first off-campus apartment with the Barbies and fell back into the familiar swing of collegiate life. So, in the beginning days of my sophomore year, when my roommates began to pick on me, I brushed it off like I was reading too much into it. I told myself that we were all just transitioning from our summers back home. And when they'd throw catty remarks my way, I'd chalk it up to me being sensitive. I must have just taken it the wrong way, or maybe I had done something to upset them. When I lost thirty pounds, stopped showing up for class, and wanted to stop breathing, I felt all alone. I'm not one to explain why we go through the things we do, but if there is any way to give purpose to the things I've battled and the things I've felt, it's in sharing my stories. In doing so, I hope you'll see that it gets better.

I didn't have a big sister I could stay up late with and talk about makeup, boys, parties, and how sometimes I felt sad for no reason. We're all trying to pretend that we have it all figured out. The last thing I wanted to do was to admit to my peers that I had doubts. I'm writing this book because, when I was sixteen and falling in love for the first time, I wished I had an older sister to talk to about it. The same for that time when I was seventeen and swore my heartbreak had left me beyond repair. For those times I locked myself in my closet and cried until I wished I didn't exist anymore. I'm writing this to tell you that you are not alone in the thoughts you think. Somebody else has felt the way you feel right at this very moment. I'm here to tell you that, despite what you've been told, your problems are not unique. Your struggles have been a part of everybody else's life, too, and the battle you're fighting right now involves a bigger army than you know. I hate to break it to you, babycakes, but you're not special. The upside is you're not alone.

dating

YOU CAN'T UNSUCK A DICK.

chapter 1

things i wish someone
told me about dating

Dating sucks. Anybody who tells you differently is either in a relationship that they're longing to get out of, or they're that lady from *Million
Dollar Matchmaker*. Now, I don't detest first dates; honestly, I think they
can be kind of exciting. They're brimming with possibilities, and despite how cynical I claim to be, I think they offer an unquenchable
spark of hope. (Gag me.) It's once you get to date two, and three, and
sixteen, that it starts to turn sour. Suddenly you're stalking their high
school lacrosse statistics and praying you don't accidentally double tap
on a captionless picture of their dog from four Christmases ago. Or
maybe that's just me. (You liar.) In my lifetime I've probably had over
a hundred crushes (on both real and fictional characters). I've cried
countless times over boys I claimed I would never get over. I've used
phrases like "the one that got away" and I swore to myself that I would
never feel those feelings again. I'm all for validating emotions, but I do
wish that somebody would have just put it all in perspective for me. I
grew up reading fairy tales of princesses who fell in love with princes at
first sight, despite some *obvious* flaws (um, Beast). Then we graduate to

romantic comedies teaching us that our true love has been right under our nose the whole time! We have it engraved into our brains that finding your "soul mate" occurs in ninety minutes and concludes with a Hall & Oates song. All of the above is a load of bullshit. Sometimes the guy right under your nose is a douchebag and you should lose his number. Sometimes the person who meets your eyes across the room is a creepy perv who deserves nothing more than a swift kick to the balls. Sometimes you're with the world's greatest person, and it's just not it. Dating isn't simple. It's complicated, it's confusing, and it's shades of gray nothing like the movies. While I can't prevent each of your heartbreaks, or tell you the secret place all the good ones are hiding, I can offer some insights I've come to learn while crying on my bathroom floor over guys with last names I've now completely forgotten.

You bring in what you put out. Not *that* kind of "put out" (or, yeah, that kind of "put out"—get your sexual consensual needs met!). What I mean by this is derived slightly (slightly) from that crystal healing kind of stuff. Now, I don't fully subscribe to that mentality of destiny and fate and the "secret," but I do believe that the kind of energy you put into the world attracts a certain kind of person. Let's say you're jaded, angry, and standoffish. You're going to attract like-minded people. So when you suddenly start complaining that every person you're dating is an asshole, take a step back and evaluate the kind of persona you're giving off. I am totally 100 percent guilty of being a little more than closed off. I'm way more insecure than I let on and I compensate for that with building 40,000-foot brick walls around myself. It's taken me years to stay aware of when my tone slips far from who I really am beneath the surface. When I first started dating in LA, I portrayed myself as this cool-girl, confident, black-leather-wearing thing who drank vodka sodas with lime and laughed at jokes that weren't funny. No surprise when every guy I'd start dating was boring and too cool to laugh at a fart joke. That doesn't necessarily mean they're bad people or that dating is fucked. It just means that the energy I put out into the world that I claimed as my own attracted somebody who could relate. I'm not expecting you to walk into a bar in sweatpants and admit you haven't washed your hair in four days. But try letting your nerves slip away for a bit and let your real, honest, and true personality show. If you're one of those cool girls behind closed doors as well . . . I'm sorry, but we just can't be friends. I don't relate to anyone who sleeps in a bra. Mostly because I don't have tits.

Someone can be perfect without being perfect for you. Oh, holy hell, I wish somebody had told me this one hundred times over. For some reason I find that, despite the fact that my generation has so many opinions on so many things, we fall incredibly silent when it comes to the people we date. Some part of me wants to blame dating apps for this, but I think it dates back to Rory Gilmore and her pro-and-con lists I've sworn by since the sixth grade. In the current surge of dating digitally, we're supplied with an abundance of prospective partners, and suddenly we all feel like we're on *The Bachelor*. Someone can be unbelievably great on paper or in a profile and we assume that they must be great for us. I think we forget that feelings aren't rational; we don't make logical decisions or choose who we fall for. If that were the case, fuck boys would be going extinct. But alas, they're terrorizing our minds and DMs like there's no tomorrow. I find that so many of my friends end up dating these guys who are perfectly nice and genuine, but they're just not right for each other. And that's okay. It's okay to meet someone awesome and great, and then look at them and not feel that feeling in your stomach that makes you blush. It's okay to hold out for somebody who feels like they were made just for you (which still might not work out).

Character traits are not mutually exclusive. What I mean by this is that the good qualities someone has aren't possessed only by them. I find so often that we'll spew out a list of positive traits to counter the obvious negatives of the person that we're dating, and those positive traits are not only vague, they're not special. Being a "nice person" shouldn't be a pro; it should be a prerequisite. To praise and cherish these character traits as if they'll never occur in another person ever again is ridiculous. You'd never become friends with somebody who didn't support your career and your future, so why are you settling to date somebody with those same issues? The number of times I have found my friends liking guys just because those guys like *them* is insane! Just because somebody likes you, doesn't mean you should like them. Their feelings shouldn't sway you if you didn't feel it to begin with. We need to drop the idea of a pro-con list and instead think of it as a scale. Ten pros and eight cons don't fall in favor of the positive if those cons carry a heavier weight. Let's say the pros consist of the fact that they've got a sense of humor and their use of emojis is never overkill. Then, in turn, the cons are that they're controlling and have a temper. When you write those down on a list, they cancel each other out, but put them on a scale, and their favorite emoji skills weigh far less than their possessive nature. I think the idea that love is hiding right under our nose sends us into a hide-and-seek frenzy where we try to fit any person handy into that mold. We're scared that if we don't give everyone 101 chances, we might miss the one. Honestly, I find that notion to be bullshit. Dating and love isn't a multiple-choice test; there is no right combination of answers to check off. Just because someone is nice and finds you funny doesn't mean that they're the only person in the entire world who will be nice and find you funny. You're nice and you're funny! Stop praising and rewarding people for something so standard-issue. You don't applaud a fish for swimming.

Red flags are blurry stop signs. This is one I'll admit that I struggled with the longest. When we start to fall for somebody, we tend to have tunnel vision. Our sights are set straight ahead and it's like we're speeding at 80 miles an hour and singing along to our favorite song in a convertible with the top down. We're concentrating on the road ahead when our blind spots might be filled with red flags and pleading stop signs. The difficulty with this is that we only realize we've taken a wrong turn down a one-way street when it's too late. Those warning signs we missed were there all along; we just chose to ignore them to preserve this feeling of happiness. I'll admit that there was a point in my life where I became pretty jaded when it came to signs and signals. I'd look for those warnings unprompted, just searching to find something terrible because I expected it. We all have skeletons in our closets and things we'd rather not advertise on our LinkedIn page. But those skeletons aren't always red flags; sometimes they're just souvenirs of the past. Now, obviously, if said skeletons are, like, actual dead bodies buried under his house, then, yeah, get the fuck out. Find a balance between the two. Don't be so jaded that you're wary and skeptical of every moment, just waiting for it all to crash and burn. Conversely, don't be so blissfully ignorant to the signs for the sake of preserving your pride and this narrative you've created. It's about being cognizant, living in the moment, but taking your time on the drive. Enjoying the journey but referencing your directions and following roadside signals. And, yes, it's easier said than done. Sometimes you'll get your heart broken and realize you could have prevented it all along, and sometimes somebody good will slip away because you doubted something really genuine. But that's the thing with this extended driving analogy: there are endless roads to take you to limitless destinations. You just gotta keep going.

You cannot change people. Despite that we widely accept this line as a cliché, we're still under the impression that we can be the one to flip that switch. Every girl (or boy or gender nonconforming queen) wants the bad boy (or girl or gender nonconforming queen) who'll be good just for them. Unfortunately, life isn't *A Walk to Remember*. We all want to be the Jamie to somebody's Landon, but you cannot change somebody; they can only change themselves. It doesn't matter how badly you want them to change or how much you love them or how much they love you. The only thing in the world that you can control is yourself, your actions, and your feelings. It sucks. It really fucking sucks but you have to let those people go. Sometimes we talk about the people we date not as humans but as programmable Sims. We'll say things like "Alex is great; I mean, he says he doesn't want a girlfriend but he'll come around," and we nod and smile like we know the cheat code to unlock Alex's commitment issues—when in reality the morals or choices people stand by need to be acknowledged as something that's all their own business. Think of it flipped: you'd never want someone to consider their future with you under the condition that they can change something fundamental about you. My best friend Sydney once dated this *terrible* guy named David. (I can say this because at this point she has dated four Davids in a row and *they're all terrible*.) I could write a separate book chronicling all the awful things about David, but the one that applies most in this context was the fact that he also fell for the myth that people can be molded and changed. Even on paper (profile) Sydney and David were pretty different, but with the pool of eligible Jewish bachelors shrinking in San Francisco, she gave the nerdy conservative kid a chance. They went for drinks and I woke up the next morning to a text message play-by-play as she explained that he was smart, cute, a little socially awkward, and way more conservative than his JSwipe bio let on. When I pressed her for more information, she explained that he was a Republican and that their first-date conversation consisted of him asking her views on abortion and gay marriage, and he proceeded to critique her answers and explain just exactly why her opinions were not valid. I will admit that I can be overly critical about the types of guys Syd dates, but to me this was a pretty clear deal breaker. She proceeded to date him for the next three months. She explained to me that while she's set in her own opinions, she liked that he wasn't afraid to challenge her, and we're entitled to have different views as long as they're respected. David obviously did not feel the same way. He broke up with her over the phone, explaining to her that he looked at dating her as a riddle to solve. He had originally set out to change her views on pretty much everything, and when he realized she was in fact confident in her own beliefs, he was over it and over her. Fuck David.

Don't be like David.

Your feelings are valid because you feel them. This is something I think every kid needs to grow up hearing. Instead, when we deal with pain and heartbreak we're reminded that we're young and our emotions are overblown, and that someday we'll understand what true feelings feel like. This is fucking bullshit. At twenty-six years old I can still remember exactly how I felt in seventh grade when Adam Taylor told me he couldn't be my boyfriend because Kathy Carmichael liked him, too, and he didn't want to make Spanish class awkward. Yeah, at this point in my life I've been through things that have hurt me much more than that moment, but at the time it was the most pain I had ever felt. The most upset you've ever been at twelve is, up to that point, the most upset you've ever been in your entire life. You have no fucking idea about the most upset you'll be at thirty-eight, so that gauge is irrelevant. That spectrum doesn't even exist yet. Your adolescent feelings are not unwarranted and they are not unimportant. I loved my first boyfriend the most I could love anyone at sixteen years old. Ten years later my capacity to love somebody is much greater, but I can still look back at my teenage self and recognize those feelings as honest and true to the ones I feel today. I guarantee that a few years down the road the spectrum of what I am able to feel will change again and again and again. When I get married, and when I have kids and grandkids, I'll discover a kind of love that I don't know about right now. But that doesn't mean that every emotion and feeling I've had prior to those moments has disappeared. Your perspective on life isn't like drawing a line on a whiteboard and erasing it every day. It's more like walking on wet cement: your past is permanently preserved but you keep walking forward. You can stop and pause and look behind you and remember those feelings, but once you've walked a few miles, those first few baby steps are a distant memory. Sometimes I think adults lose sight of that; they forget what it's like to be twelve and have your heart broken in a thousand pieces. They forget how your first crush feels like nothing you've ever felt before. I hope I never lose sight of that, and one day, when I'm a mom and my kid is going through that, I can flip back to this sentence in this book and remind myself.

Every relationship ends. Literally every single one. They end in breakups, divorce, or death. It's morbid but it's true. I'm not saying that relationships are pointless or not a crucial part of growing up; I'm not even saying that you should only date people who you can see yourself marrying. All I'm saying is that I wish I could tell my thirteen-year-old self that my heartbreak was just the first of many and to learn how to get through it, because it's a lifelong skill. Think of it like every person you let into your life has a "sell-by" date printed on their forehead in invisible ink. Sure, you can drink the questionable milk after its FDA-approved date, but at that point you're just asking for trouble. It's no longer good for you. I'm not a big believer in fate or anything of that nature—I like to think that I've got at least some say in where I end up in life—but I also like to believe that we invite people to come into our lives for a reason. That reason may be unbeknownst to us at the time, but everybody plays a supporting role or a cameo in the story of your life. I find that when I talk to my friends about their relationships turning sour, they reminisce over how great it was at the beginning and how they have no idea how they ended up where they are now. Every story has a beginning and a middle and an end. You wouldn't read your favorite book if the final chapter and the prologue were exactly the same—and you wouldn't watch a movie with the first ten minutes on a loop for an hour and a half. That's just not how it works. The end of anything is always unavoidable. It can come after a slow-burning anticipation or when you least expect it. And, yeah, it sucks. It's like the first time I read the final Harry Potter book, and I so desperately wanted it never to end, so I savored the chapters and the words and I took as much time as I could to feel that feeling that I knew I would never get to experience again. But eventually I was on the last page, reading the last words of the last sentence, and despite that I wish I had more, I was happy that I had what I did. Relationships, even the "failed" ones, teach you something, which I guess doesn't really even make them failures. If I could go back in time and spare my heart, I wouldn't even be tempted. Sure, in the heat of the moment you can claim to regret something and write it off as a complete waste of time, but I guarantee you, even if you don't realize it immediately, you've learned something from it. Which I know at a point can be exasperating when it feels like you've been stuck in the school of dating for an eternity, but let me just say this: it will fail 99 percent of the time until it doesn't. It's all wrong until it's right. Think of your dating life as a casting call: you've been auditioning people for the co-star role in your life. Some people don't get past the first round, others get callbacks, and some get further and further along but something doesn't click and it's just not "it." So you hold out for whatever "it" is, and it might feel like it's taking forever with no end in sight, but suddenly one day it just clicks and it's "it." But until then you'll get your heart broken and you'll break some hearts along the way. And it will feel like you'll never get through it, but you will because that's the only option. Find it in yourself to recognize your worth and realize that you're not alone in those sentiments. Know that one day down the road you're going to realize that every other crappy relationship and bad date and heartbreak has led you to this moment when you look at this person and realize that everything before them brought you here. Every relationship ends in heartbreak until one day it does not. It all sucks until it doesn't. It's that simple. And I know that's asking you to have a lot of faith in something that seems so far-off and intangible, but sometimes you just have to trust.

chapter 2

2005 was a great
year for dating

I never once thought boys had cooties. I'm pretty sure I actually came out of the womb thirsty (and not for breast milk, if you know what I mean—heh heh heh). I had my first boyfriend when I was three years old. His name was Gabe. We were neighbors, and our parents were best friends, and I may be biased, but we were seriously the cutest preschool couple ever. Gabe would carry me if my feet hurt, tell me jokes to make me stop crying, and I'm pretty damn sure that three-year-old would have taken a bullet for me (even if it was just from a Nerf gun).

When elementary school rolled around, I dumped Gabe for a younger man. His name was Brad. I called him "pip-squeak" and he called me "scary." Brad was my first case of unrequited love. He was blond, played soccer, and had an underbite. I was smitten. I used to chase Brad around the playground trying to pin him down and kiss him, which really wasn't fair, because I was twice his size. And you know, consent. I'm sorry, Brad.

As you may be able to tell, subtlety was not really my strong suit (and still isn't). While it didn't necessarily pan out for me and Brad, new love opportunities did come my way. Brad ended up dating my best friend Mia. He then pawned me off on his best friend so we could go on double dates to Frankie Muniz movies with talking animals. I remained optimistic about my romantic future in the mystical land of middle school: slow dances and coed parties where all the boys smell of Axe body spray and the girls discover the magic of lip gloss. The mid-2000s were magical.

Did you ever know that one girl who was so incredibly pretty at eleven years old that her face looked like one of those porcelain dolls they sell on TV at three a.m.?

You know, the one who all the boys drooled over at the playground?

The one who was great at soccer and long division and even managed to evade the chubby phase, all the while stuffing her face with pizza at Chuck E. Cheese?

The cool girl?

Yeah?

Well, that wasn't me.

That was Mia. At eleven years old, Mia was like if Angelina Jolie and Mia Hamm had a baby and gave her black eyeliner and an acoustic guitar. She got any guy she wanted. I got his less cute friend. I realize this may sound bad, but I'm totally not complaining. Otherwise I would have remained "the chubby girl with the weird transition lenses who won't stop talking about Harry Potter." Instead, I was able to be "the chubby girl with the weird transition lenses who won't stop talking about Harry Potter and I think she's dating Matt?!!" See? Everybody wins!

I won't claim to be great at dating at that age. Through those three years of middle school I "dated" three different boys. Like most preteen relationships, we hardly spoke, avoided eye contact, and MAYBE held hands once for .3 seconds. We'd date Monday through mid-Friday; then, during sixth period on Friday, I'd pass them a note, breaking up with them, so I could be single for the weekend, and AIM my (very, very gay) community theater crush. I am fully aware of how horrible this is, and anybody out there reading this should know that I have (almost) grown out of this mindset.

By the time I was heading into high school, I had this fantasy that when the first day rolled around, an upperclassman with an uncanny resemblance to Chad Michael Murray (à la *A Cinderella Story*) would spot me across the quad and suddenly fall madly in love with me. Overnight, I'd become the most popular and envied girl in the school! Alas, I wore thrifted Hollister head-to-toe and I still hadn't discovered the beauty that is skinny jeans . . . or contact lenses. My dream crashed before it could even get off the ground.

My first two years of high school went by pretty much boy-free, aside from the time Sam Machado asked me to homecoming, which I must say, *Sam, if you're reading this, I regret everything, because I'm on your Facebook page right now and you are so pretty.* Then there was that time when this guy from my homeroom with bleached hair and a puka shell necklace asked me out. But I was, like, his seventh option after every other girl in class rejected him, so I declined the offer.

I missed the simplicity of middle school when the pool of girls was smaller and teachers forced boys to ask us to dance. High school was all about free will and making your own seating assignments. I knew giving boys those options would never play in my favor. This was still the age I thought I was going to be a Broadway star, so the dramatics were on high. Immediately after entering high school, my friends were all French-kissing boys, and bases now meant something unrelated to PE class. I pined after seniors in the drama department. I swooned as they recited Shakespeare to me in a required class assignment. I lived vicariously through my friends and their romantic hand-holding endeavors and even over-the-shirt accidental boob grazing (gasp!). Then, it happened . . . just like the Nicholas Sparks books had told me it would. I went to camp in the summer of 2009 as an ugly duckling, and I came back with BOOBS!!!

With my newly acquired confidence and tits in tow, the ladies and I made our debut at my friend Emma's barbecue. (Cue the optimistic music and flattering lighting.) There I met an older guy from a different school, and he was athletic and tall and blond, with a face so angelic it belonged on a lunch box from Claire's. We spent our summer nights eating ice cream at deserted playgrounds. You know, the kind of stuff fifteen-year-old dreams are made of. On the night before my sixteenth birthday (after the Jonas Brothers concert), he kissed me. I, Meghan Rienks, was no longer a kissing virgin. I was ecstatic. He, on the other hand, never called me back.

I was initially devastated that the angel-faced boy and I would not grow old together, raising obscenely tall blond-haired babies. On the other hand, I owed my newfound confidence in dating to him. I mean, maybe using the word "confidence" is a stretch. Realistically, I was just overjoyed that I no longer had to lie when playing ten fingers. For the first time since I traded in my glasses for contact lenses, I was actually excited about going back to school in the fall. I envisioned myself sauntering through the hallways of Sir Francis Drake High School as a new woman, a mature, cultured female specimen who now had a solid handle on how to make out with a boy. I was unstoppable. I would waste no time before hopping into the bountiful pool of high school dating. The rise in popularity of the Justin Bieber haircut was well represented among my male classmates. My life would feel like one giant Las Vegas buffet, except instead of lobster and a fountain of chocolate, I had my choice of every newly braces-free, floppy-haired, hormonally charged sixteen-year-old boy my school had to offer. I was elated. Elated but also delusional. Despite my deepest fantasies, every boy in my grade looked less like Justin Bieber and more like Coconut Head in *Ned's Declassified*. Except for this one guy named Owen, but he told me that I looked like an uglier version of Hermione Granger—and, no, not Emma Watson's portrayal. He explained to me that I resembled a more heinous version of the bucktoothed, bushy-haired character in the book. I'm still holding a grudge on that one.

With my standards set about as high as my push-up bra propped my tits, I widened my horizons. I set my sights on the far cuter boys from neighboring schools. Their impressions of me were untainted. They had no memories of my transition lenses or my side bangs phase. It worked. I found my guy. Or, rather, he found me while stalking my friend Emma on Facebook. (Seriously, E, I owe you all my boy experience. Remind me to send you an Edible Arrangement.) She set up a classic meet-cute. She would invite him to attend my school play with her, and she would introduce us after the performance. If this was a movie, I would have been appearing in something romantic like *Romeo and Juliet*. I would have looked out into the crowd while reciting my final monologue and locked eyes with him, our hearts bursting with love at first sight, as a song by the Script swelled in the background. But this was real life. The play was a rip-off of *The Odyssey* and I was wearing a sarong. But we did meet after the play, and within weeks we started dating. In the three months of autumn in 2009, I lived what I can only compare to a YA novel come to life. We spent our weekends having picnics in the park, our nights falling asleep on video chat, and our days filled with an excessive number of emojis—every sixteen-year-old girl's dream. He even once snuck me out of my house to watch a midnight meteor shower on the hood of his car. When he ghosted me out of the blue, I was devastated. He was perfect. I mean, he also came in his pants once when we were making out, but honestly, I was just really flattered. He was one of those too-good-to-be-true guys who ended up being true. I got vindicated a few years later when he told me he'd dump his girlfriend to have sex with me (I declined), so my ego is fine.

I remained single up until spring. My life seemed to be lived from heartbreak to heartbreak. Pivotal eras of my adolescence were marked by the boys who dumped me at the time. To say I had given up hope would be an understatement. My daily uniform consisted of sweatpants that had "Wildwood, NJ" spray painted across the butt in a neon graffiti font, a men's Hanes XL T-shirt, and Birkenstocks (before they were "ironic"). I had put a face to the term "not giving a fuck." Believe me when I say I fell in love by accident. It wasn't a truck I didn't see coming. It was the Hogwarts Express appearing out of thin air, plowing straight through Platform 9¾ and promptly smacking my helpless muggle body. It was nothing like the movies I had spent my youth praying would materialize in my small-town life. No, instead it was the outcome of one too many shots of Captain Morgan and a drunken voice mail from my friend Molly informing me that she told my best friend Jasper that I was in love with him.

Everybody always stands strongly against dating your best friend. They warn that, no matter the outcome, things will never be the same between you two. And they're right. But does that mean I regret any of it? Do I wish I had played it safe and fallen in love with a convenient classmate, where the only risk was losing a lab partner in physics? No. Because if you play it safe for the rest of your life, you'll end up like one of those lavender-sweater-set-wearing Stepford Wives living in a house straight out of Sims with a life you hardly recognize. That's not the life I want. Plus I look horrible in pastels.

Charlotte York famously summed up my feelings regarding dating in season three, episode one, of *Sex and the City*, with "I've been dating since I was fifteen. I'm exhausted. Where is he?"

Over my fifteen years of dating I've learned which flavors of Ben & Jerry's contain magical properties that heal a broken heart (Phish Food), what Taylor Swift song should be the soundtrack to throwing eggs at your ex's car ("Should Have Said No"), and how exactly to converse with your crush without (obviously) drooling. I've decided that instead of hoarding all of this to myself and letting my embarrassing flubs go with me to the grave, I'll share them—maybe it's educational, or maybe it's just amusing.

chapter 3

my first heartbreak

Jasper and I dated. We broke up. The end. Kidding!

I mean, not kidding because that's what happened, but kidding because three short sentences do not count as a chapter. I'm not necessarily dreading writing this because I still have a lot of emotions tied to the person or even the situation. My hesitance about being honest in this chapter about heartbreak is rooted mainly in the fact that pieces of that seventeen-year-old girl are still inside me. (Gross.) Despite that I'm way beyond happy and I wish nothing but the best for him, the feeling of your first heartbreak isn't something you easily forget. Yes, I can take a step back and look at my life and see how far I've come from point A to point B, but point A still exists. When you're seventeen and your world begins and ends with a school bell, your little reality is the only thing you know. For me, that reality resulted in a terrible breakup and a rebound and feelings that lingered far longer than I care to admit. So, yeah, this is the breakup chapter. In order to get to the end, we have to start at the beginning.

His name was Jasper. He was smart, lanky, and he liked scarves more than millennium Hilary Duff. Jasper and I met in the sixth grade when he, like every other male and female at White Hill Middle

School, fell head over Heelys for my friend Mia. Jasper didn't even cross Mia's radar. I'll admit that Jasper went largely unnoticed by me as well. My sixth-grade notebooks were crowded with doodles of Henry and Matt. But somewhere between starting seventh grade and my first boy-girl dance, Jasper and I became an "item." I wish I had more of a memory of what sparked our flirtation, but, honestly, my only memories of our seventh-grade fling consist of a typical group "hang" at the mall, where we sat in the bell tower eating burritos, after which I proceeded to hide from him in the Macy's handbag department. (The reason why remains a mystery to me. Playing hard to get?) There's also the final preteen memory of us where I avoided participating in the boy-girl "snowball" dance at Winter Formal and hid from Jasper in the girls' bathroom. The overall theme here seems to be hiding and avoiding my "boyfriend"—you know, all positive signs. Like most middle school relationships, Jasper and I probably lasted for a total of three weeks. It ended as memorably as it began (as in, I don't remember at all).

Time passed and our paths naturally diverged as we attempted to navigate the social hierarchy of high school. Just how were we going to identify ourselves for the next four years? Somewhere on that timeline, Jasper decided he hated me. It could have been a long time brewing as the result of our tween romance gone south. Truthfully, I didn't notice until we were assigned to sit next to each other in AP Composition our junior year. As our teacher read my name and seating assignment aloud, Jasper audibly sighed and tossed an exaggerated eye roll to his best friend, Cody. What the fuck? I was so confused. What in the world had I ever done to this kid except ditch a slow dance when we were twelve years old? When I brought up the awkward encounter to my friends at lunch, I was met with responses of "Ohhhh, yeah. You didn't know?" "Yeah, he's always hated you." "I don't remember a time when he didn't hate you!" A lot of people would take this personally—I probably should have—and they'd rack their brains to pinpoint the exact moment that it all went awry. They'd then devise a plan to get back in their enemy's good graces. I, on the other hand, decided that I would just hate him too. Ha! Take that, Jasper.

They say there's a fine line between love and hate. What they don't tell you is that that fine line is friendship. Somehow, Jasper and I ended up walking that line, and it was all thanks to the death penalty. It was about three months into the school year when fourth-period AP Composition began the debate section of our curriculum. Our teacher created teams solely based on their seating proximity, assigning us topics and an argument to present on. Much to our initial dismay, Jasper and I were paired together to argue in favor of the death penalty. I don't know what my teenage self was more torn up about: advocating for death or cooperating with my nemesis. We put our less-than-fuzzy feelings toward each other aside as we prepped our unwinnable debate. Our lunch hours were spent in the library sifting through articles rather than scarfing down bagels and bubble tea alongside our peers. We traded in our late Facebook-stalking binges for productive instant messenger sessions rife with links to various sources backing up our arguments. Without even realizing it, we forgot to hate each other. We started to crack jokes and laugh and reference things other than case trials and lethal injections. Any bad blood between us suddenly vanished without question or complaint. Oh—we totally lost the debate, by the way. We weren't mad. I think I'd be more alarmed if a group of soon-to-be voters switched political and moral leanings solely based on a presentation of facts mostly found on Wikipedia. Plus we might be the only two people able to say that the death penalty brought us closer together. (Too far?)

We took all the energy we had used for hating each other and channeled it into our friendship. We scolded ourselves for letting petty issues prevent our friendship from rekindling sooner. Come winter, our friends, our classmates, and even our teachers hinted that they sensed something more between us. We were both quick to shut those rumors down and defend our friendship, claiming that we were the perfect example of what it meant for a guy and a girl to be just friends. I honestly believed that. There wasn't a part of me that drifted off into the what-ifs or dwelled on the possibility of taking it one step further. I just couldn't see Jasper like that. I couldn't picture what it would be like to cross that line once again. Until I did.

It was a cold California night over winter break. A group of us had decided to climb the hill behind our friend Claire's house, a place we frequented to drink vodka out of plastic cups. High school was glamorous. A few too many shots later, my footing was clumsy and Jasper's arm was around my waist, steadying me as we crawled through the barbed-wire fence back toward suburbia. As the knee of my distressed low-rise True Religion jeans (gag me) caught the wire, he wrangled me free with a tug that sent my body stumbling into his. I'm not sure if his lips broke my fall or if in that moment I decided that it was the most fitting way of saying thank you for sparing my overpriced white jeans. But it happened. And we never spoke of it again.

I've never been a big believer in love at first sight, mostly because I've met Channing Tatum, and if I didn't feel it with him, it doesn't work with anybody. I mean, I definitely have that instinctive attraction where I find a guy cute right from the get-go and develop an innocent schoolyard crush. But, more times than not, those butterflies fade when I realize he takes shirtless mirror pics and he puts protein powder in his cocktail as a "healthy balance" (true story). That being said, while I'm not gonna marry that douche, I'm not opposed to hooking up. But I'm talking about beyond that initial desire to jump someone's bones, and beyond that level of drunkenness you need to let your standards slip. I'm talking about those actual real, feelingy feelings. The kind where you're so far gone and so over your head, you're past drowning, and no hot lifeguard can rescue you from the black hole you fell down. The slow-burn feelings. The kind that don't just sneak up on you; they crawl low to the ground like firemen going through a burning building. And you wake up with your lungs filled with smoke and you're dying because you can't breathe because this is so beyond a crush. The kind that makes you pay attention in science class because you're sure something is up with gravity because the weight of it all feels way heavier than any textbook could explain. Do I sound completely batshit insane? Good. Because that's how I felt the day I was told that I was in love with Jasper.

Even though Sir Francis Drake High preaches an all-inclusive mentality among its students, one of the age-old privileges of prom still remains reserved exclusively for the upperclassmen. So while 75 percent of my junior year revolved around the SATs and the ACTs, the last 25 percent revolved around talk of taffeta versus silk, party bus check collecting, and, finally, the most important, prom-posals. The first step of it all, and frankly the most important, was selecting a date. While attending any other Drake dance with a date was unheard-of and reserved for foreign exchange students or the transfer kids who used to be homeschooled, prom was a whole other story. Getting a date to prom was not optional; it was a prerequisite.

Friday nights were spent huddled in a circle with your closest friends as you flipped through the yearbook, ranking your potential options with as much thought and insight as a fantasy football draft. From there you'd devise a plan, assigning one of your friends who happened to be lab partners with your target to subtly but forcefully drop the hint that you two would be "oh so adorable together in formal wear." Once that seed was planted, your potential date would ask your friend to feel out the situation on your end, to which they would happily agree. Despite their feigned "discovery" of the perfect match, in reality this elaborate plan has been in the works for months. So while you play dumb and practice the surprised face you'll make when the moment comes, it's your friends who are the true masterminds behind the night that seventeen-year-old you has deemed the most important of her life.

Prom season at Drake was like Christmastime for Buddy the elf. It was like the administration slipped the potion Puck used in *A Midsummer Night's Dream* into the drinking fountains. Everywhere you'd turn, another potential couple would pop up. The student body arranged itself into pairs at the utmost convenient time. While in some instances this sparked jealousy between classmates, more often than not, the prom spirit got into all of us.

"What about her?" I said, pointing to an underclassman practicing tai chi in the courtyard. That suggestion earned me a swift elbow to the shoulder and a "Fuck you" from Jasper. We were perched on the steps where we ate lunch. While Jasper started on his fourth sandwich of the hour, I surveyed the pool of potential dates within eyesight. Prom was more than three months away, and I liked to remind him that with his lack of urgency he'd be forced to take a fourth-corridor pariah (the students who hung out in the farthest hallway were notorious for wearing cloaks, playing *World of Warcraft*, and hexing you if you stared too long), the point of no return for his social standing. I'd then remind him that if he started playing *World of Warcraft* again, I'd be forced to fake amnesia with regard to our friendship.

"You've vetoed nearly every girl you've ever talked to. You're fucked," I said.

"I just don't see what the big fuss is over me finding a date right now. Who knows what'll happen between now and spring," Jasper responded, brushing off my impatience.

"Okay, okay, I'll put a pin in it till February. But then you have to pick someone before your only option is that girl in my PE class who groped me to find my chakras, because that's a deal breaker for our friendship. She weirds me out," I warned him, shaking my head.

"Meghan, she hasn't gone to school here for the last two years," Jasper replied, staring blankly at me.

"And that's the last time I went to PE," I said, and shrugged.

By the time February rolled around, Jasper had decided to ask a senior from our drama class. I was on my third round of pro-con lists, deciding which of my ex-boyfriends' new girlfriends would be the least likely to kill me if I took their current significant other to prom. Thinking back on it, I have no idea why I remained so calm at this point about my own plan. For some reason the worry and wide range of what-ifs didn't faze me one bit. Then again, I was also convinced a casting director was going to discover me at the Westfield mall for a new Disney Channel show so I'd never have to go to college. Delusional thoughts were pretty much my forte. I somehow felt that my situation would work itself out, so I set my sights on helping Jasper orchestrate his prom plans.

Her name was Aurora. She was a senior, hilarious, and the poster child of the unique brand of popularity Drake High fostered. She was one of those cool girls with that cool group of friends who at any other school would be deemed complete and total freaks. But at a school that celebrated the abnormal and scoffed at anything that could be considered mainstream, she was the crème de la crème. I was terrified of her. She was far cooler than I'd ever be, and she and I both knew it. I had tossed her name out as a suggestion to Jasper back in December. While he wasn't sure in the moment, when we regrouped in spring he agreed that she'd be a fun date. "I think I'm gonna ask Aurora," he told me as we rounded the corner from the theater after drama class one day. After months of pestering him and feeling frustrated by his indifference, I waited for that feeling of excitement and wingwomanship to kick in. It didn't. Instead, I felt a tug at my stomach that made it a little harder to pull off the smile I gave him.

Let me make this really clear: I had no idea that this meant I had feelings for Jasper—which probably sounds like a complete load of bullshit, because now it's completely obvious. But in that moment I had no fucking clue. It was so far off my radar that I didn't even have feelings to put aside, because I didn't register that I had any sort of feelings at all. It was my assumed duty as the best female friend to help him plan it all, so I began to put feelers out to Aurora about her feelings toward Jasper. I dropped subtle hints that she saw right through. She was completely for it, and I gave Jasper the green light to go ahead. The only thing left to do was wait.

I spent that Friday night at my friend Alexis's house, and that morning I woke to the sounds of Lauren and Heidi's latest blowout as the TV blared the '09 MTV hit we forgot to turn off the previous night. After I sleepily fumbled through the sheets, attempting to find the remote and slip back into a few more minutes of slumber, the TV went black. Alexis tossed the remote back on her bedside table and rolled over.

"What time is it?" she mumbled to me as I reached across her for my bedazzled LG Xenon flip phone.

"Ten," I read aloud to her. "Molly drunk dialed last night," I continued with a laugh as I slid my phone open to listen to the three a.m. voice mail my friend Molly had left.

"Put it on speaker," Alexis replied.

"Shmmeeeeeeggg!!!" It started with a high-pitched slur barely audible over the party sounds behind Molly. "Iiiiiiiiii diiiid sumafhinggggg . . ." She trailed off. "Yooooooooou pretttayyy were naaahht my numero unooooo drunkie cawl tooonight . . . I mighhhht haff towlldd Jaspper that you luffffff heeeeem." With this slurred statement Alexis and I both sat straight up. Molly wrapped up the voice mail with "Shhhhhh, don't tell!!!!!" The message clicked off and a robotic voice recited, "If you'd like to listen to this message again, press 1." I pressed 1. And when that one ended with the same earth-shattering words, I pressed 1 again. And again. No matter how many times I pressed 1, the message never changed. And no matter how many times I heard her say it, I still couldn't believe it.

It took Molly five voice mails, eighteen missed calls, twenty-three unread text messages, and three full episodes of *Life of Ryan* to resurface. She answered my call on the final ring with an annoyed grunt. "What. The. Fuck. Do. You. Want," she growled, her voice raspy.

"Do you have any idea what the fuck you did last night?" I snapped as I paced around Alexis's living room.

"I literally do not want to know. I'll call you la—"

I cut her off with a snarl. "You called Jasper and told him I was in fucking LOVE WITH HIM, MOLLY!" I screamed into the phone. I clenched my hand into a fist and waited for her to respond. She said nothing. I attempted to steady my breathing, but with each passing second of silence, I clenched my jaw tighter and tighter. "Molly, did you hear me?" More silence. "Molly, are you even going to fucking say ANYTHING?!" I yelled. I heard her exhale on the other end of the line. "MOLLY!" I screamed again, my frustration building into some other emotion I didn't recognize.

She cleared her throat and finally spoke. "But, Meghan . . ." she started, "you *are* in love with him." And that's when the world stopped spinning.

It wasn't as if the moment she said it everything suddenly clicked. It wasn't like I hung up the phone with the realization and acceptance of these feelings I was completely unaware of. I turned to Alexis to deny it all, and I was met with a look that confirmed Molly's words on the phone. I opened my mouth to protest, but Alexis shook her head and said, "Meghan, we *all* know." I stared back at her blankly as my chest began to tighten and my eyes welled up with tears. I felt that wall I had built up around myself start to crumble. Logically it made sense; I could see that. It would explain why my face involuntarily lit up like a goddamn Christmas tree every time he texted me or laughed at one of my jokes. It would explain why in the past six months I had traded in my uniform of leggings and oversized hoodies for sundresses and winged eyeliner. It would explain why I couldn't muster up that same excitement my classmates had for prom, why I didn't have a preference for which ex-fling would be my date for the evening, and why the idea of Jasper slow-dancing to Train with Aurora made me want to throw up. Suddenly the insinuations of our classmates, teachers, and that one guy who worked at that boba place all seemed justified. The pieces were all there, like a giant jigsaw puzzle of my life that everybody else around me had solved months ago, and only now was I finally seeing the finished product. In that moment it hit me bigger than a double-decker London bus. It hit me bigger than any metaphor involving any mode of transportation. It hit me like a girl who missed every episode of her own show and tuned in for the season finale. It hit me like a girl who fell head over heels in love with her best friend and had no fucking idea until she was in way too deep.

The rest of the day was a blur. If I remember correctly, Jasper had called Molly to inquire if the contents of her message were the lies born of too many mixed drinks or the truth spilled by liquid courage. Unbeknownst to me, she confirmed the latter. I was in a complete and total fog. My feelings toward him had been public domain and I was the only one out of the loop. When you're so used to burying your feelings and sweeping those sparks of emotion under the rug, the second they've been placed in front of you, you don't even recognize them as your own. I felt like I was in this *Freaky Friday* moment, trapped in a body flooded with foreign thoughts and feelings. What the fuck do you do when you're the last one to know that you accidentally fell in love for the very first time in your life? Answer: you drink. Or at least that's what I did.

It was a Saturday night, so a craving for lukewarm flavored vodka from a Camelbak backpack wasn't out of the ordinary. My best friend Sydney was my usual voice of reason (and sobriety) in the times I tried to solve my problems with blacking out. But Sydney happened to be out of town. I commanded that Alexis and our friend Emily join me that night in getting belligerently drunk. I told them to invite whoever they wanted and not to ask any questions. We'd begin on the hill behind our friend Claire's house and we wouldn't stop until I forgot all about that day. The moment the sun dipped below Mount Tam and no one could claim it was too early for cheap vodka, I attempted to drown my feelings. They wouldn't fit back into whatever Pandora's box I had locked them in before.

By the time 5:30 p.m. rolled around and everyone's parents bought the lies they were told about our not-so-wholesome plans for the evening, I was already, like, four shots in. My parents were never home on the weekends and had far too big of a booze cabinet to keep track of the levels. Out of the three of us, Alexis was the only one with a license, and she offered to pick me up and take us to Emily's house, where we'd pregame before we went to meet everyone at the field at seven o'clock. Now, while this isn't something I'm proud of *now*, at the time one of my party tricks was my ability to be excessively inebriated without anybody noticing. So as I popped a piece of mint gum into my mouth and locked the door to the empty house behind me, I made my way down the driveway and into Alexis's car. Deceptively, there was nothing but the pungent smell of spearmint on my breath.

If pregaming were an Olympic sport, high school Meghan would be the most decorated medalist the USA has ever seen. With the latest DJ Earworm remix blasting on Emily's not-so-portable speakers, we crowded into her bathroom. We had the kind of enthusiasm exclusively reserved for tipsy sixteen-year-olds getting ready to go out. Alexis was behind me, flat ironing the pieces of hair I missed as Emily sat on the counter, eyes wide as she blinked on yet another coat of mascara. It was the routine we had gotten down to a science in our years of friendship. "Okay, you're good," Alexis said, smoothing my hair down as she shut off the straightener. "We ready?" Emily nodded and hopped off the counter, and they made their way downstairs to slip on their shoes. I promised I'd be right behind them. I turned to my reflection in the mirror, bent over, and shimmied my C minuses past cleavage to the brink of nip slippage. I straightened up, flipped my hair to one side, and gave myself a final once-over. My eye caught Emily's and Alexis's abandoned half-empty drinks. Alexis yelled up the stairs for me to hurry up. "I'm coming!!!" I shouted back, and chugged them.

Now, if you've been keeping track of the amount of alcohol I had consumed (stop judging), you'd probably assume that this is the point in the night where my memory starts to fade out. You'd assume right. I'm not quite sure how long it took us to get up the hill, though it's safe to say that my "party trick" of fake sobriety was still effective. My pace of drinking once we got to the field continued steadily, and nobody cut me off. I'm not going to lie and pretend that I had no idea Jasper would show up. I think it's pretty clear that this night of drinking was influenced by that inevitable outcome. While I never directly suggested to Alexis or Emily to invite him, our circle was tight-knit, and the options for a night of underage drinking in Marin County were pretty slim. The idea of facing Jasper for the first time since "the revelation" was terrifying. If I could drink enough to dissipate that gnawing feeling in my stomach and simultaneously spare myself from an awkward (and sober) encounter on Monday morning, I was all for it. That being said, I had no master plan. Truthfully, I had no plans or intentions of addressing it at all. I just knew I couldn't do it sober.

Do you remember how in high school every party ended coupled up? Like New Year's Eve, but without the countdown or disco glasses? We were at that point in the evening. One of the last clear memories I have of the night was right before everyone began to break into twos and fade into their respective corners. I remember sensing the impending divide, panicking, and crawling (yes, literally army crawling) to the backpack full of alcohol. I remember looking over my shoulder to make sure nobody saw me and I chugged the remainder of a bottle of Captain Morgan.

That's when it went dark.

Let me make a quick segue here for a second. I feel the need to state the fact that I most certainly had a problem with alcohol in my younger years. It took me quite a while to recognize it, and writing this book has made it even more abundantly clear to me. So while, yes, I tell funny stories about getting drunk and the hilarity that ensued, I also don't want to suggest that I think my heavy reliance on alcohol growing up was normal or healthy at all. There are tons of excuses I could throw out there, like Marin County has the highest binge-drinking rate in California, latchkey kids have distant parents who don't put locks on the liquor cabinets, and my parents drank a lot and I grew up with the notion that drinking hard alcohol daily was nothing noteworthy. Or that I used booze as a crutch to help with my social anxiety and deep-rooted insecurities. I could sit here all day long and play the blame game. In the end, it doesn't matter why I was that way; it just matters that I was. There's no glamorous way to spin it other than I had an unhealthy and dependent relationship with alcohol. That's it. So as you continue to read this chapter about my attempt to piece together one of my regularly occurring blackouts, please keep in mind that it's not cool to lose control. It's dangerous and it's a slippery slope.

I woke up the next morning in Emily's bed with no memory of how I got there. As I attempted to sit up, I was met with a surging pain on the back of my head and a full-body ache. When I reached for my head with my hand, I felt blood. My hair was in a French braid and matted with blood, dirt, vomit, and gravel. I slowly peeled the covers off to inspect the rest of my body for damage. I was still wearing the jeans I had gone out in, but they were stained with the same sediments as my hair. The buttons weren't aligned, and my belt was missing. My tank top was on backward, my bra was only clasped at one hook, and the lining of the right side of my bra was gone. I wasn't wearing shoes, but my once-white peds were a greenish-brown and wet. I wish I could say that in this moment I was shocked. I can't say that, because it's not entirely true. I mean, I wouldn't say this was my regularly scheduled programming, but it was in that vein. As I went through the post-blackout morning routine (YouTube video request, anyone? Kidding . . .) I patted my pockets in search of my phone, so I could see the call log and text chain of whatever damage I had caused the night before. My phone was nowhere to be found. At least, nowhere within arm's reach, because I was most definitely still lying in bed. I was waiting until the last possible second to move the lower half of my body and potentially discover something as equally gruesome as the gash on my head. The rustling of my sheets woke up Alexis and Emily, who were in much better states than me. Emily offered to go get me some water, and Alexis volunteered to rifle through the house in search of my phone. I was instructed to sit tight and remember as much as I could, which wasn't a lot.

With a cup of water in hand and still no cell phone to speak of, Emily and Alexis told me the story of my night. They confirmed that my last memory of the group breaking off into pairs had happened at about eight p.m., and that our night didn't wrap up until far past midnight, a couple of hours past the time we promised Emily's mom we'd be home. There were more than four hours that I couldn't account for. At sixteen I was already pretty well settled into my party girl reputation, so my antics weren't surprising to Alexis or Emily. They also confirmed that Jasper and I were among those who trickled off into couples. They had absolutely no idea what happened or what was said between the two of us.

At about eleven p.m. everyone rounded up to head home, and that's when it became abundantly clear to my friends that I was far drunker than they anticipated. It took over an hour to get me from the field where we were drinking to the paved road, which is about a six- to seven-minute walk sober. Alexis explained that once we had gotten to the road, we were far past the town curfew, and the best solution seven drunk sixteen-year-olds could come up with was having one of the boys carry me piggyback. It took less than five minutes for me to lean a little too far back, fall more than six feet onto the asphalt, and hit my head. They said I was knocked out unconscious for what felt like forever. They all had no idea what to do, so they just stood there in silence waiting for me to come to. I woke up vomiting on myself, and they were pretty confident that I had a concussion. Emily said that they were afraid that I'd fall again, so instead of carrying me, two of the boys acted as crutches on either side of my body. It took us three times as long to get down the hill and into town. As we approached civilization, we came across a classmate who offered us a ride. He was a senior, he was popular, and he was stupid hot. I told him this right before I barfed in his passenger seat.

We made it back to Emily's house two hours past the curfew her mom gave us. When I stumbled through the doorway, it was abundantly clear that we had not gotten away with anything. Her mom was livid. To make matters worse, my drunken racket woke up Emily's little brother, who might have witnessed me vomiting in the bathroom sink. While Emily attempted to calm her mother, I begged Alexis to French braid my hair as I barfed (thankfully now into the toilet), insisting that "nothing says sober like a French braid." To this day, an iconic quote I will never live down. When I was pleased with the braid in my hair and I stopped retching, Alexis put me to bed. That's how we ended up here. Oh, and nobody knew where my phone was. Or my belt. And they were pretty sure the dampness of my socks was due to my bad aim while vomiting into the toilet. Cute!

I profusely apologized to the two of them for my behavior. I asked Emily if I should say sorry to her mom in person, but she nixed that idea pretty quickly. It's been ten years and I'm pretty sure she still hates my guts. So we hid out in Emily's bedroom until we were sure her mom had left for the day. We made our way downstairs to ransack the kitchen for mashups to satisfy our hangover cravings. I peeled off to the computer in hopes of gaining some insight into the blank spots of the previous night's story. I logged into Facebook and sent out a generic "Hi i got drunk last night and lost my bedazzled phone, does anyone have it?" status update. It received far too many likes and far too little productive information. My cursor blinked over my empty inbox, and before I could talk myself out of it, I started to compose a message to Jasper. I gave zero fucks. I was hungover, my body was throbbing in pain, I was pretty sure I had a concussion, and I had no idea what had happened between Jasper and me the night before. "Legit feel like death. Also zero memory of last night. Care to fill in the blanks? Also do you have my phone?" I pressed "send" and waited out *Jasper is typing* . . . I felt the weight of the couch shift as Emily and Alexis sat on either side of me. They silently handed me a burnt bagel slathered with whipped cream cheese. The only sounds between the three of us were the crunching of carbs and the pounding of my heartbeat as we waited for his response. "Haha oh shit. Don't have your phone, might still be up the hill. What ru doing today? Can we meet up?" My breath caught and my stomach felt like I was on the Ring of Fire at the county fair. "Say yes!!!!!" Emily exclaimed, nudging my shoulder, and Alexis nodded in agreement. "Okay honestly I know what Molly told you and I know you guys talked about it and I'm sure I said something last night and can you just tell me how you feel right now because otherwise I need to move to Tasmania," I typed, then took a deep breath and hit "send." And waited. And waited some more. *Jasper is typing* . . . Before I could steady myself or confirm that tissues and ice cream were within arm's reach, it popped up: "I like you Meghan. I like you like that." And suddenly it didn't matter that Emily's mom thought I was a bad influence, or that I told the hot senior that he was hot, or that I had lost the phone I had spent three days bedazzling, or that I had a pretty severe concussion and had walked in my own vomit. None of that fucking mattered, because he liked me too. We went on our first date that night. We got high, went to go see *Clash of the Titans*, and he kissed me. And this time I remembered it.

We kept "us" quiet for a while. We had spent the first half of the year defending our friendship to our peers, and the idea of having them say "I told you so" was a satisfaction we weren't ready to give them. But actually I think taking baby steps with it was also a great way to ease ourselves into us becoming an "us." Our seventh-grade fling aside, we didn't know how to relate to each other on a level past friendship. It's not like when you get set up on a date and you walk into the situation with your best foot forward and your hair perfectly done and that excitement of getting to know somebody new bubbling inside you. Dating a friend is like skipping all those steps and diving headfirst into something way more serious. It's fucking terrifying. The stakes are higher and there's a lot more to lose. Until we were sure that we could handle the inevitable outcome most teenage relationships have, we lay low. Plus sneaking around our friends, sharing knowing glances in the hallways, and ditching class to make out in storage closets was pretty hot.

One day, about two or three weeks into our secret rendezvous, I was lingering by the door of my statistics class, waiting for the bell to excuse us for lunch. I was out the door the second it rang, and I was met by a nervous-looking Jasper standing outside. I whipped my head around to see if anybody had taken notice of the gesture, but Jasper didn't seem fazed by that possibility at all. "Could you walk me to the library?" he asked me, hands fidgeting.

"What? Walk you to the library? Why? I'm going to lunch," I said, shaking my head with confusion as I continued my way toward the parking lot. He reached out his arm to stop me and asked again, "Meghan, please? It'll just take a second." I was too lazy and honestly too confused to object. I hastily told him that I would if he promised to stop being so weird and that it would only take a second, because I really wanted to get to Barton's Bagels before they ran out of the sundried tomato ones. He chuckled nervously and agreed, and we walked toward the library. About three feet before the doors, Jasper stopped walking and looked at something behind my head. I turned to him in exasperation, and as I started to vocalize my frustration about whatever he was trying to pull, he stopped me. "Turn around," he said. I rolled my eyes and turned around. The entire window display of the library was transformed. The usual poster board backdrop cluttered with announcements and pinned flyers was replaced with cascading gold fabric. On the stand where the latest book releases usually resided was instead a giant red gummy bear dressed in a tiny little tux and holding a tiny little sign that read: "Meghan, Prom?" I let out a gasp as I threw my arms around Jasper's neck and pulled him into a hug. "I'll take that as a yes," he said into my hair as he kissed me on the top of my head. I felt like I was in a goddamn Disney Channel original movie.

To state the obvious, the grand gesture of a prom-posal took us from sneaking our relationship past our peers to fully waving it in their faces with gold lamé and supersized candy. The gossip spread as rapidly as always, and then suddenly everyone knew. Including Aurora. If you grew up in the era of Formspring (formally known as Formspring.me), I just want to say that I feel for you. If you have no idea what I'm talking about, consider yourself lucky. Formspring was a website that hit its stride in the late 2000s as a platform where people could submit anonymous questions and messages to your profile. With their user demographic being middle schoolers and high schoolers, you can only assume the nastiness that took place. The day word got out that Jasper and I were dating, my Formspring inbox was flooded with scathing messages about the terrible person I was and that I should do everyone a favor and just off myself. The next day at school I asked Aurora if we could talk in private, and surprisingly she agreed. I tried to explain to her that I had never had any evil intentions when I agreed to help Jasper ask her to prom. I told her that at the time I was completely and totally unaware of my feelings for him, let alone his feelings for me. Her response to my ten-minute heartfelt apology? "Fuck you," plus a slew of colorful and creative insults only a theater kid could come up with. It's safe to say those "cool" kids never liked me after that. And homegirl holds a grudge too. Ten years later and she's still got me blocked on Facebook. Now, that's commitment.

There is something to be said about your first love. As time and life move on, we tend to belittle those hormone-induced feelings of "love." We embark on new relationships and forge new paths and each love we fall into makes the others look like puddles. As teenagers we're told that there are some things in the world we just won't understand until we're older. These things that mean so much to us right now won't cause us a thought down the road. While in the grand scheme of our (hopefully) long lives that's true, it's almost as if we're expected to put our lives on hold until a quarter of it has already passed by. Falling in love at sixteen is much different from falling in love at twenty-two, but they share the same root emotion. At sixteen I loved Jasper as much as a sixteen-year-old could. He was smart—the kind of smart that saw right through my ditzy reputation and pushed me to take more pride in the left side of my brain. He was the kind of confident I longed to be. Even as a teenager he carried himself with such self-awareness and worth that he commanded every room. But most of all he made me feel special.

What's ironic about your first love is that it's usually your first heartbreak. Every story, both good and bad, concludes in some way or another. This story is not an exception to that rule. Jasper and I broke up a little over a year after we first got together. There was really no one event that imploded us; we just ran our course. Little habits I never noticed before began to get under my skin. That confidence I was so drawn to at the start now just read as pompous arrogance. I decided he chewed way too loud, and I hated the way he got moody before lunch. I hated that the jokes he'd whisper in class were at somebody else's expense, and I hated that I used to laugh at them. I hated the stupid scarf he wore, and I hated how cool he thought he looked. At the time it was hard to wrap my mind around it. I just couldn't understand how we had deviated so far from that path. All I wanted was to go back and be who we were when we started. In the span of a few months we went from googling the miles between our top colleges to arguing over anything and everything. No matter how much we fought it, our time was up.

It started with a text. I had left school early that day, claiming I was sick, when in reality I was actually sitting on Sydney's couch with our best friend Jake, watching *Barefoot Contessa* reruns. I don't even remember what sparked this specific fight between Jasper and me; I just don't think we ever stopped fighting. Whatever this one was about led me to text him something like "Can we talk at school tomorrow?" I can admit that in my adolescent years I was prone to instigating drama in attempts to get a reaction, which validated me and made me feel loved and desired. (I'm aware of how completely fucked-up that is.) In that moment I'm not sure if I said it because I felt insecure and wanted him to prove his love for me, or if I really did see the end of us approaching. Whatever my motive may have been, my phone vibrated with his response: "You want to break up? Fine. We're broken up." He had brought a gun to a knife fight. My empty threats and thirst for validation were met with a very harsh and very real conclusion. For hours I cried on the couch to the soft murmur of Ina Garten and Jeffrey bantering over nuts in brownies. At some point Jasper and I talked on the phone but I blocked out most of that conversation. I stayed home from school the next day. This time I actually did feel sick.

Our breakup was messy. We were vindictive and vengeful and were able to hurt each other in ways only close friends could. About a week after our breakup, Jasper asked our mutual friend Katie to prom. He did it in the middle of the quad right as school let out on a Friday. I walked out of physics class and straight into an original song Jasper and his band were performing in front of the entire school. As the music came to a swell and Jasper's lyrics hinted at the question he was about to ask, the crowd turned to me. Then he ripped his shirt off and sang the name Katie. In that moment I swore I could actually feel my heart break.

A week after Jasper asked Katie to prom, he texted me and asked if I could meet him by the library after school. I'd be lying if I said there wasn't still a totally deranged part of me that wanted him to try to win me back. Instead of the heartfelt and genuine apology I was looking for, Jasper told me I was depressing and dramatic and that I needed to get over it. I had told myself that if he acted like an asshole, I'd punch him in the face and it would make me feel better. I didn't punch him. I just cried.

I got asked to prom the following week by my friend Sawyer, who was far too attractive to attend any high school not on television. Like the kind of hot guy you see on TV and you're, like, *Wait, why don't the guys at my school look like him?!?!* Sawyer looked like that guy, except he actually did go to my school, and he would be in a tux in my prom pictures. It was a much-needed win. Plus, Jasper hated Sawyer, which made it all the sweeter. It was the perfect rebound. He had just gotten out of an equally long relationship with a similarly sticky ending. We were both frustrated and angry, and we found a way to productively channel that together. AKA we started fucking. As it always does, our exes caught wind of the news. And I kid you the fuck not, Sawyer's ex-girlfriend, Paige, and my ex-boyfriend, Jasper, started dating. I fucking *wish* I was making this shit up.

The day before prom, Sawyer got suspended. He had loaded a shopping cart at Safeway full of alcohol and condoms and attempted to just ride it out of the store without paying. Naturally, this didn't work. I said he was pretty; I never said he was smart. The real kicker, though, was that he had done it on a school day, during school hours. Because he was under eighteen, the police were automatically forced to hand over all disciplinary matters to the school. Our douche lord of a principal decided that the most fitting punishment for Sawyer would be depriving him of senior prom night. The prom that I had bought a dress for five months earlier, the success of which was completely and totally riding on my date who could no longer attend. I spent my senior prom rotating between five situations: (1) crying alone in a bathroom stall, (2) asking the sketchy kids if they had any drugs, (3) getting the hired face-paint artist to paint a narwhal named Sawyer on my back, (4) stealing my friend Jake away from his date "because I needed him more," and (5) my personal favorite hell: hiding from Jasper and Paige, who (rumor has it) had popped ecstasy on the bus ride over and had seemingly made their mission of the night to follow me around and hook up in front of me. Their pupils wide and their tongues down each other's throats, they rubbed their sweaty half-naked gyrating bodies on each other. It was one of the worst fucking nights of my life.

So, yeah. This was the breakup chapter. I hope you rooted for us and I hope you fell for Jasper as hard as I did. I hope that when I told you that it ended, you felt unsatisfied at the outcome. I hope you felt all those things, because that's the shit they cut out of movies. The lights go dark and the credits begin to roll and we're left with closure; we're fulfilled and under the impression that everything always works out.

I fell in love with these two characters and I wanted it to work out but it didn't. It didn't because they were seventeen and their worlds were bigger than their adolescent dalliance. It didn't work out because they had lives to live in different cities and states, with different friends and different memories and different people to break their hearts. It didn't work out because most of the time it doesn't. He was (quite literally) a chapter in her book, and she was one in his.

This particular story didn't end happily ever after, but I don't want a happy ending until I'm about to go, on my deathbed, surrounded by the people I love. To me, that sounds like a happy ending. A kiss scored by a Maroon 5 ballad is not an ending. It's a beginning, really just a moment. We have those joyous periods of our lives and assume that they must be the last and only great things we'll ever come across. Then eventually, when it does end, we think we're right back where we started at square one. As if that period in our life was an unproductive detour. Just because something ended doesn't mean it was a waste of time. It's like skimming a book as fast as possible just to read the last sentence.

If we can't make light of and learn from our failed relationships, how are we supposed to succeed in one with the one we want to? You're not Cinderella. Your shoes are not made of glass, and your "one true love" might not be just one. Your life has many great love stories. Some you leaf through casually, some you pick back up on a rainy day, and some you've packed up in boxes, never to touch again. One day you'll pick your favorite story and you'll read it until you don't. Maybe it ends happily, maybe it ends on a cliff-hanger, or maybe it ends with a to-be-continued. You're the one who has to write it.

spackle your heart

If getting over a heartbreak were a science, Bill Nye would be all over that shit. There's no equation or cheat sheet or methodology to get you through a breakup; each one will be different from the last, and the next will be entirely its own. So if you were looking for a secret to fast-forward your feelings and bounce right back, I apologize. You won't find that here. Or anywhere, for that matter. Because that secret doesn't exist. Or it's Victoria's, and I don't think she's looking to share.

In my twenty-six years I've mended my heart of both hairline fractures and seemingly terminal shatters more times than I can count. And while I'd never claim any of them were easy, or that they didn't come with their own set of unique turns, they all met the same end. While I don't have a foolproof system in place or a timeline I hold myself accountable to, I do have steps I take to get me in the right direction. My own set of rules I consistently break.

7 (Totally Unreliable) Steps to (Attempt to) Follow to (Potentially) Repair Your Heart All the While Remaining (Under the Illusion That You're) the Mature, Composed, and Hotter Half of the Split

Step 1: Purge. This is not an invitation or suggestion to partake in your own rendition of the blockbuster movie. Purge your ex's presence from your life in a legal and humane manner. That means removing yourself from as many instances and situations where in-person interactions occur. There's no way to get over somebody if you continue to slip back into old routines and attempt to pretend that you have no feelings on it all. We interact with our significant others in a totally different way from anyone else in our lives; trying to backtrack into casual friendship or acquaintanceship after everything else just isn't realistic. I can't unsuck your dick. Now, obviously if you're in school together or you work together, this poses an obvious obstacle. While it may seem dramatic, I don't think it's going overboard to switch shifts, change seating assignments, and bail on events where you'll be in close quarters. It's not necessarily about erasing all evidence of this person from your life; it's just about doing everything in your power to detach yourself from the person and their prior role in your life. If unfollowing them on Instagram seems too vengeful, mute them. They'll have no idea you've hidden them from your feed, and you won't be hit with a selfie while mindlessly scrolling. Same applies to Snapchat, Twitter, Facebook, and any other social platform I'm forgetting about or that hasn't been created yet. I advise unfollowing your ex on all of them, especially if their profiles are private. It takes away the temptation to check in on their whereabouts at the tap of a finger. Plus, more likely than not, your friends are still following them. So if you *must* see something, they're the ones you have to plead your case to. Speaking of friends, inform them of your decision to put some distance between you and your ex. You don't have to ask them to purge them out of their lives in the same way; just let them know that you'd prefer they don't bring your ex up in conversation until you're ready. Looping them in not only gives you support in your endeavor; they also hold you accountable to the claims of separation you're making in attempts to make it to . . .

Step 2: Wallow in it. I don't care how many pseudo-inspirational quotes you add to your Pinterest board about how your mascara is too expensive to cry and how you're a boss-ass bitch whose tears are made of glitter. Everybody needs to wallow. Even Rory Gilmore learned to wallow. While it's seemingly unproductive and a waste of your energy, it's a crucial part of the process. All losses deserve a mourning period. While breakups are (hopefully) much less tragic than death, the adjustment and finality of them remain quite similar. You owe it to the relationship and to yourself to indulge in those feelings and conclude that part of your life. Go ahead: Eat ice cream with no pants on. Don't wash your hair and sleep in past noon. Watch Christmas movies in July and send every call straight to voice mail. Cry at commercials for pet adoptions, cry when your laundry is done, and cry when you spill the milk you poured to eat with your cookie dough you were too lazy to bake into actual cookies. Bask in your misfortune and stew in your self-pity. Wallow and mope and sulk and brood and grieve and agonize over it all. Then stop. Wipe your tears, pull on your big-bitch panties, and pledge that you'll never waste a tear or lose sleep over this one again.

Step 3: Hate 'em. At the risk of sounding like a raging bitch, this one is the easiest for me. It's quite simple, really—a natural progression. We dealt with our sadness, we put our heartbreak on a pedestal, and we've grieved the fact that our lives will no longer be gifted with their presence. Now is when the reality, albeit salty, sets in. You begin to recognize their flaws and those tics you never quite learned to love. You point out their tendencies that drove you up the wall and their bad habits that you're thrilled you never have to deal with again. You no longer have to put up with their bullshit, and all those shitty things you hate about them are somebody else's problem now. This is where you finally admit that you hate their favorite band and that they weren't the greatest kisser. This is your freebie for you to say all those terrible things you never thought you thought. Take advantage of this step, as it's quite cathartic. Just make sure these sentiments of yours are expressed to only your closest friends, your therapist, or the pages of your angsty Tumblr blog. The cashier at Trader Joe's does not want to hear how many orgasms you faked with Alex.

Step 4: Treat yourself. Because you deserve it. You're a boss-ass fine specimen of human and you need to remind yourself of that. So treat yourself to something that ignites that feeling in you again. Buy yourself some flowers. Get a manicure and opt for the extra-long hand massage. Buy that top you've been eyeing for weeks, and ask the lady to gift wrap it for you. Order a cookie cake and have them write something in icing. Get yourself something that represents that feeling of empowerment and independence in you. Just don't max out your credit card doing it. Oh, and treat yourself in the other sense of the phrase too. You are your own buffet: Go ahead and help yourself. (Masturbate.)

Step 5: Boost your ego. Now that you've refreshed your own memory about what an amazing person you are, it's time to be reminded that your captivating charm and devilish good looks are not unnoticed by others. Yep, you heard me. We're seeking validation in the eyes of others. Before you scold me and preach that self-love is the only kind that really matters, hear me out. I'm all for self-love, mentally and physically (mostly physically). But at the end of the day we're not all self-pollinating creatures. Sometimes you just want to get dressed up and feel pretty and flirt with people you'll never see again just because you can. Reassure and remind yourself that there are in fact more fish in the sea, those fish think you're fine, and they are pretty fuckable.

Step 6: Learn from it. Ugh, learning. Learning is the worst. Kidding (kind of). This is the part in the lesson where the teacher is, like, "Well, kids, what did we learn today?" and everyone groans and says, "Nothing," to avoid actually thinking. This is the step where you break down the positives of your previous relationship and reflect on their importance to your next relationship. Decide what traits you'd like to see your next partner have and others you'd never settle for again. Relationships, no matter the heaviness or the duration, all serve the purpose of teaching us a lesson—a lesson about love and dating as a whole, but also a lesson about ourselves. In the eyes of another person, we discover parts of ourselves that we might not have been privy to. Both our good and our bad traits are thrust into the spotlight, and it's our job to interpret our mistakes as well as our triumphs in order to move forward. No matter how much your pride claims your ex was a useless piece of shit, his only use to you was to teach a lesson, so you might as well let him fully fulfill his purpose.

Step 7: Get back out there. Go get 'em, tiger.

chapter 4

my date with a GDI: the worst date ever

It was 2012 in Riverside, California. I was a freshman at UCR (also known as "Ratchetside," or which some people fondly referred to as UC–Reject, and by "some people," I mean myself). I was a sorority thot, and I thought I was the fucking shit. I gained, like, the freshman thirty, and my insistence on wearing bodycon dresses four sizes too small left me cosplaying as an overstuffed andouille sausage. I was living life on the edge. My tits could not be tamed. I was killing it. And by "killing it," I mean slowly drowning my liver in tequila and my stomach in two a.m. Mexican food. But, alas, nineteen-year-old Meghan was blind to low-rise shorts and a bad dye job. I was blond, my tits were huge, and I was Greek royalty of the Inland Empire.

Now, I'm not going to bash the Greek system (yet), but let me just say that I fit nearly every stereotype of a sorority girl portrayed in straight-to-DVD movies. I was perpetually decked out in some screen-printed tank top advertising that I paid for my "friends," my empty-besides-gum book bag was a rhinestone-embellished *vintage* tote from my big sis, and I could be quoted saying things like "Ugh, I got, like, so blotto at the

Phi Psi date auction I legit bought that, like, foreign exchange student pledge and idk what language he speaks but he's, like, def like a solid seven so I'm gonna make him clean my dorm shirtless so I can gram the whole thing" (for as much as you hate me right now, I hate myself more). The only thing that really set me apart from my *sisters* was my major. While they pursued far more realistic goals of owning Etsy soap shops with a communications degree, I was naively convinced that my way to the Hollywood big screen was with a degree in theater from UC–Reject. In my efforts to take the appropriate steps toward stardom, I sought out auditions for student films. After weeks of refreshing the student bulletin, I finally found one that posted those three words I longed to see: "Caucasian/Blonde/Dumb." My heart skipped a beat. Finally I would be recognized for being the girl I was (quite literally) born to be!

The auditions were held that day in the library on campus. As I rummaged through my closet for something to wear other than the beer-soaked bandage dress I had passed out in the previous night, I realized that in my drunken state not only did I fail to change into pajamas, I also failed to put my monthly contact lenses into their proper case. Instead I opted for sticking them on the stucco wall, right next to my bid card and the menu for questionably dangerous Thai food. I racked my brain for what to do. I knew I couldn't be caught dead wearing glasses to the audition. Um, like, helloOoOOooo, they made me look *super*smart—deff not the right character choice. I couldn't even risk wearing them to the library and then just taking them off for the audition. I needed to be committed to this role, to my craft, to my destiny. So I did the only logical thing in my mind. I forced my academically driven (and way-too-nice-to-me) roommate Ava to ditch class and accompany me to the audition to be my eyes as I went into the audition (quite literally) blind.

In the movie version of my life, this moment would be in slow motion and set to one of the songs from the *Twilight* soundtrack. So just keep that in mind. I walked into the study room where they were reading the actresses, and even with −4.5 in each eye, I knew the fuzzy out-line of the man behind the table was a solid 9. Like not even a Riverside 9, which is like a 5 or a 5½ anywhere else. No. He was across the board a 9. His voice was deep and his tone was brooding and his vocabulary was robust in the way only a GDI who spent his weekends studying instead of chugging from the boot could be. He was a mystery to me, unaffiliated, untainted by horny Gamma Phi bitches and AChi hoes; he was uncharted territory and I was entranced. My brain turned to mush as I performed the obscure indie dialogue of the horror/comedy/drama/musical this blurry man (whom I was pretty convinced was Zac Efron) had written. Once I finished, I thanked him for his time and hurried out of the room as Ava tackled me in front of the encyclopedia aisle. "OMIGODOMIGOD, PIPER, HE IS SO CUTE!!!" (Side note: "Piper" was the only name she referred to me by, because in her words on the first day we met, "Meghan is a boring name. You look like a Piper. I'm gonna call you Piper.") "Like he's CAHUTE," she continued. "Like, not even just 'Oh, he's white, and you're white, and you'd have cute lit-tle white babies' cute. He's like *cute* cute!!!" she squealed, slapping my Jergens self-tanned arm. "I KNOW, RIGHT!?!?!" I exclaimed. "And we TOTALLY had a connection! Did you see how he was looking at me? But, seriously, did you see it? Because I'm like one hundo percent blind right now." As Ava reenacted a silent version of five minutes prior, I basked in the oxytocin from stumbling upon the hidden hottie of the 909. The only issue: I had no idea what the fuck his name was.

I didn't get the part. Which was surprising—not because I'm talented or anything, but solely based on the lack of blond Caucasian students. I was shamelessly much more upset that the hot and blurry GDI had slipped between my thirsty grasp than I was about losing the role to a girl in a Party City Hannah Montana wig. I mourned the loss of Hot Blurry GDI for approximately as long as my oceanography night class—and by the time the pregame of sugar-free Red Bull and lukewarm Smirnoff commenced, I had almost forgotten all about him.

Fast-forward to my spring quarter, and I had already dated every guy I was even remotely interested in (or bored enough/drunk enough to pretend to be interested in—except Ian, who refused to give me his virginity no matter how hard I tried). Dating is time-consuming, exhausting, and a full-time job. I had no idea how I was supposed to pursue an "education" while I was hunting for dick. Seven months into my *short-lived* college career (RIP), my bench was barren. I had exhausted my options. As I scanned the university lawn for fresh-faced fraternity boys, I was met with a bad rerun starring my former flames. With no one to distract me from the $25,000-a-year education (that I wasn't participating in), I had no excuse but to actually go to class. (Cue tiny violins for unappreciative and entitled former Meghan.) After a few entrances to wrong classrooms, I finally managed to find myself in the familiar makeshift theater in which Acting 102 was being held. As I attempted to fit in with my classmates I hadn't seen since the last time I got bored enough to go to class, I realized that my senile teacher couldn't tell the difference between my attendance and a wildebeest stampede. Just as I was about to sneak out the back, it happened. The earth stopped spinning, my hangover vanished, and I was in the presence of an angel—a crystal-clear angel in the form of the hot (no longer blurry) GDI. And just like it does in every free Kindle romance novel, our eyes met across the room and sparks fucking *flew*. He walked toward me, his hand extended, and before I could reintroduce myself and tell him why I looked familiar, he cut me off with "Meghan. You have no idea how good it is to see you."

I Die

Needless to say, my academic career at UC–Reject flourished as a result of my crush. Okay, maybe "flourished" is a strong word to use here, because it was a 2-unit class and it didn't even count toward my undergrad requirements. His name was Nathan. I found out that Nathan had taken his sweet time with his education, which extended well into his twenties to my baby-faced eighteen years of age. An older man = sexy. George Clooney = SEXY. Dennis Quaid (especially in *The Parent Trap*) = SEXY. Al Gore = SEXY. You get my point.

It took weeks of push-up bras, ass-cheek-baring denim shorts, and countless high-pitched fake laughs before Nathan finally asked me out. As class wrapped up one day he caught up to me as I headed for the door, his arm extended to prop the door open for me (I'm swooning at this point) as he nonchalantly said, "What's your number? Let's do something this weekend."

I Die Again

Now, I tend to think I have the first-date routine on lock, and while that routine has defiantly matured in protocol at my age, at eighteen this ritual involved a lot of vodka, some glitter, and very little clothing. Naturally, I had to skip the whole day of school to prepare for the six p.m. dinner date Nathan had planned. My nails were painted an offensive neon shade of coral, my hair was curled in ringlets circa Taylor Swift "Our Song" days, and my cleavage resembled that of a large, large ass. The perpetual Riverside heat was in favor of my outfit choice.

As I'm blasting Rihanna, scream-singing "we found love in a hopeless place," downing my fourth shot, and blending a frosted white eyeshadow on my lids, I get a text from Nathan.

Nathan

> Hey! So I have to go see three school productions for my Film Studies class and turns out the last performance of the last play is tonight :(So either we can rain check dinner, or you can accompany me to the play & we can grab dinner after. Either way!

Meghan

I'm down for the play, let's do it!

I pressed "send," downed the last of my vodka Red Bull, and proceeded toward the campus theater.

As the theater comes into view, I see Nathan standing by the ticket booth waiting for me. He turns to me, and his face breaks into a smile as he picks me up (literally—*Bachelor*-style) into a hug. Let us note that it's no easy feat, because my boobs could be considered flotation devices for an entire economy cabin. He leads me into the dark theater with his hand on the small of my back, and we find our seats just as the opening music begins. Within the first few seconds of this play, I am reminded why UCR's theater department is not recognized by anyone, including its students, as anything but laughable. I fought back an audible snicker as the shit storm commenced in front of me, and as I leaned in to whisper some remark to Nathan about the atrocious and culturally offensive plotline, he stuck his hand out in front of my body and without even looking at me, released a sharp and annoyed "SHHHHH." I flinched and retracted back in my seat. This guy had zero sense of humor. His arms resting on his knees, he began to lean forward in his chair, seemingly entranced by the "performance" in front of him. Meanwhile, I was stifling my vodka-infused laughter and counting down the minutes until intermission. Plot twist: there was no intermission. After a solid two hours of what I can only recall as being the worst play I've seen since my fifth-grade performance of *Frampton* (a locally written musical about a three-legged cat), it was finally over. At this point I now knew better than to crack a joke to Nathan, so I kept my comments to myself as we exited the theater.

When we made it outside, Nathan turned to me and stated, "We're going to wait until the cast comes out so we can congratulate them on their performances."

"Uhh . . . okay!" I responded, trying to force a smile over my instant reaction.

So there we stood. In complete silence. Waiting.

After what I can only describe as the longest and most awkward silence of my life, the cast finally came out to do the rounds. (Let it also be noted that they stayed in their costumes—which, if my memory serves me right, resembled *Star Wars* meets Death Eaters meets *O Brother, Where Art Thou?*) When they made their way toward the corner where Nathan and I were standing (an awkward distance apart), he ran toward them with open arms, offering his congrats on their "remarkable" performances. I lingered awkwardly beside him waiting for an introduction to his friends, yet none came. Now, I'm not being a diva here. I'm not saying I need him to formally bow and wave his hands around and round up a trumpet and announce my presence through every door I walk through. Though I wouldn't object. Not only is Nathan not just making measly introductions, he is completely ignoring my presence. It's as if he attended the atrocious two-hour-long play alone. I am less than arm candy. I am like arm gum. Stale arm gum that you want to stop chewing and you're not sure where you got it from in the first place but you can't find a trash can within eyesight to throw it away and you would never litter because you're not Satan.

At this point the booze is wearing off and I'm trying to decide if Nathan is hot enough to make up for his complete and total lack of social skills. After about fifteen or so minutes of small talk, I had managed to peel off all my nail polish, plan my outfit for the next day's philanthropy event, and decide that Nathan was in fact hot enough to try to make this work. As if he could read my mind, he grabs my hand, giving it a reassuring squeeze. I snap out of my mental to-do list and tune in to the conversation as I hear Nathan assure the group that we'd love to grab drinks with them at the campus bar as we had absolutely no other plans. So much for dinner. I muster up a smile and remind myself that Nathan is a 9. A real-time, big-city, honest-to-God 9. I can't give up that easily.

"I can fit five in my car, Meghan can sit in the middle," Nathan says to the group of twenty-two-year-old men dressed in cloaks, squeezing into his mom's Honda. This was going to be harder than I thought.

There are few things worse than when your date doesn't live up to your expectations. Like when your date invites the entire cast of the school play to tag along. And when he forgoes dinner and your grumbling stomach for beers at the campus bar. And when he doesn't sit next to you or acknowledge your existence or remember that it was his idea to take you out in the first place. For some reason unbeknownst to my current self, I stuck it through. I managed to justify that I was sitting in the middle of a beer-soaked couch, sandwiched between two juniors doing various magic tricks as my date struck up a conversation with a senior with prosthetic elf ears. I was somehow rationalizing his actions as being close to okay, chalking them up to his GDI pedigree. Maybe this is how people outside the cult do it . . . I had no idea. I was an AEPi whore through and through.

"Pick a card."

I snapped out of my self-pitying spiral as I reached for the clammy deck of cards and drew a joker. Fitting. He continued on with his trick and I politely smiled and nodded as he fumbled his way through it. Maybe this weekend I was just particularly lonely, or I believed in the Mayan calendar and needed to land a 9 before I died at a solid 7.5. Whatever my reasoning, I was there, and I wasn't giving up on this one easily. Plus the dining hall food sucked this week and I could desperately use a free dinner.

Amateur Criss Angel's bar-side performance was cut short when the waitress tapped me on the shoulder and asked to see my ID. For the first time in my life I proudly (and loudly) announced to both her and my party that I was the ripe ol' age of eighteen and I could show my vertical ID to prove it. Getting kicked out of the bar meant no more group hang, which meant alone time, which meant tacos (literally) and chemistry homework (not literally). As I got up to leave, Nathan firmly placed his hand on my shoulder, keeping me in my seat as he turned to the waitress and began to scream at her. Yes. Literally scream at her. For doing her job. I wish I could tell you what he said, but all I remember is that, despite how bat-shit crazy this guy was turning out to be, I was still kind of turned on. (Gross.)

When we were finally alone, Nathan and I walked back toward his car in silence, enjoying the dry, polluted desert air. Now, I'm all for silences—I can totally jam with a pregnant pause, a moment to ponder, all that shit—but this was the kind of awkward silence that makes me want to crawl back into the womb. Neither of us even looked in the other's general vicinity; hell, for all I know, Nathan stayed back at the bar and I was walking alongside the actual Criss Angel as he set batons on fire and stuck them up his ass. In the walk between the bar and the car I took exactly 320 steps and not one of them in the direction of this date ending well. We got into his car. More silence. He started to drive. More silence. Great. He's Ted Bundy. But then it finally happened. Somewhere between the 79 gas station and the Phi Psi front lawn I had barfed on, he spoke.

"Can I play you my favorite song?"

I wanted to tell him yes, under the condition that he promised not to murder me, but instead I just said, "Sure," and hoped he wasn't as strong as he looked. He pulled out a burned CD with illegible scribble attempting to note its contents. As the first few chords echoed through his prehistoric sound system, I realized what song he was playing. I burst into laughter, covering my mouth as I tried to maintain any sense of composure. I turned to Nathan, smiling from ear to ear as I realized his sense of humor was so much more complex than I ever imagined. And in that moment our eyes meet, and I realize Nathan is not fucking with me. His favorite song is "Bleeding Love" by Leona fucking Lewis. Fuck. My. Life.

I had probably sung "Just Keep Swimming" in my head about a hundred times before Nathan pulled the car to a halt. I scanned the parking lot looking for our dinner destination just as he pointed toward a liquor store. "I thought we'd ditch dinner, grab some bottles, and go to the cast party. You're a sorority girl, drinking is your major." He didn't wait for my response before he exited the car. I wasn't even going to fight him on the last part. I just really wanted tacos.

With three handles of flavored vodka in hand, Nathan and I made our way toward the eerily quiet house where this cast "party" was allegedly being held. Before I could make some snide comment on this pathetic attempt at a social gathering, he turned to me and said, "Did I ever tell you about the time someone I knew was brutally murdered?" He said it like "Oh, hey, did I lock the car?" or "Did I turn my flat iron off?" I struggled to find words and I shook my head no, only to realize that he had already gone inside. So there I stood. Me and three bottles of vodka. And in that moment, I knew. The only way to get through this night would be to drink. Heavily.

There are few times I wish I had a GoPro strapped to my body more than I did in the first moment I walked through those front doors. Instead of being met with the usual cloud of smoke and a Tyga song, I was met with the *Lord of the Rings* soundtrack playing from a record player at a responsible volume and about a dozen kids in cloaks, capes, and prosthetic ears drinking two-buck Chuck red wine out of Solo cups. As I stood there in my bandage skirt, arms filled with pastry-flavored vodkas, I realized where I was. This was my own personal hell.

I tried to make a friend when I saw a girl from our acting class headed toward the bathroom and I intercepted, asking if she wanted me to go with her. She looked at me as if I had just offered her a golden shower. She passed. I was denied a girls' *bathroom trip*!?! I was out of my element; I was in uncharted water where girls preferred to attend the bathroom alone and being trilingual in Klingon was the norm. I was outnumbered, alone, and far too drunk to care as a decently cute guy (by Inland Empire standards) proceeded to pour me tequila shots, introducing himself over the lightsaber fight in the living room.

"I'm Ben," he said, extending his hand. "Have we met before?"

"Nice to meet you, Ben," I responded, ignoring his handshake and question and reaching for the shot glass in his left hand. "I'm drunk," I added as I slammed the now-empty glass on the countertop.

Ben seemed to be relatively normal in the scheme of things. For starters, he was wearing civilian clothes, which was pretty much my only criterion for a drinking buddy that night. He, too, had been brought to the cast party begrudgingly by a friend, and he, too, knew not a single word of Klingon. Ben had rushed his freshman year but dropped out in the pledging process and survived UC–Rachet as a GDI for the past three years.

"So, what about you? What's your story?" he asked, pouring us another drink.

I give him the hit-clips version. "My name's Meghan, I'm a freshman, I moved here from the Bay Area, I'm majoring in acting. I'm in a sorority, and I have no idea why the hell I'm here," I rattle off.

He smiles into his drink. "I have no idea why the hell you're here, either, Meghan. But I won't lie. I'm glad you are."

It took about three games of failed beer pong before Ben got drunk enough to let his curiosity get the best of him and he began to try to piece together why I looked so familiar. Now, at this point I was on YouTube, but I was pretty sure this failed fraternity boy was not refreshing his feed to see my latest Target haul. That being said, my online presence was not a secret at UCR, but it certainly wasn't something I brought up in casual conversation over a beer pong table with a guy I met that night. I let him deduce it himself. "Okay, so you're in a sorority . . . and you're a freshman . . ." he says slowly, as if he's profiling me à la *Criminal Minds*, ". . . and your name is Meghan . . ." As he said my name aloud, it began to click. "Meghan Meghan Meghan Meghan . . . Meghan Rienks?" he says as the lightbulb goes off. I nod, confirming that indeed that is my last name, and I wait for the internet reference to come. But instead I get a surprise much more awkward than his admission that he watched a video of me getting ready for prom. "You're Josh's ex-girlfriend!" He claps his hands together, proud of his low-tier-UC-level deductive reasoning. I, on the other hand, am drunk, thinking of my ex-boyfriend, and wondering how in the world did a school of 21,000 start to feel so damn small.

I (attempt to) keep my cool as I confirm that I am in fact *that* Meghan, hoping that if Ben and my ex are close, he'll relay the fact that I was totally not crazy, completely over him, and way hotter than the last time he saw me (which was maybe a solid seventeen hours ago). "This is so crazy. I can't believe he dumped you. You're so hot." I don't know whether to say "Thank you" or "Fuck you," so I combine the sentiments and do that smile where you raise your eyebrows and nod passive-aggressively. "Did he ever talk about me?" he continued. "Me and him and this other kid have all been best friends since the dorms freshman year. Actually, I think he's here right now." Ben must have noticed all the color draining from my face before he clarifies, "Oh, no, not Josh; our other friend." And before he can finish the thought, he sees said friend across the crowd and motions him to join us. "Meghan, I'd like you to meet Nathan." And you didn't think this date could get any worse.

So there I am, shaking my date's hand as I flirt with another guy who happens to be his best friend and their other best friend just happens to be my ex-boyfriend who dumped me over the phone while I was drunk and crying on the floor of a twenty-four-hour Mexican restaurant. Life is fucking great. We stand in silence for a minute before I realize I am still shaking Nathan's hand and I am still not saying anything. I ease into it with an uncomfortable chuckle as I explain to Ben that Nathan was actually the boring dickwad sorry excuse for a date that I came here with tonight. (I said most of that in my head.) "Ohhhhh, are you guys dating?" Ben asks, attempting to hide his disappointment (surprisingly I was a hard 8 in Riverside).

As I shake my head and begin to explain that this is only our first (and last) date, Nathan cuts me off, slinging his arm around my shoulders, saying, "Yep. And if she plays her cards, she'll be my girlfriend by next week." What. The. Actual. Fuck. This kid was straight-up delusional. In what alternate universe is he living in that he would classify this "date" as anything other than great material for a satirical advice book!?!? It's official. Nathan had just crossed the line of being 60 percent hot and 40 percent crazy to 99 percent crazy and 1 percent hot. Okay, maybe, like, 10 percent hot, because I was pretty desperate and I wouldn't have rejected an over-the-bra-feel make-out session if he initiated it and promised not to talk for the rest of the night.

Even I knew when to stop lowering my standards, and with that, I picked my dwindling standards up off the floor, mustered up the politest tone I could, and said, "You can take me home now. I'm done."

Sadly, the night was far from done. After Nathan informed me that he was far too intoxicated from the sip of a lite beer he had had three hours earlier to drive me home, he suggested I go inside while he and Ben "talked it out." You might be asking yourself, *Talked* what *out?* I have no answer to this question because I didn't even ask this question. Nathan was crazy and Ben wasn't that cute and Josh had dumped me. What else did I have to lose? I let the boys talk about their feelings while I proceeded to rip a three-foot bong and nap on the couch of this stranger's house while watching *Adventure Time*.

Just as I was drifting asleep, a partygoer poked me on the shoulder. "Yo, you're Connor's ex, aren't you?" he asked, chuckling to his friends.

I stared him dead in the eyes, unblinking, emotionless. "Yep," I replied, and rolled over, shut my bloodshot eyes, and willed myself into a dreamless, ex-boyfriendless sleep. I woke up two hours later to a nearly empty house and Netflix judging my current state with its "Are you still watching?" screen. No, Netflix, I am not still watching. I fell asleep because I am crossfaded and stuck at some random person's crappy house, waiting for two guys I don't even like to hash out their drama so my "date" can take me back to the dorms so I never have to see him ever again (until class on Monday). I got up and wove my way through the house looking for the boys, half expecting to catch them in a crying embrace, swaying to the soundtrack of *The Sisterhood of the Traveling Pants*. To my disappointment (and honest surprise) they're bro-ing it up on the patio chairs, sealing it with a *Parent Trap* handshake. All the "drama" looked to be settled. "Not that this isn't a total blast," I begin as I walk toward them, "but can we *leave* now?"

As if it were scripted, they both stood up, turned to me, and said, "I'll take you home," in perfect unison. Very *Freaky Friday*, but I didn't give a shit if Lindsay Lohan took me home in the trunk of her limo or Jamie Lee Curtis let me ride on the Activia couch with wheels.

I just wanted to get home to my roommate, who was dead asleep and not worried about me at all. "I literally do not give a shit which of you takes me home, but someone has to take me home," I stated calmly as I made my way toward the front parking lot of the house. I attempted to tune out the hissy fit of an argument going on between the boys behind me, but I caught snippets of their reasoning as to why they should get to be what they thought of as my knight in shining armor. I stopped myself from correcting them by saying that the only real hero in this story was tequila and the guy who smoked me out. I bit my tongue until we reached their cars, the only two left parked on the street. (Seriously, though, WHOSE HOUSE WAS THIS!?!?)

I turned to them, my tone dripping with annoyance. "What's the verdict, boys?" I asked.

They exchanged a look (possibly a really short blinking contest), and Nathan offered up that he thought Ben should drive me home. "His apartment is closer to your dorms. It'll be way more convenient for him to drop you off," he stated matter-of-factly.

"Okay, then," I announced, slightly caught off guard but still no fucks to be found. "Let's go, buddy," I said to Ben, motioning for him to unlock his doors. Then I slid into the passenger seat and began what I naively thought was the end of my night.

Remember when I said Ben was normal? I lied to you. I only lied to you for the sake of the story because at the time that I told you he was normal, I was under that same impression. This car ride drastically changed my feelings. It took only about three minutes into the drive for me to realize that Ben was weird as shit too (shocker). Most of these memories are pretty hazy, as my bloodstream was filled with tequila and my mind was preoccupied with calculating the likelihood that I could survive jumping from this moving vehicle and walking home four miles in the desert without cell reception or a sense of direction. (The success of this was unlikely but utterly tantalizing.)

"You know I took Jessica's virginity, right?" he said proudly, as if he put that he deflowered an AChiO on his résumé at Baja Fresh.

"Cool?" I responded, rolling my eyes as I took a mental note to slap my friend Jessica across the face.

"What do you want?" Ben asked me, and I looked up to see the bright flashing lights of a twenty-four-hour Carl's Jr. about half a mile from my dorms.

"What the fuck!?" I exclaimed. "I want to go *home*, Ben. HOME. I don't want a goddamn SPICY BUFFALO WRAP. I. WANT. TO. GO. HOME!!!" I sat there red in the face, stewing in frustration and anger.

He was silent for a moment. "If I got CrissCut fries, would you eat some?" he said, completely unaffected by my outburst.

"Fine," I responded, flopping back into my seat. "But we eat them on the way."

Two #13s, two Diet Cokes, and a box of CrissCut fries in tow, Ben made his way back toward my dorm. It was finally coming to an end, it was nearly four a.m., the booze was wearing off, and the imminent hangover was just beginning to rear its ugly (and chunky) head. I couldn't wait to take my makeup off, strip down to pajamas, and crawl into a freshly made bed. This was not going to happen. Firstly, because I would most likely fall asleep in my current getup, makeup and all, facedown on an unmade bed. And this far into the year I'm pretty sure

I didn't have a fitted sheet, because I barfed on it, so I would instead be sleeping on a stained twin XL mattress with nothing but a DIY Pinterest blanket to keep me warm. Oh, and also because Ben had no intention of taking me anywhere other than his pants that night. This was made clear when the car came to a halt and I realized we were not at the hallowed halls of the East Lothian dorms. Instead we were parked in a lot under some random apartment complex that I assumed Ben lived in. Without a word he began to slip his hand on my thigh, crawling toward the hemline of my skirt as I slapped his hand away.

"Take. Me. To. My. Dorm," I stated through gritted teeth. "I don't want to have sex with you, I don't want to kiss you, I certainly don't want to spend the night, and I don't even want to share fucking Criss-Cut fries with you. I want you to take me home and I want you to take me home NOW."

He looked more surprised than hurt. As if he was floored that I had rejected his suave advances. Ben started the car, and we drove back to the dorms in complete silence. When the car slowed to a halt, he turned to me as if to offer some final attempt, but I was out of there. I flung open the door, jumped from my seat, collected my belongings, and ran all the way up four flights of stairs to the comfort of my barf-stained bed.

I had survived. And I had stolen the soda.

I woke up the next afternoon around one to the threat of the previous night's regrets in regurgitation form. I ran to the bathroom and promised myself I would never drink on an empty stomach again. When I finally stopped heaving, I shuffled back to my room and grabbed my phone to alert my friends to how the date had gone. I was met by the standard morning notifications, a few Instagram likes, some group chat activity, Facebook alerting me to somebody's birthday that I forgot I was even friends with on Facebook to begin with, and then something out of the ordinary. Among the expected "Tell us everything" texts from my girlfriends, there were ten missed texts from Nathan, marked from four a.m. until about twenty minutes ago. The following is written from memory, as iCloud did not exist in the era of iPod Nanos:

Nathan

> Hello Meghan. I just wanted to let you know that I am extremely disappointed in your actions tonight, namely the choice you made to have Ben take you home.

Nathan

> You were my date last night and I had not been on a date since my ex and I broke up a year and a half ago. My heart was broken but spending time with you I felt the pieces slowly finding their way back together again. I thought you were something special and I thought what we had together was pure, beautiful and so very unique.

Nathan

> You crushed my dreams tonight Meghan.

Nathan

> You broke my heart again and I don't think I will ever be the same again.

Nathan

> We could have been great.

Nathan

We could have been it.

Nathan

You could have been the one for me.

Nathan

But you blew it.

Nathan

I am so angry with you.

Nathan

My heart is broken and I will never be the same and it is all your fault. –Nathan

He deleted me on Facebook that night in 2012. He re-friended me on Facebook four years later.

I still haven't accepted.

chapter 5

i think i'm
allergic to you

Contrary to popular belief, I have in fact been the dumper as opposed to the dumpee in a few of my previous relationships. I have let crushes down easy, I have politely rejected dinner requests, and I even once turned down a date to homecoming. (I must reiterate, Sam Machado, if you're reading this, I regret that deeply because you're really hot now.) I am not trying to portray the image that I get asked out a lot, mainly because that's just not true. I'm weird as fuck. But that's beside the point. The point is that I'm not Kendall Jenner, I don't have boys fawning over my every move, and I've never rejected a spin on a private jet because I knew I'd have future opportunities. Some kids blessed with the Beckham gene pool grow up with a mental bank of polite rejections ingrained in their genetically perfect skulls. I, on the other hand, was a chubby kid with transition lenses. I thought hot pink was a neutral and cheetah was a shade. My toddler years weren't a baby Gap ad, my tweens were not a Limited Too catalog (RIP), and my high school years were closer to a before picture than an after. What I'm trying to say is that I didn't grow up with a steady stream of romantic attention.

Regardless of my socially inept nature and my eternal awkward stage, even I, co-headmistress of the Harry Potter club, have experienced what it's like being on the instigating end of a breakup. That, and I've been dumped enough to tell you what hurts the fucking worst. Don't worry, I'm totally not bitter at all.

timing

I get it, you're fired up. You just met a hot slice of meat on the subway, and your feelings for your current relationship are already a distant memory. You've had a few too many sips of liquid courage, and suddenly the urge to split is greater than your pants at a Vegas buffet. You may have been identifying as single for the last few months (despite the initials in your Instagram bio), but the only title changes your (soon-to-be) ex is aware of is the presidential election. Ending a relationship requires the same two people who started one. Except for extenuating circumstances, like catching your significant other at a romantic dinner date with a zaddy fifty years her senior (this is a true story from my Uber driver Oscar), there is a time and a place for everything. This includes when to break up with someone, and the following are not the times or the places:

1. On a voice mail
2. With emojis
3. On Valentine's Day
4. On their birthday
5. On your birthday
6. In a DM
7. In a MySpace message (Is MySpace still a thing?)
8. In a Snapchat (direct *or* story)
9. Over a Never Ending Pasta Bowl
10. While swimming in open water

11. On a tandem bike
12. While driving through a thunderstorm on the Pacific Coast Highway
13. At the DMV
14. Via smoke signal
15. On a Scantron test
16. In Morse code
17. After they've watched *Marley & Me*
18. During a commercial break
19. On their deathbed
20. During the finale of *Game of Thrones*
21. In the frozen novelties section at the grocery store
22. While they're having acupuncture
23. On a bank holiday
24. At the bank
25. On April first
26. After they've finished a series on Netflix
27. At a funeral (unless it's your own)
28. After they've just finished the final Harry Potter book
29. While tripping at Coachella
30. In front of a claw machine at a twenty-four-hour Mexican restaurant
31. During childbirth
32. While sharing a single piece of spaghetti à la *Lady and the Tramp*
33. On an international flight
34. While they have diarrhea
35. On the jumbotron
36. Over a loudspeaker during school announcements
37. Through choreographed dance
38. In an assembly
39. On a road trip
40. In a YouTube video

do your own dirty work

Don't ask someone to break up with your significant other *for* you. Extenuating circumstances (like safety) aside, you got yourself into this mess; you best believe you're the one getting yourself out of it. This may seem like a "duh" moment, but to eleven-year-old me, it had seemed like a perfectly good option. I also broke rule #1.

I was dating Henry for a total of three weeks. It was just long enough that he sent me a Candygram on Valentine's Day, which made me feel *really* cool. That's obviously the intention, because if anyone says they want candygrams for the actual candy, they're lying. Don't trust anyone who enjoys the taste of conversation hearts. Those are soul-sucking, Voldemort candies.

Prior to age eleven I never had to break up with any of my boyfriends. I would just sit next to someone new in the sandbox and then they knew it was over. But middle school is all about the dramatics. Preteens live for passing notes, quick comebacks, and "your mom" jokes. So naturally breakups are done on a much grander scale. After I finished off the box of Russell Stover chocolates that Henry had also given me for Valentine's Day, I enlisted my friend Mackenzie to help me cut him loose. Word travels fast between eleven-year-olds whose parents don't let them have cable or cell phones. Before we knew it, our table at the library was fifteen girls deep. It was covered by dozens of crumpled-up pieces of college-ruled notebook paper as we tried to formulate the best breakup "note" ever to have been passed in the hallowed halls of White Hill Middle School. It was like a bad game of telephone. What started off as a straightforward breakup note turned into a lost letter from *The Notebook*. I really wish I could ask Henry if, for some self-loathing reason, he decided to keep the note so I could insert it here as a visual aid. But we're not friends on Facebook and

I'd have to use the phone book, which requires a lot more effort than I'm willing to put forth. We'll have to make do with the summary my goldfish-sized brain has created over the years of telling this story as an icebreaker at holiday parties:

Dear Henry,

It's over. There's just no chemistry between us anymore.

—Meg*

CHEMISTRY!? REALLY, MEGHAN?!! YOU HAVEN'T EVEN TAKEN CHEMISTRY YET! NOR HAVE YOU KISSED HIM OR HELD HIS HAND OR EVEN SLOW-DANCED, FOR THAT MATTER!!! WHY ARE YOU USING THIS WORD?!

DO YOU EVEN KNOW WHAT IT MEANS?! (I didn't. Mackenzie wrote it.)

It's important to know when to be honest and when to lie. Everyone knows that "It's not you; it's me" directly translates into "It's not me; it's really just you."

Growing up, we're told that honesty is the best policy. While I do agree that in most cases being up-front is better, sometimes the truth can do more harm than good. Are my shoes totally last season? Probably! But don't tell me that right after I've had a big meeting and I'm on my way to a blind date. Instead, balk at my question and reassure me that my fashion choices are always stellar. The same goes for breakups. I'm 99.9 percent sure your soon-to-be ex doesn't want to hear that the real reason you're dumping him isn't because you need time to "focus

---

* This was the age I insisted I was going to go by Meg for the rest of my life. The "-han" was just so 1993.

on yourself." You don't have to tell him you really just need more time to focus on dating someone else.

Sometimes the truth just hurts. It's better to spare feelings than list every single trait you dislike about your partner to their face. But some truths are what they really need to hear. If the truth is that your feelings have changed, it might be better to let them know that. Don't keep them waiting on the sidelines for you to "figure yourself out" or whatever lie you used to avoid admitting that you just don't feel the same way about them anymore. But if the truth is that you now find them utterly repulsive and you're embarrassed to have touched them . . . maybe fib a little. If it's not constructive and not something they can keep in mind with their next relationship, don't say it.

There isn't a strict black-and-white way to figure out when it's better to lay it all out in the open and when to fudge the truth a little bit. It's more of a (fifty shades of) gray area, but that's the beauty of relationships. You live and you learn. (Or you don't, and you become the next Amy Dunne.)

taking a break vs. breaking up

I'm hoping by this day and age, anyone reading this book has seen *Friends*.

Forever marked as one of the most memorable episodes is when Ross and Rachel go on a "break." If you are one of the few who refuse to watch *Friends* and you're still not familiar with the concept, I'll break it down for you:

A "break" is an arbitrary term used to describe when a couple decides to put things on hold for a while. Sounds vague, right? *Precisely!* Because it's not exactly crystal clear what the parameters actually entail, it's really up to the specific couple to discuss and decide what it means for them. But to be blunt, I think of taking a "break" as the prequel to breaking up. The foreplay before the big act. The sweatpants you buy before your holiday weight gain. The training wheels of singlehood. It eases you into the idea of breaking up for good. Whether it's getting your feet wet with the idea of being single again, or easing a clingy ex into the friend zone. If you can gradually take a step back to reevaluate where your head is at, you can think it all through before you make any rash decisions. Just make sure you've learned from Ross and Rachel's mistake. Clearly define what is and is not acceptable during this hiatus. Personally, I usually give it a two-week window of completely severed ties. No in-person meetings, phone calls, text messages, smoke signals, or telepathic mind conversations. If I'm wanting to hold off seeing them longer than that, chances are I don't want to be in this for the long haul.

break up in person

Break up in person, unless they're crazy. This is rich advice coming from a serial ghoster, but do as I say, not as I do. We live in a day and age in which you can order groceries, buy a new outfit, get laundry done, and maintain strong friendships with people thousands of miles away—all without leaving the comfort of your couch. Technology has essentially eliminated the need for human interaction. As an avid homebody, I completely revel in this fact. But your cell phone is for pretty filters, playing Candy Crush, and perfecting your Instagram aesthetic. It's not for breaking up with your significant other who lives down the block. Your computer is for watching my old nose job vlogs, getting lost in sexual gifs on Tumblr, and WebMDing your weird rash. It's not for breaking up with the person who sleeps in your bed. Obviously, if you're in a long-distance relationship, you might have to resort to breaking up via a phone call. But please do it in person if you can. As much as you want to evade the imminent awkward silence followed by the possibility of seeing your boyfriend ugly cry worse than Kim Kardashian, you owe it to them to break the bad news in person. Take it from someone who has been dumped over the phone (me).

I hadn't even been in college for a month before I started dating someone. He was exotic. By "exotic," I mean he was one of fifteen Jewish guys in all of Riverside. (This was in my "I'm going to marry a Jewish guy so I can convert" phase, largely influenced by the fact that my best friends are all Jewish and I was feeling left out.) He was an upperclassman fraternity man (better deemed a frat boy) who swept me off my naive freshman feet with his dad bod and knowledge of Harry Potter. The first few months were great. I upgraded from the "walk of shame" my peers were doing to the much less embarrassing "drive of shame." Imagine my surprise when, after a particularly strong batch of jungle juice, I woke up to a text message from him saying, "I think it's just better if we're friends right now." After that, he avoided me for a year and a half. To this day I could not tell you why, how, or even exactly when we broke up. Rumor has it he did it over the phone while I was drunk-crying underneath the claw game machine at the twenty-four-hour Mexican restaurant. Moral of the story? Breakups are to be done in person, and my friends were shit for letting me lie on that fucking disgusting floor, crying over a boy with a small dick.

don't keep putting it off until it's too late

Breakups are not like fine cheese or wine. They do not get better with age. They're more like an infected cut: you have to get it dealt with before the wound starts to fester and ooze. Otherwise you'll look like a mutilated house elf and you have to amputate your whole arm instead of just applying an antibiotic twice a day. Breakups aren't fun. If they were, Taylor Swift's albums would be pretty damn boring. The longer you stay in a crappy relationship with someone who isn't right for you—or as Phoebe Buffay would say, who isn't your lobster—the farther off you are from finding a *great* relationship with the *right* person. It takes two active participants to make a relationship, so if you're just not feeling it anymore, then essentially it's already over. Trying to spare their feelings by putting it off just makes it worse, and it isn't fair to either of you. Before you know it, you've put it off so long, you've got three kids and a 401(k) plan, all the while dreaming of what your child's PE teacher looks like naked. So save yourself now, before your dating pool consists solely of people who take their teeth out at night.

The goal in breakups is to approach them with as much empathy, understanding, and maturity as you can muster. Regardless of how sticky it gets at the end, be the bigger person and rise above petty drama better suited for a Bravo pilot. This will not only cast you in a way more flattering light; it'll leave you with a sense of pride at your capability to handle less-than-stellar situations. This means listening instead of defending, as well as accepting whatever role your ex thinks you've played. Is this the advice you're going to take? Probably not! That's okay, you can always set your standards lower (my life motto). Move on to the next best option: Set out to do it in the manner you'd like to be broken up with. Would you love to discover your newfound singledom through a DM? Most likely not. Would you rather your significant other have the decency to do it in a quiet, private spot where your hysterical sobs won't be mistaken for a screaming goat? That's valid and also completely doable. I don't expect you to always take the high road, also because I certainly don't hold myself to that standard. Sometimes the high road is really steep and really far away and you get altitude sickness. Sometimes you just take the second-highest road. Or the third. Or the one right before the lowest. What's that saying? Aim for the moon and you'll land among the stars? How about: Aim for a tree and get caught in a shrub a few feet above the ground?

Now, hopefully some of those helped you, but maybe you were just looking for suggestions of lines to memorize and regurgitate the next time some bro named Trent asks for your number. These are some of my go-to excuses, phrases, and responses to gently (or not so gently) let someone down, listed in order of delicateness:

When Someone Wants to Buy You a Drink

Thank you so much for the offer! But I'm good for now! I'm actually here with friends. But thank you anyway!

I'm seeing someone.

I'm married.

I don't drink alcohol.

I don't drink anything except the trendy water that comes in cartons.

I don't even drink the trendy water that comes in cartons.

I only drink things that resemble blood or tears.

Daddy, is that you?

When Someone Asks for Your Number

I don't give my number out.

I don't have a cell phone.

If you give me yours on this napkin, I totally won't throw it away as soon as you turn around!

If it's meant to be, we'll be able to guess each other's numbers.

Are you referencing the Anna Faris movie? Because I haven't seen it yet.

I only give my number to guys with lightweight bolt-shaped scars on their foreheads.

Daddy, is that you?

When Someone Asks You on a Date

I'm busy that day.

I'm busy every day.

I think I'm allergic to you.

Unless you own a helicopter, I'm not interested.

I only date former members of One Direction.

I'm doing this thing called the Duggar Detox where I don't date until I'm married.

Daddy, is that you?

And if all else fails, and your milkshakes keep on bringing the bitches to the yard, and you still can't go a day without being showered with marriage proposals and promises of grandkids and retirement funds? Give me their number. I'll slide into their DMs.

how to talk to your crush

Sometimes when I'm driving alone in my car, I pretend like I'm on *Ellen* and I answer interview questions out loud to myself, saying things like, "Oh, Ellen, that's hilarious! Thank you for asking! Yes, winning my Oscar was such a surprise! That music really does creep up on you!" I am not kidding. You know what's not nearly as embarrassing? Talking to your crush. If I can admit to every person reading this book that I'm possibly insane, then you can go ahead and say "grool" to your Aaron Samuels. (Just don't vomit on him.)

I have never been shy when it comes to the boys that I like. By no means am I trying to humblebrag or anything like that. In all actuality, I could probably stand to be a bit more demure in regard to crushing. I really embrace the word "crush" in all its senses. Take Brad, my first instance of unrequited love, as an example. I fondly referred to him by the pet name I gave him: "Pip-squeak." Which now, as an adult, has me wondering if I was taking a not-so-subtle jab at his then-fragile birdlike physique. We'll never know. We were in the same kindergarten class, and he also happened to be my neighbor. This meant we carpooled to school, where we spent six hours a day knitting and singing and talking about our feelings and all the other bullshit you do in alternative-learning kindergarten. Then, once that was done, we carpooled to gymnastics, where he excelled on the parallel bars and I excelled at convincing my coach to give me an extra blue Otter-Pop. From there we were shuttled back home, where we (finally) parted ways. This kid couldn't fucking escape me no matter how hard he tried. I had about ten pounds on him (which at five years old means, like, I basically looked like I had eaten two Brads for my recess snack). My sole form of exercise was chasing this poor boy around and begging him to kiss me. I was beyond boy crazy; I was a savage. (Again, Brad, if you happen to be reading this, I profusely apologize for my actions.) Thankfully, I've toned down my technique over the years.

Despite that I've always had a soft spot for romantic comedies, I've never been able to wrap my head around one consistent plotline: the female protagonist wishing she knew what her Patrick Dempsey was thinking. I've always stood behind the idea that the quickest way to get the most accurate answer is to ask the question. Now, I'm not saying go up to Harry Styles and be, like, "Can I have your babies?" But if you've been seeing someone for the past three months and you're sitting at home with your roommates, stalking their tagged pictures on Instagram to see why they've been too busy to text you back, all the while wondering if they saw the #tbt pic of you on spring break in a bikini, save yourself the headache and just ask them what's up. I hate that, in this day and age, half of what dating has become is just a thing to gossip about between friends. We've immersed ourselves into creating these confusing and vague dramatic relationship situations that we don't try to fix, just so we can discuss them over red wine during *The Bachelor* commercials. My friends and I have wasted hours of our lives obsessing over what the person we like is thinking or feeling when in fact all of this could have been avoided by just asking the damn question! I think a part of us is hesitant in those situations, not just because being honest and vulnerable is completely terrifying, but because sometimes we're scared of the answer. And when we're scared and unsure of that answer, sometimes it feels better to live in denial and blissful ignorance and put off that hurt until a later date. And, yeah, sometimes it's going to suck, sometimes you'll find out that you've wasted the last three months investing in someone who hasn't factored you in at all. But you either find that out now, or you find out the hard way in three more months. If your heart is about to shatter, wouldn't you rather walk into it with a dustpan in hand rather than be caught by surprise? Better now than later. You got better things to do. Screw the other fish in the sea (literally, if you're down). You want to find your lobster.

chapter 6

pimp yo profile

I'm fucking great at (the digital component of) dating. I can make an Oscar-worthy Tinder profile, formulate the perfect combination of cheeky yet engaging messages on Bumble, and compose a seamless response to every text that leaves the recipient completely and totally enamored. When it gets to actually going through with it and meeting someone face-to-face, I can't help you. I'm all lead-up and zero follow-through. I'm slightly ashamed to admit it, but I treated dating apps like bored preteens treat TikTok. They were a mindless game of swiping and scrolling and tapping and instant validation. I'm aware that this is terrible. Thankfully, I am no longer on said dating apps, so we can just look at it as a fault of my past. Despite that I no longer have a need to pursue a guy via an iPhone application, I will admit that I live vicariously through my single girlfriends—not because I want to see what else is out there, or because I'm unhappy in my relationship (I don't and I'm not); I do it because it's still a fun game. There's a formula to win, cheat codes, and ways to level up that nobody else is utilizing. In this digital age, it's natural for people to go about dating like it's a video game. We're normalizing the use of these apps. We want to meet great people and embark on healthy and stable relationships, but because dating apps are so much about first impressions, many chance encounters and matches slip through the cracks. You could be the nicest and most normal dude, but your profile reads like a police blotter. You could be the most chill and sweetest girl, but your profile reads like Megan Fox from *Jennifer's Body*. One of my favorite midweek activities is convincing my friends to relinquish control of their dormant dating apps and let me make them over. It's like *Pimp My Ride* for Tinder, *Extreme Makeover* for Hinge, *Botched* for Bumble. I'm drawing a blank on any other makeover shows but I think you get the point. As much as we preach that love is blind, at the end of the day we're scrolling through potential partners like we scroll through BuzzFeed Tasty videos. Since it's all about first impressions, you might as well make a good one.

pictures

Let's start with pictures. Whether we like it or not, the pictures on your profile are the first things that anybody looks at. You can try to dispute that and say that your eyes naturally instead go to the 8-point Arial font in the lower corner, but that's just bullshit. I accidentally discovered my formula for profile pictures through my own judgment of the guys I was swiping through. I started to take note at what point I lost interest and swiped left and what combination of pictures kept me scrolling for more until my interest sparked a right swipe and (hopefully) a match. After I realized what I liked to see in a guy's profile, I started to supplement my profile with the same things. It was only when making over my friend's Tinder that I realized I had developed some sort of system, which I now refer to as the Four *F*'s (trademark pending). They are as follows, in this exact order:

The Four F's

1. Face
2. F(ph)ysique
3. Friends
4. Fun

1. Face. This may sound obvious to you, but indulge me for a minute. This is your *first* profile picture, the *first* of the first impressions, and it needs to speak volumes. This picture is in focus, from the waist/shoulders up, and it is the best goddamn picture you have ever taken. If the last great picture you have of yourself is more than two years old and you hadn't discovered the importance of eyebrows yet, enlist a friend to snap some pics of you candid-laughing by a hedge somewhere.

2. F(ph)ysique. I'm a tall girl. I clock in at about five-eight, and as totally superficial as it is, I never really date guys shorter than me. So when I scroll through seven profile pictures and don't discover that some guy is five-two until I stalk his tagged pictures on Instagram, I'm exasperated. At the same time I'm not trying to hide the fact that I'm tall. My excessive vertical trajectory is as much out of my control as the next person's. Now, I'm aware that this is coming off as incredibly shallow, and at the end of the day I genuinely do believe that love is blind. We fall in love with people because of a million little things. In the grand scheme of it all, your height doesn't really play a part. But what definitely does factor in is your candid self-awareness and honesty, even on these dating apps. As we scroll through hundreds of Facetuned pictures, cropping and tweaking and trimming, there is something so attractive and enticing about owning who you are. They've already seen your first picture of your face and they're scrolling to see more, so show more! Not like "birthday suit" more (unless you actually wore a three-piece suit to celebrate your latest year). It can be a picture of you from a family vacation to Italy, or a heavily stylized #OOTD picture from the days you attempted to be a fashion blogger. Whatever your body type is, just own it. If some ass-lord swipes left because your thighs touch, is he really the dude you want to father your children? Fuck no. Every single part of you will attract somebody who is attracted to every single part of you.

3. Friends. We all have at least one friend, family member, or a Disneyland employee who is obligated to accept our request for a picture together. Now is their shining moment. If you're anything like my friends, you're probably heavily protesting that your first two pictures are solo shots. (Did I make that clear enough before?) In that case, I would probably tell my friends to shut up, but since you and I are not close friends (yet), I'll explain my reasoning to you. Whoever you're trying to attract on a dating app, you're trying to attract them to *you*, not to your friends. Think about how annoying it is when you're scrolling through somebody's picture and you're forced to pull out your goddamn magnifying glass and your Sherlock Holmes hat to try to decipher which guy in a polo shirt is "James P." That shit is annoying. If I can't tell *who* you are within the first three seconds, I'm out. This isn't to say that pictures with friends are a complete and total deal breaker; it's quite the opposite, actually. While I'm not in favor of the buddy system in full force in every picture, showing that you're (seemingly) socially adept and normal (enough) to have friendships is important. It means that (a) you're most likely not a serial killer, (b) at least some people in this world enjoy your presence for at least as long as it took to snap the picture, and finally, (c) I have some sort of leads to show Nev if you catfish me, so I can get my revenge.

4. Fun. This is your freebie, your wild card, and your chance to stand apart. The first four pictures have been purely to captivate and establish interest; your final picture is to separate the people who swipe right on every pretty thing from the people who actually have personalities. Go fucking ham. Post a picture of you skydiving in a hot dog costume. Post a picture of you as a fat baby with your face covered in peanut butter. Post a picture of you dressed in a full Hogwarts uniform. You can use this picture to convey an interest of yours, a hobby, or just something random and fun that you're passionate about. If your hobbies include binge-watching television with a face mask on (my soul mate), feel free to display that with a photo booth selfie, or just opt for something completely random. This is your opportunity to let your freak flag fly and poke a little fun at yourself in the process. I'll leave you with this nugget of inspiration: when I dabbled in the world of dating apps, my final picture was a photograph of me one day post–nose job, with two black eyes and a bloody, bandaged nose, with the caption "You should see the other guy." Fucking fire.

captions

I always joke that I'd be a great pickup artist. At any time you can scroll through my phone and see about three text message conversations I have going on with my friends and their crushes. Hate to break it to you douche-bags-of-my-gal-pals-past, but those impeccably well-crafted text messages you received that read like movie-worthy banter? Me, all me. This is the area of my life where my inability to shut up, my self-deprecating humor, and my vast backlog of pop culture references all come in handy. I have a response to everything. My library of comebacks and comments is never-ending, and this is the only sector in life that not only accepts them, but they also flourish here. I live every moment of every day like I'm starring in my own reality show. Every conversation is a stand-up performance and every moment is a movie montage. Crazy? Yes. Helpful? Yes.

Now, I may be a self-proclaimed wizard, but ultimately I am not Harry Potter. (Cries.) There are a few basic things that need to be set into place before I can start going all millionaire matchmaker Amy Dunne (pre-psycho, like the cute her from that one flashback) and every stereotypical "cool girl" from every manic pixie dream girl movie. So ask yourself these three questions, and we'll take it from there:

1. Have you ever talked to your crush?
a) Yes.
b) No.
c) Does fanfic count?

If you answered (a), amazing! Move on to question #2. If you answered (b), can you change this? If yes, move on to question #2! If not, move along. If you answered (c), no, it does not count but I would like to read it.

2. Is your crush attainable?
a) Yes.
b) No.
c) I have front-row Shawn Mendes tickets.

If you answered (a), great! Move on to question #3. If you answered (b), firstly, don't belittle yourself. The basketball star falls in love with the science geek if you're in *High School Musical*. That being said, if your crush has 50 million followers on Twitter and your username is in their honor, I'd say now would be the time to explore other interests, possibly one involving face-to-face human interaction. If you answered (c), no, it does not count but I would like to join you.

3. Is it kosher?

a) Yes.

b) No.

c) They're not a hot dog.

If you answered (a), flawless! If this were *American Idol*, I'd be handing you a golden ticket. If you answered (b), this one is kind of a big deal. The use of the word "kosher" in this context is to mean proper, legit, or fine, not anything to do with salt curing, BTW. Let's dive through some examples of what would be considered not kosher: your sister's ex, Marilyn Manson, your English teacher, or any relationship you'd describe as being "complicated." While I thoroughly enjoyed playing Romeo in my seventh-grade class's adaptation of *Romeo and Juliet*, I'd rather not live it. Pursuing a relationship with a person who you're already aware might not be the best choice isn't too promising for its future or sustainability. Sure, there are movies in which the girl falls in love with her best friend's boyfriend, and he happens to love her, too, and they get together and live happily ever after without burning a single bridge. But that shit was scripted by a wistful NYU grad attempting to actualize her own fantasy. While all people come with baggage and all relationships come with their respective bumps, if there are major obstacles preventing you two from being together, it's probably not worth the uphill battle. If you answered (c), Amber D'Alessio made out with a hot dog.

If you've read this far, I assume that means you've passed the qualifying questions. Otherwise, you're just a rebel who's ignoring my advice and continuing on your quest to bed the latest CW heartthrob. I'd scold you, but I do admire the dedication. Now that we've established that the doodles you've made on your notebook with hyphenated last names might actually come to fruition (or that you're just delusional), it's time to move on to phase 1.

phase 1:
make contact with the target

The first step is always the hardest one, and this is no exception. Whether you've been staring at the back of your crush's head in Econ all semester or you've been silently pining after one of your best friends, there's no way to take your relationship to that next level without them knowing. If you don't talk to your crush, chances are you won't be dating them anytime soon. Putting those feelers out isn't just for them to begin to see you in that light. Think of it like a trial period, like a thirty-day free subscription where you test the waters and see if the feelings you've built up in your head stand up to the real deal. Now, don't think you have to go from zero to one hundred in ten seconds flat. If anything, I think taking it slow is usually the way to go. (Use this motto the first time you have sex too.) In the digital age, this step could mean a multitude of things, including but not limited to: an unprompted follow-back on Instagram, sliding into DMs, a shared academic class, or a group hangout with mutual friends. Your goal of phase 1? Leave an impression. Whether that means that your name is the most recent search on their Instagram or they asked a friend about you, leave the thought of you in the back of their mind.

1. Compliment. Everybody loves a (genuine) compliment. I'm not suggesting you turn into the starfish earrings from *Aquamarine* and spew pointless praises, but well-thought-out and unique verbal admiration does not go unnoticed. Compliment your crush on something special— something that reflects them as a person, not just the cocktail of their DNA. For example, if your crush has piercing blue eyes, I'm sure they've been told they're remarkable their whole life. They had no say in the shade of their eyeballs. They did, on the other hand, have a say in the shirt they picked out to wear this morning. These compliments don't always need to be from a material standpoint, either. Maybe it's the way they spoke passionately in class about a topic they cared about, or maybe their interaction with a random old lady on the street was noteworthy. Say it, smile, and saunter on off. That brief and unexpected compliment surprises them with flattery, and the walking away leaves them yearning for more. Make sure that your walk away includes a little swish of the hair, a little booty, and a lot to remember.

2. Leave a cheeky comment. This one requires a little cyber confidence and possibly a friend to press the "send" button for you. Now, to be frank, I'd steer clear from Facebook, which is at this point the land of distant aunts who sign off comments with a dash followed by their name. I'm assuming you'd rather not have their verbal responses to your winky face on your crush's selfie. Also, if I'm so blissfully out of touch with the world and Facebook is dead, please just ignore my previous statement. Venture on to your other various social media platforms, some of which I'm sure are still just embryos of ideas growing in the brain of some soon-to-be-somebody in Silicon Valley. Did your crush just post a #tbt of summer camp? Did they snap a selfie with their mom for her birthday? Did they repost a relatable quote about the latest episode of the hottest HBO show? Skip the lazy internet slang and leave an abbreviation-less comment. Give your relevant, genuine, and above all nice commentary to their post. You won't just stand apart from the haphazard "likers"; you'll establish that you not only like it but might even *like* it. ;)

3. Make up a reason. I attribute my entire dating life to the practice of this technique. I still used it well into adulthood. I can make up an excuse for anything. I can justify an expensive pair of shoes, I can reason with myself that having three bowls of popcorn is healthy, and

I can think of a reason to text my crush when the only real reason is that I want to. A made-up reason is the safest and easiest way in the world to bridge the gap with your crush without leaving you feeling too vulnerable. Do you have a class together? Ask if they've got the homework assignment. Do you work together? Ask if they know who got Monday off. No direct connection? Text them and say you thought you saw them at the grocery store and made a total ass of yourself saying hi to a stranger. Is any of this true? Probably not. But now you're talking, so you're welcome. Will they see through it and realize it's all a ploy to spark a conversation? Maybe. Does that matter? Not at all. And in true moments of (possibly wine-induced) flirtation, "accidentally" double-tap one of their pictures from sixty-four weeks ago. You're welcome, young grasshopper. Now, go tag me in your kissing selfies and invite me to your wedding. I'll be waiting.

chapter 7

100 things that are worse than a broken heart

1. A broken bone
2. Walking in wet socks
3. Getting your period in white pants
4. Trusting the wrong fart
5. Losing an unused gift card
6. *Cats*
7. Walking in on your parents having sex
8. *Mean Girls 2*
9. Drinking orange juice after brushing your teeth
10. When your takeout order is wrong but you don't realize it until you get home
11. Falling in public
12. Accidentally deleting an assignment
13. Working for Miranda Priestly
14. Losing the Apple TV remote
15. Finding out you're the Miranda of your friend group (Side note:

The older I get the more I realize Miranda had her shit together and Carrie was actually the worst.)

16. Soft grapes
17. Donald Trump
18. Being trapped in an elevator
19. Getting a ring stuck on your finger when you're in a store
20. Taxes
21. The plot of *The Boy Next Door*
22. The season finale of *Lost*
23. People who say Hermione and Harry are OTP
24. Death
25. Being constipated
26. Clogging the toilet at a party
27. People who bring babies to movie theaters for non-baby-appropriate movies
28. Transition lenses
29. People who pronounce milk "melk"
30. The hot chocolate that comes out of a machine at the bowling alley
31. Bad sushi
32. Shattering your phone
33. World Wars I, II, and III (I assume)
34. Tight bra straps
35. Appendicitis
36. A lost sneeze
37. Tomi Lahren
38. The end of *My Sister's Keeper*
39. Kim Kardashian's musical career
40. Drinking vodka when you're expecting water
41. Delayed flights
42. Hangnails
43. Having something in your teeth all day and nobody telling you

44. Oversleeping
45. Over-plucking your eyebrows
46. When somebody eats your leftovers in the fridge
47. Calling your teacher/boss "Mom"
48. Calling your teacher/boss "Dad"
49. Food poisoning
50. Piers Morgan
51. Public speaking
52. Not finishing your frozen yogurt before it melts
53. Getting a cavity
54. Getting water up your nose
55. Small talk
56. Strangers who share too much
57. Sitting next to someone who eats tuna salad on an airplane
58. Sweating in sneakers with no socks on
59. Advent calendar chocolate
60. Dropping your food on a dirty floor
61. Locking yourself out of your house
62. Unsolicited dick pics
63. The post office
64. Movies in which dogs die
65. The hiatus in the Olsen twins' acting career
66. Getting a zit in a place you can't reach
67. Peeing in a bodysuit
68. My grade in high school physics
69. Losing money
70. Spam emails
71. Every day that isn't Christmas
72. People who don't like french fries
73. Friends who tag you in pictures when you look bad
74. People who play videos on their phone at full volume in public places

75. Buying something full price and seeing it on sale the next day
76. People who use the wrong version of "their"
77. Nicolas Cage's acting career
78. Accidentally eating moldy bread
79. Stale cereal
80. Middle-of-nowhere rest stop bathrooms
81. Falling asleep on the random passenger next to you on the plane
82. When somebody mistakes you for another person
83. When you think someone is waving at you so you wave back, but they were waving at someone else
84. Nuts in cookies
85. Ikea on a Saturday
86. Ikea on a Sunday
87. Rose not scooting over for Jack
88. "Baby on Board" stickers
89. Any bumper sticker that asks you to honk if you relate
90. Anti-vaxers
90. People who bring black lights to hotel rooms
91. People who say "lit fam" earnestly
92. Gender inequality
93. Racism
94. When your clothes shrink in the dryer
95. When your iPhone updates without your consent
96. Mondays
97. Breaking a nail
98. People who leave puppies in boxes on the side of the road
99. Old white men
100. Flat-earthers

friends and frenemies

UGLY BUILDS CHARACTER.

chapter 8

toxic friendships

By "toxic" I don't mean the Britney Spears hit that inspired my twenty-first-birthday outfit. Sadly, in this context, it's far less sparkly. The first time I ever heard the term "toxic friend" I must have been in high school. I don't know if I read it somewhere or heard about it in a movie or on an AOL headline, but it really resonated with me. Ironically enough, one of the first advice videos I ever uploaded to YouTube was how to deal with toxic friends. At the time I thought I had experienced my share of these people and I was ready to dish out what I had learned. Little did I know that I'd spend the next five years of my life in and out of tumultuous, scarring, and manipulative friendships.

A toxic friend is a bully in disguise. Most of the time, the friend-ship doesn't start out that way, or at least it doesn't appear to. There really is no standard for what kind of person is a toxic friend. They come in all different packages and they are each volatile in their own unique way, like snowflakes, except made out of acid and nunchucks. Sometimes, when we're young, these friends are the ones our parents and our teachers classify as "bossy." They thrive on telling people what to do, how to do it, and when to do it, and before you know it, you're a minion. Other times a toxic friend could be somebody who comes across as incredibly shy, soft-spoken, and self-conscious. That intense insecurity can manifest itself in them putting you down to make themselves feel better. Moral of the story: toxic friends are about as hard to spot as carbon monoxide leaks. I also just had to google if those are hard to detect. They are. Go, me.

The first friendship of mine that I'd consider toxic spanned my freshman year of high school through midway of my junior year. Like most bad relationships, I really had no idea that it was bad until I was out of it. We shared almost an identical class schedule, the same taste in movies and books, and a love for making stupid videos. We met the first day of freshman year—we had gone to different middle schools—but our friend groups merged instantly, and only a few weeks into the school year I felt as if I had found my place. I don't remember exactly when the first red flags started to appear, most likely because I had rationalized them for so long, but it probably started earlier than I'd like to admit.

One of the major things we had in common was that neither of us drank, did drugs, or partied at all—which, considering that we were fifteen, shouldn't have been such an anomaly, but it was. We grew closer as other members of our friend group began to explore the world of high school house parties and the substances they had to offer. While I had no animosity or judgment toward any of our friends who chose to do so, she did. She'd whisper these terrible things, prefaced with "Just between you and me . . ." or "Don't tell anyone, but . . ." She said these nasty and negative things about people I considered my best friends, but she did so in a way that made me feel like I was being let in on a secret. I was the exception; she'd only confide in me about it. In a weird and twisted, fucked-up way, she made me feel special. And I knew that if I ever disappointed her and did something she did not approve of, I would no longer be exempt from her judgment. At the time I really felt that I was making my own decisions. I didn't think I was being pressured or even influenced by her, but that's manipulation for you.

After a while the list of things I could not do included more things than just not partying. I could not eat less than she did. I could not work out for as long as she did. I could not weigh less than she did and I could not look better than she did. When I was forced to go on birth control after a six-month-long period (fun, I know), she made sure to tell me that she wouldn't ever go on it because "obviously it makes you fatter." I'm sure she said it with a smile, which confused me even more. She would phrase these personal attacks in a way that made me feel as if she had my best interest at heart and she was just trying to be a good friend. When I started to date, she had been dating my best guy friend for months. Yet any headway in the romantic department for me was quickly shot down by her for various reasons. Some guys weren't cute enough, others weren't smart enough, some were just plain weird, others she had "history" with, and she even nixed some without any reason. In her mind I existed for her to feel better about herself. I had a supporting role to play and I was not allowed to go off script. I played that part for almost three years, until one day I didn't want to play it anymore.

Since she got a boyfriend, my evenings and weekends were freed up a bit and I was able to get some much-needed distance from her. With my newfound freedom, I began to date a guy I 100 percent knew she wouldn't approve of. When she found out, she lectured me in the way a strict parent would scold their pregnant teen. She gave me the ultimatum between choosing him or her, and I chose him—not because I had some new strength or sense of worth instilled in me, but mostly because he was really cute and I didn't want to die a virgin.

I think there was also a part of me that didn't think she would actually follow through with that threat. Despite all the signs, I just so desperately did not want to believe that our friendship was contingent on me fulfilling her checklist. I was wrong. After she ended our friendship, I didn't go to school for a week. I listened to "Breathe" by Taylor Swift on repeat and I cried until my eyes swelled shut. I begged her to change her mind, to trust me that he was a good guy and that I should be allowed to date him if she just met him and gave him a chance. She refused. Two weeks after our friendship ended, I stopped being sad. I forgot that I was upset because I was happy. I had forgotten what it felt like to be unapologetic—how easy it felt to feel good when you weren't constantly being pushed down. When I stopped asking for it, she gave me a second chance. To her surprise, I didn't take it. I didn't need her.

The next run-in I had with toxic friends occurred in college. They were so terrible that they got their own chapter. Refer to the table of contents for that one. The shitstorm I endured in college left me a little worse for wear when, afterward, I embarked on a less-than-glamorous move to a cockroach-infested apartment in West Hollywood. You'd think after the torment of the previous year I'd be jaded when it came to friendships, but I was the polar opposite. I had been accepting terrible bullying from my roommates for so long that my standard of how I should be treated was completely warped. I was so used to their abuse that anything that didn't match that intensity was more than I could even dream of. This was a rather lengthy period in my life in which, to put it bluntly, I just was blind to shitty people. I was being walked all over left and right and I accepted it because I knew firsthand that it could always be worse.

I was in a really unique situation when I moved to LA. A huge part of the reason I went to school in Riverside was because of its close proximity to LA, the mecca of the entertainment industry. The move to LA was bound to happen at some point; it just happened a little earlier than I had expected, and under far different circumstances. I hadn't dropped out of school for a nine-to-five job or any sort of steady career. I dropped out of college because I was incredibly depressed and it just so happened that my YouTube channel could sustain me financially. Moving to a new city in general is terrifying, but most of the time there is something you're moving for, whether it's a job, a relationship, family, school, or friends. I didn't move for any of those things. I didn't know a single person who lived in LA and I didn't have a job to go to on Monday morning. I had a laptop and a DSLR camera. If I choked on a pretzel, Twitter couldn't check up on me. Don't get me wrong, I had spent quite a lot of time in LA. For the last half of my stint in Riverside, I was commuting to various parts of the city for different shoots and jobs. I could navigate the 405 and I knew not to go to the Third Street Promenade at four p.m., but socially the only regular friendly face I came across belonged to the gas station clerk at the PCH Mobil. Great guy.

My first few weeks were lonely, but that was ordinary. I was so used to being alone that I don't think I even realized I was until I wasn't. One of the few depictions *The Hills* got right is the surplus of teenagers and young adults living on their own in LA. So while I had no "real" job to speak of and no classes to attend, I fit right in with the rest of them. This unique culture draws in a colorful collection of characters and puts us all in a very weird social experiment. It's rare to find somebody with a "normal" job or schedule or anything of that sort, so the circumstances in which we foster relationships are much different. For the first time I was not a slave to any sort of routine. I could get brunch on a Tuesday. I could hang out with people for five days straight without calling it summer camp. The immersion you have in these friendships is far greater than any other solely because you have no other set routine or obligations. This isn't to say that LA is a city of unemployed losers; it's not—or at least I'm not one of them until I finish this book. Then I'm unemployed. #Sequel?

I'm sure you can assume what sort of chaos would ensue when a bunch of underage kids move to LA with credit cards and nobody to report to. I was all for it. I was so ready to go out and be social and pick my life back up post–freshman year as if sophomore year never existed. That didn't happen. I fell into a situation that felt far too familiar. I had been hanging out with a few different people. Honestly, I'd hang out with whoever wanted to hang out with me; I wasn't picky—pathetic but not picky. And thus history repeated itself. Again, I didn't really make the connection or notice anything out of the ordinary until years later. My friendships with these people started out normal enough. We'd order takeout and watch movies, buy random things from Target we'd never use, and gossip about the celebrities we saw at the Coffee Bean & Tea Leaf. We were all still in that very green phase of moving; none of us had established our place in Los Angeles, and it felt comforting to know that we were all taking off together.

All the friends I had at this time were toxic in their own way, thus making their toxicity much less obvious. If we were all together, I was the butt of the joke. Actually, the only time I wasn't the butt of the joke was when there wasn't somebody to justify it with laughter. Everyone gossiped about each other, coaxing rude remarks out of one another to use against them. Once again I was sworn to secrecy, naively thinking that meant nobody was talking about me behind my back. When they started saying things to my face, I didn't have to speculate about that. Again, this should have been a deal breaker, but I was ready to accept any form of friendship I could get, and they knew that—knew it and milked it. Individually they all made it clear where I stood in relation to them and how I was so lucky that they had given me the opportunity to be graced with their presence. And I ate it up. I took whatever I could get. I truly believed it when they said that if they were mean to me, it meant we were really friends.

I let them institute a ridiculous set of "rules"; for example, if I appeared with them in public—which seldom happened, I might add—I had to walk six steps behind, speak when spoken to, and oh, so help me God, if I even *thought* to flirt with a boy . . . I accepted their lame excuses for why they never invited me to the parties they went to, and I believed them when they said that, despite their ample Instagram presence, their phone had died and, besides, "you wouldn't have had fun anyway." I didn't bat an eye when I was instructed to change my outfit when someone requested to borrow the top off my back or if they just thought it made me look too good. When my phone didn't ring for days on end, I made up the excuses that they were too lazy to give me. I was a figurative and eventually a literal punching bag. I wish I could say in all of this there was a moment when it all got to be too much and I finally stood up for myself, but I didn't. Each of these friendships ended on their terms, not my own. I spent months agonizing over why I was left behind and what I could do to get back into their good graces. It pains me to recall a time in which I was so lost and so broken that I accepted scraps of acknowledgment and confused them with love.

Sadly, the story doesn't end here; it just gains a new star. Would you believe me if I told you that I have even narrowed it down to only the true crème de la crème of the terrible friends of my past? Because that's the truth. I've always justified shitty things I've gone through as material for my book, so at first it was pretty frustrating when I realized I did not have the time or the stamina to go into detail about every bitch from my past. But that's beside the point; let me get back on track. The good thing about this toxic friend is that she was the last one. And I'm not even going to add any sort of ominous "for now" to that, because she is, without a doubt, the last one. Seriously. I broke the cycle with her and now all my friends are great and I don't need or want any more friends. Unless Ina Garten wants to hang out. Or Michelle Obama.

Thankfully, for the first time, I wasn't nearly as blind and naive as I had been before. I wouldn't go so far as to say I was as jaded as people claim I am now, but I was somewhere in that ballpark. I had been burned by nearly every friend I had made in LA. After putting my trust in the wrong people time after time, I finally just stopped searching for Southern California versions of my childhood friends. So although this particular friend was the most toxic of them all, she (thankfully) didn't affect me the same way. There is no real nice way to put it, but to be frank, at the time I knew her, she was just, to me, a bad person.

She was insanely moody. She'd go from laughing hysterically to slamming doors and screaming at the top of her lungs. She was possessive to a point of codependency where if I did not accompany her for all my waking moments, she'd throw a tantrum. In one specific instance, I was three weeks into a three-month-long shoot. One evening, when I told her I didn't want to go to the grocery store, since I had food at home and I had work to do, she lost it. She screamed at me that she had let me go to work all day and she waited for me and now it was time for me to do something for her. Maybe a few years ago this would have worked on me, but at that point I was pretty well versed in this kind of behavior. I just rolled my eyes and let her scream it out.

We spent nearly every waking moment together, mostly at her request, which I'm sure eventually got to her as her frustration grew with my "lack of effort" in the friendship—which, I'll admit, was somewhat true. I wouldn't go so far as to say that I was an inactive participant, but as time went on and she treated me worse and worse, I fought less and less to please her. She was perpetually negative and critical of every aspect of my life. She hated my boyfriend, my other friends, and every other thing she could find. She'd go out of her way to say rude things to me loudly in public, and even on lazy nights in she'd attempt to put me down in any way she could. Again, I was pretty unfazed by this, which I think just irked her even more.

When her verbal commentary didn't get the reactions she wanted, she'd smack my arm with enough force to hurt, rather than just get my attention. Everywhere we went, she would play goalie to my every move: stepping in front of me, bumping shoulders, nudging me from behind, constantly ignoring any sense of personal boundaries. Instead of succumbing to her controlling tendencies, I called her out on it. In doing so, I was now the bad guy. She claimed I was overreacting and that I couldn't take a joke. She chalked it up to her favorite insult, my "sensitivity," accompanied by a lengthy eye roll. If not wanting my friend to push me "playfully" made me sensitive, then fuck it. I guess I'm starring in *Inside Out 2*.

I was checked out of our "friendship" for a really long time. Considering I had kept her at arm's length since we first met, that transition was pretty smooth. Despite my ample experience with these telenovela-like friendships, I myself am the least dramatic person when it comes to relationships. And I'm just really lazy. I had no intentions or plans to "dump" her as a friend—not because I wanted to be her friend, or because it sounded like it would be a lot of work on my end (which it did), but it just seemed so silly to me. I think if you treat something like a big deal, that makes it a big deal. Why on earth go through the dramatics of an epic blowup when I knew it would meet its maker on its own? Which it did. It happened on my twenty-second birthday. I had invited her to Disneyland during the day, drinks that night, and Vegas the following weekend. She stood me up at Disneyland, was a no-show at drinks, and neglected to wish me a happy birthday. I heard from her days later with a bitchy text about how I should have wanted to spend my birthday with only her and how she refused to be one of my "many" friends. I was to be only her friend or she would be forced to walk away. As you can imagine, I let her walk away. Took me far too many tries, but at least I learned my lesson.

As I look back on this chapter, there is a part of me that is so disappointed and embarrassed by that blind and pathetic doormat of a person I was. But there is a bigger part of me that remembers that feeling of worthlessness, desperation, and loneliness as if it were yesterday. Even though I came out better for it, if I had a Time-Turner necklace or that thing from *Clockstoppers*, I would 100 percent utilize it. But because (as far as I know) the Apple Watch has yet to introduce that feature, I'll instead opt for a much more rewarding (vom) act. In channeling my experience with unhealthy friendships, I've compiled a list that can hopefully help you break any cycle like the one I was stuck in for so long. I present to you a list of red flags and warning signs that your friendship is about as toxic as Febrezing with asbestos:

20 Red Flags and Warning Signs That
Your Friendship Is Toxic (in No Particular Order)

1. Jokes are consistently made at your expense, without your consent.

2. There are certain "rules," spoken or otherwise, that you know to abide by.

3. You are not allowed other friends, or are only allowed a select few.

4. You are held to a different standard than they are.

5. You are the target of insults, hateful words, or other jabs.

6. You are expected to be at their beck and call, with no reciprocation.

7. They go out of their way to embarrass you or make you feel less than they are.

8. They acknowledge your friendship only when it is convenient to them.

9. The way they treat you in public differs from in private.

10. They treat you differently, depending on their audience.

11. They won't be seen or associated with you in public.

12. They hide you from their other friends or they segregate you.

13. They talk about you behind your back but deny it to your face.

14. They blame you for their shortcomings and point the finger at you for their faults.

15. They make you work for their friendship.

16. They detest seeing you happy and will do anything in their power to stop it.

17. They make negative comments about you.

18. They make you do things you are uncomfortable with.

19. They make you question your character, your own morals, and your self-worth.

20. They are physical without your consent.

chapter 9

bullies should dress like cruella de vil . . . or mufasa

My family didn't have cable TV growing up. Not in the, like, "We all slept on a single mattress like *Charlie and the Chocolate Factory*" kind of way. More like my mother was convinced that watching *The Power-puff Girls* would ignite some underlying serial killer gene and turn me into a violent, cartoonish fighting machine. (I really wish I was kidding.) She also convinced me that the radiation in the microwave would shoot out and kill me if I stood near it while it was on. Up until I was about sixteen, I'd sprint out of the kitchen and hide behind the couch while my popcorn popped. My mother is an erratic combination of research analyst and drama queen, so, needless to say, she kept me on my toes.

We had the most basic of all basic TV packages: the local news, PBS, and by some strike of luck a channel that exclusively played reruns of crime shows. I remember sneaking behind my mom's back to watch *Criminal Minds* with my dad. (It's a vastly underrated show, by the way.) I have this distinct memory of sitting on the couch with my father as he briefed me long and hard about the potential content of the show we were about to watch: "It'll get violent" and "It might get bloody" and "Are you sure you can handle this? I don't want you to get night-mares." There was a sensation of rebellion running through my veins the first Thursday when my mom had a meeting and my dad finally caved, letting me watch Special Agent Hotchner and Dr. Reid (swoon). They dove into the minds of sociopaths who drugged and dressed up their victims like dolls and made them have tea parties. I was hooked. I don't know what caused more of an adrenaline rush: the hot Behavioral Analysis Unit agents (Derek Morgan can get it) or that I knew I was watching something my mother had forbidden and deemed dangerous, something my young eyes needed protecting from.

Growing up, we are taught to be afraid of kidnappers, guys who drive unmarked white vans offering candy, and the serial killers plagu-ing the lives of my beloved fictitious *Criminal Minds* characters. We are not taught to be afraid of our peers, cliques of girls, or nineteen-year-olds who look like they could grace the cover of an American Eagle catalog. At twenty-six years old I can sit alone in my empty apartment and binge-watch hours of every mentally twisted crime show known to man and Netflix, and then promptly turn off all the lights and fall asleep. But put me in a room full of bubbly sorority girls? I'm quivering with PTSD in my Sam Edelman booties.

Aside from the few natural hiccups of being thirteen and reading the Clique books one too many times (I'm still placing the blame for my bitchy streak on Massie Block), my childhood was more or less bully-free. I mean, a kid named Drew in my fifth-grade class discovered the silent *h* in my name that my father had added in tribute to his Irish heritage. This gave birth to the nickname of "Meg*ham*," highlighting my chubby appearance at age ten. But that was pretty much the extent of it.

I did not have the traditional American high school experience. Our football team was a joke, cheerleading was for social pariahs, and when one of my guy friends came out as gay, he got more prom invi-tations than the entire Duggar family. Composting was "cool," as was volunteering on weekends and being passionate about nerdy things like Harry Potter. (This one not so much, but it's wishful thinking from my fanfic days.) We played hacky-sack on the quad barefoot, singing "Kumbaya" and holding hands with flowers in our hair. (That last part is a joke . . . sort of.)

I took for granted growing up in a town where quirkiness and individuality were celebrated. I watched shows like *The Secret Life of the American Teenager* and laughed at their vast "misinterpretation" of high school social conduct. Now, I wasn't totally out of touch with what growing up outside hippie-land was like. I went to summer camp. (Side note to parents: Summer camp is where your kid learns all the bad stuff, will inevitably have their first kiss, and then some. Just a friendly warning!) Unlike my "cool" Jewish friends who spent their summers in canoes making friendship bracelets, I attended theater camps with kids who could only be themselves two weeks out of the year. They spent the rest of their collegiate days deepening their voices and unpinning Michael J. Fox key chains from their JanSport backpacks in attempts to stand a little straighter. I thought I had dodged a bullet. I silently thanked my father for finding this tiny little town where social norms went to die. I continued my blissfully drama-free life, never once pausing to think that maybe the train was just a little late coming.

I was nineteen years old when the shit hit the fan. I still hate using the word "bullied." Try saying "bully" without sounding like a whining seven-year-old. It's hard. Bullying seems like something that is reserved for preteen girls with body glitter and snappy comebacks they got from Judy Blume books. Nobody will sit with Suzie because Timmy and the other boys say she has cooties! For some reason we've rationalized that "kids can be mean" because they'll just naturally grow out of it. Like, the second you turn eighteen, a switch flips in your head and suddenly your morals are crystal clear and your intentions are spun out of pure gold. I call bullshit. Bullies do not only exist in high school, middle school classrooms, or elementary school. Bullies come in every shape and at any time. The sooner we start acknowledging that fact, the better equipped we'll be to handle it.

I think a common misconception is that bullies are always your archenemies, villains like Georgina Sparks who you can sense from a mile away. They're the popular kids at school who thrive off throwing you into your locker and writing nasty things about you on the bathroom stalls. We're taught that it's easy to spot a bully, as if it's as obvious as night and day, but sometimes bullies can take the form of boyfriends and friends and even the sweetest-looking of girls. Sometimes you don't even know when it's happening to you. It took me a while to admit I was being bullied. For some reason, admitting it left a bad taste in my mouth. I felt as if saying those words not only made it true but also made me weak. Who gets bullied at nineteen years old? It sounds preposterous. It sounds childish and outdated and something that must have happened only to me. And that's what I thought. I convinced myself that I had to be a fluke, the exception to the rule. It wasn't until I finally talked about it that I realized I was not.

My bullies came in the form of my two college best friends: sorority girls that I had pledged to be "sisters for life" with. We were inseparable from the first week of our freshman year. You couldn't find one of us without the other, and our classmates even dubbed us the "Barbies." We spent every waking moment together, we dated guys in the same fraternities, and we coordinated Halloween costumes. We talked about where we'd end up postgraduation and how we'd be sisters forever and ever and ever. (Gag me.) After a strangely distant summer, we reunited in our new apartment, where it became abundantly clear to me that our trio was now a twosome and I was the odd one out. It began with paying rent: they said it was my responsibility to cover way more than my share of the rent each month because they said that they had measured the rooms and mine was much larger than theirs, though it was only bigger by a few square feet. I couldn't wrap my head around what they were saying. The lease we had signed for the three-bedroom apartment was apparently relying on the assumption that I would pay hundreds of dollars more than each of them for the biggest room, but it was hardly bigger at all. I had expected to pay maybe fifty or a hundred dollars more, not basically half the rent of the entire apartment. My parents were flabbergasted. My mother spent the next two weeks on the phone with my roommates' fathers, until I finally caved. I agreed to pay thousands of dollars a month just so I could live with them. I didn't want anything to change. I could already sense them drifting away, and I didn't want to lose my college best friends. As we moved into the apartment, I held my breath, hoping I dodged a bullet. It was all smiles and small talk while our parents moved us in, but the second the last goodbye was exchanged, everything shifted.

It started off small. They'd "forget" to invite me to their dinner plans; it "slipped their minds" that we were going to carpool to class together. By the end of September they refused to acknowledge my existence. As a kid, when people asked me if I'd rather have the ability to fly or to be invisible, I always said I wanted to be invisible. I wish I could go back in time and tell my childhood self that there is no worse feeling in the world.

For weeks they ignored my presence, let their eyes glaze over as I walked by, and silently stared off into the distance as I tried to make conversation. I kept telling myself that I was being crazy. I didn't tell anyone about it. I would show up late to sorority meetings, and my sisters would ask why I didn't drive with my roommates. I'd make up some excuse that didn't reveal that they hadn't spoken to me in weeks. When sisters would compliment my weight loss, I'd thank them, as if crying so hard that I became physically sick was something to be proud of. When my mom called and asked if things had gotten better, I broke down. I bawled on the phone to her about how I was feeling so left out and I couldn't figure out what I had done wrong. She reassured me that sometimes friends go through rough patches and that, with a little more effort on my end, things would all go back to normal. All I wanted was for things to go back to normal.

Just as it would in a Lifetime movie, it all came to a head on Halloween. For the first time in months my roommates shouted up the stairs,
asking me if I was going out that night. I was recovering from a nasty
combination of bronchitis and strep throat, but—spurred by sheer joy
that they had actually spoken to me—I happily obliged. After attempting
to dull my hacking with a hot shower and applying layers of makeup, I
went downstairs. I made myself a cup of tea before putting the finishing
touches on my mermaid costume. Much to my surprise, I found my living room filled with frat boys and sorority girls taking shots and selfies.
I explained that my bathrobe was not in fact my costume. "Oh, I'm not
ready yet," I said, poking fun at my attire. "I didn't know we were host-
ing a pregame; otherwise I would have gotten dressed sooner!" I smiled
at my roommates, silently forgiving them for breaking the "Nobody is
allowed over unless we all approve it" rule they enforced. With perfectly
glossed lips they smiled back at me, eyes sparkling as they said, "*You're*
not having a pregame . . . WE are." Their laughter chimed in unison
while their catty remark went unnoticed by the gaggle of drunken college kids in our living room. Writing it all down makes me realize now
how atrocious this all was, but at the time, I was so desperate for things
to even resemble something close to how they used to be, I just took it.

I rushed upstairs to put my costume on and came down to them
screaming "ROOMIE PICTURE!!!" as they handed me their phones to
take pictures of . . . the two of them. I then let them take my key to
the apartment "in case we split up." I went along with it, saying that
it was totally fine if they could just let me into the apartment complex
when I called. When four a.m. rolled around and my hundredth call
was ignored, I finally got confirmation from an Instagram picture that
the girls had in fact been home for hours. I bummed a ride back to the
apartment from one of our sisters, silently irate in the passenger seat.
After attempting to scale the fifteen-foot-high gate, I made it through
our front door only to be greeted by a haze of smoke, the stench of
cheap liquor and vomit, and a room full of people I'd never even seen

before. So, in my most composed fuming mom-like tone, I told the half-naked superwoman and the rest of her scantily clad posse that the party was over. They loudly objected to this, slurring that "it's not your party, so you have no say when it starts or ends." This commotion woke one of my incoherent roommates, who then stumbled out of her bedroom spewing a string of crude words in my face. I excused myself to my room saying, "We can talk about it tomorrow. You're too drunk to be rational right now, and I'm too upset to even form words." She continued going off, digging into me with every insult she could think of. I just kept repeating myself, saying "We will talk about it tomorrow" as I managed to get up to my room. They followed me up the stairs, along with their alcohol-induced courage to spit the nastiest words in my face as I attempted to hide my tears. I locked myself in my closet as they banged on the door, screaming every vile thing they thought about me. They drunkenly slurred how worthless I was to them and just exactly what they thought I should do about that. I slept in a pile of scarves that night, no longer muffling my sobs as I left my mom a voice mail finally admitting what was really going on. I moved out of the apartment less than two months later and dropped out of university that spring.

It's remarkable to me how much I grew up in that year. It was like I had spent the first eighteen years of my life on autopilot and suddenly hit a wall. I had to figure out how to fly again. These days I put on a brave face when I stand at podiums and sit in meetings and dig my fingernails into my palm to keep from crying. I regurgitate a rehearsed string of sentences to address the topic but promptly move past it instead. It happens every time someone asks me to tell the story of how my YouTube channel came to be. Despite being an actor, I hate to lie. Don't get me wrong, I'm alarmingly wonderful at coming up with elaborate stories. I once told a riveting tale to my entire preschool class about my family's recent trip to China—much to my mother's dismay when my teachers asked to see photos of me on the Great Wall. She had to admit that I, her adorable, chubby-cheeked, angelic-looking bundle of blond joy was too creative for her own good. So I'm honest when people ask how my channel got me to where I am today: "It was a hobby through high school and my freshman year of college. Then it was a distraction when I was getting bullied my sophomore year, and it ended up succeeding enough to become my ticket to dropping out of college." Then I make some self-deprecating joke about how I never planned on graduating anyway. And UCR is more like UC-Reject, am I right, ladies?! All the while, I'm pinching the skin of my closed fist and trying not to let my voice quiver. That's the dead giveaway that I'm about one more prodding question away from tears.

I wish someone had told me that bullies don't always have glowing red eyes and fangs. I wish somebody had told me that I wasn't crazy, I wasn't being sensitive, and I wasn't the only one who had gone through something like this. I wish I had had somebody to tell me that I was worth so much more than those girls made me believe. I deserved love and there was nothing wrong with me. So that's what I'm telling you now. I'm telling you that your worth is not determined by what other people think of you. Your value in this world is not resting in the hands of your enemies. You don't have to take it. You don't have to let it slide as something that "comes with the territory" of growing up. You have the power. Don't let them win. If I could go back in time and tell myself all of this, I would. I can't, so instead I'm telling you. Stand up to your bullies and take charge of your own life.

Do not let yourself become a target. Bullies are like vicious dogs—in more ways than one. They can smell fear. Do you hate your red hair and freckles? Are you embarrassed about the way you stutter? Are you ashamed of your after-school job? First of all, you shouldn't be. Own your insecurities and wear them like a medal of honor. Poke fun at yourself, and take pride in the quirks that make you you. By doing that, you take back control. You take away anyone else's power to make fun of you. Bullies seek out victims who will give them the greatest reaction. They feed off breaking other people down to build themselves up. So don't break down. Put on a brave face and grin and bear it. Who knows? Maybe you'll fall in love with your freckles after all.

The English language has countless words that can be strung together to make endless sentences and questions and start a limitless number of conversations. **Use your words,** just like they taught us in kindergarten. Take a note from those quintessential teen flicks where the nerd finally stands up to the quarterback with some eloquent speech about how he actually pities him, because if he's going so far out of his way to make someone else miserable, his own life must really suck. While you might not look like Logan Lerman or have an empowering soundtrack to back you up, you don't have to bow your head and let their words eat you away. Chug a Red Bull, do some Sharpay Evans vocal exercises, and grow some (figurative or literal) balls. But if your bully is built like Dwayne "The Rock" Johnson, forget everything I just said.

Tell somebody. A friend, your mom, a teacher, a counselor, anybody who will listen (maybe not the guy working the McDonald's drive-thru window, though, because he's evaluated on his turnover speed). Don't say it in passing like it's not a big deal or it's something casual. Tell them in a way that makes them understand just how serious it really is. Be uncensored and be honest, and don't stop telling them until they really listen. Getting bullied has such a stigma attached to it, and people are quick to blame the victim. Nobody wants to believe that, outside of the movies, people can be even crueler than the actors playing villains. I hear from people all the time that their parents or friends won't listen when they confide in them that they're being bullied. Getting the brush-off doesn't make what's happening to you okay, it doesn't render your feelings invalid, and it just means you need to keep telling them until it finally sticks. Your feelings are not "your problem," and your problem is not a burden to others—ever. Once you see that, you'll feel that.

There is no such thing as an innocent bystander. Now, you may be one of the rare lucky souls who live a life of sunshine and unicorns. The biggest drama in your life is whether you're team Kourtney or team

Khloé. If so, then hats off to you! But that doesn't mean you're in the clear. I am a firm believer in speaking up for those who might not have the courage to do it themselves. "Seeing injustice and doing nothing is the worst injustice of all." People need to stop turning a blind eye to wrongdoings because they don't want to "get involved" in business that isn't theirs. As human beings with the emotional capability to feel compassion and sympathy and basic morality, making sure others abide by those basic instincts is our business. You wouldn't drive by the scene of an accident without pulling over or at least calling 911. You wouldn't witness a kid falling from his bike and breaking his arm without rushing to his aid. You wouldn't sit by and watch as someone got burned alive. Why is bullying any different? Sure, the spectacle may not be as obvious as arson, but your moral instincts to intervene and help in any way you can should be the same. If everyone only stands for the things that affect them directly, then who's going to come to your aid when you need it the most? Who's going to speak up for you? Nobody. Break that cycle, stand up against injustice just because you know it's wrong, and acknowledge that other people deserve the same basic respect that you do.

If you can get out of the situation, **there is nothing weak about knowing when enough is enough** and making a change. In an ideal world, bullies would see the error of their ways, and I could bake a cake filled with rainbows. But life is not a Tina Fey screenplay, and sometimes people just suck and we need to accept it and move on. That might mean changing jobs, switching soccer teams, moving out, or going to a new school. The number one thing people said to me when I told them I was leaving college was that I was "letting my bullies win," as if I should value my pride more than my mental health. Your bullies only "win" when you take their abuse, so know when you're still strong enough to walk away.

chapter 10

how to make friends

I was going to start this chapter by saying that if you google "how to make f," "friends" would autofill in the first or second spot. But I just tried it, and French toast, fluffy slime, fried rice, and frosting all show up higher. And when you add an *r* to that *f*, you get fried chicken. But don't worry, when you add the *i*, "friends" slides right into home. For some reason I assumed "friends" would be more googled than "fluffy slime," but maybe I'm projecting? It would probably surprise most people to hear, but I was a really shy kid. When I was in preschool and my dad used to take me to the park by our house, I'd sit on the bench with him and point out the kids I wanted to be friends with. Then my dad would walk over and introduce me as I hid behind his legs. He said it took me only a few minutes to warm up to people and let my personality shine through, but that initial moment of ice-breaking was too much for me. While I've grown out of a lot of my preschool habits (like peeing my pants, a disdain for naps, and an addiction to Otter Pops), this one stuck with me.

The steps that go into making and maintaining a friendship run pretty parallel to those of a romantic relationship. As Charlotte York on *Sex and the City* so eloquently summed it up, "Maybe our girlfriends are our soul mates and guys are just people to have fun with." I certainly thought that was true when I was single. Even now, more than four years deep into (hopefully) the last relationship I'll ever have, I still see the truth in this. The most important and life-changing relationships I have had in my life have not been romantic. The people who have shaped me into the person that I am have not been boyfriends or lovers or flings; they've been my best friends. I've had my fair share of fair-weather friends, but it's those Barbs in a sea of Nancys that make it all worth your while. While I believe that most great things take a great deal of time, effort, luck, and some pixie dust, the task of befriending is far easier and way less daunting than four-year-old Meghan thought it to be. If you don't suffer from CRBF (chronic resting bitch face), this chapter and advice probably seem obvious; but if you (like me) constantly look like you've smelled something foul, you'll appreciate this.

how to break the ice without sounding like you want to wear their skin

Dish Out a Compliment

By far the easiest way to make a friend is with a compliment. Compliments are the best icebreakers. If some girl in line at Whole Foods compliments the thigh-high boots I just scored at an amazing Nordstrom sale, you best believe I will be telling her all about it. I made it a point a few years back to give out more compliments to strangers. I came to this decision when I realized how much it brightened my day to receive an unsolicited and out-of-the-blue statement of admiration. At first I was going out of my way to hit that self-imposed quota, but before long I found it to be second nature. Not only could I strike up a conversation with someone in line for the bathroom at a party about how much

I loved their hair color or their T-shirt, but when I was introduced to somebody, I had an automatic go-to. I could break the ice and prove that my resting bitch face was all bark and no bite. Offering a compliment not only shows that you're not in fact a raging bitch but also makes the person you're talking to feel good about themselves, thus opening them up for conversation. Just don't compliment them on something weird.

Find a Common Thread

So you've complimented them on their shirt, and you've run out of things to say about buying clothes with intentional holes in them. That's okay, no need to panic. Now it's time to attempt to find the common thread. This could potentially be very easy, or it could not, but let's be optimistic here. Start with the obvious: Are you at a party? Ask them how they know the host. Are you in class together? Ask them what they thought of the last lecture. Do you play on the same sports team? Bring up how unflattering you find cleats on your feet. Are you both currently scanning the Ralphs ice cream aisle at five p.m. in sweatpants? Ask them what they're watching on Netflix tonight. Finding something you both share is a great way to make conversation. It creates a sense of commonality and gives you something to bond over. If you have attempted to find common ground in five-plus attempts with no reward, abort mission. Or just revert to the compliments and let them think you're cosplaying as the starfish from *Aquamarine*.

Do Your Research

This one only really works if you have some time to prepare and get intel on your future best friends. Sorry, I've been watching way too much *Law & Order: Special Victims Unit*. Some prime examples where this one would work include a wedding, a double date, or any other event where you know your audience before you get there. I probably shouldn't advertise how stellar my (internet) stalking capabilities are, but oh well. I like to be mentally prepared for everything. At first this

probably sounds like a mature and responsible way of life, but ask anyone close to me and they'll tell you it's insane. I have banned the term
"high-maintenance" and have asked everyone to use my preferred term
of "particular." In my ideal world I'd be given ample time to research
and verse myself in a whole slew of background information on whatever I'm doing to ease my anxiety. Sadly, this is not my ideal world,
because Donald Trump is president and Mondays aren't optional. The
only time my friends really indulge this terrible neurotic nature of mine
is when it comes to meeting new people. If I'm headed to meet some
out-of-towners, I'll poll our mutual friends to gain some sense of what
they like and what they do, essentially prepping myself with conversation starters that are surefire hits. This is also key to avoiding potentially
awkward situations resulting from a question that will unavoidably
hit a nerve. Attending a holiday gathering at your significant other's
house? Meeting a truckload of their midwestern cousins? Take the time
to peruse their social media to gain some sense of their interests, then
prod your partner for the land mines to avoid. Now when you meet
cousin Billy Ray, you'll ask him about his favorite cars instead of asking
him where Miley is. Just make sure you don't reference something too
obscure. Nothing says crazy like quoting their graduation Instagram
post verbatim. Be cool—or at least act cool until you know them well
enough to admit that you're pretty much room temp.

is there, like, an e-Harmony
for friends, or is that just tumblr?
where can i meet friends?

Somewhere You Spend Regular Time

I'd advise a location that involves you leaving your bed and putting
pants on. Otherwise, your options for friends are pretty much limited

to your family dog and fandom forum members (which I'm totally not knocking, by the way). This could be a place you're forced to attend, i.e., school, jail, etc. Or it could be a place you've elected to spend your free time, e.g., bookstores, the beach, a coffee shop. Chances are if you're a regular somewhere, somebody else will be too. Not only will you both have that in common, you're both pretty much guaranteed to run into each other frequently. Convenient friends are the fastest friends.

Hobbies and Activities

One of my favorite things about doing extracurriculars when I was growing up was that it exposed me to all different kinds of people. The friends I had in English class were different from the friends I made in community theater, who were all different from my friends I took dance classes with. I was able to meet and befriend people from all different walks of life. Plus, because some of my after-school activities appealed to a larger pool of kids my age, I befriended peers from different schools, some of whom I'd probably never cross paths with otherwise. Having a multitude of different friends doesn't make you a traitor or unfaithful to one particular group. If anything, I think having friends all over the place creates a healthy sense of balance and awareness in your life. When you surround yourself with people who don't live and breathe the same exact life as you, you're able to take a step back and gain perspective on the bigger picture.

Friend Setup

Think of it like a blind date without all the crippling fear of a strange tongue in your mouth or a reenactment of the date Rachel on *Friends* went on with that drug addict Steve. Did I go too far with this analogy? Have I scared you off? Let me reel you back in. A friend setup is probably one of the safest and most successful means to building a friendship. Obviously there is the convenience of the mutual friend card, when you get herded into a friend group based on one or two members you know—automatic and easy assimilation. Alternatively, there is the setup. I find this happens most often with moves and similar career paths. For example, let's say a friend of mine moves to New York all on her lonesome. I'd offer to make the introduction to some friends I have in the city, ones I could see her hitting it off with. Not only do they have a friend in common (me), but they also have a reputable source (me) who knows them each pretty well and has a pretty clear idea whether they'd get along. If the common connection you have with somebody is a mutual friend, chances are you two would get along.

how i ask people to hang out with me without sounding clingy

Invite Them to Join In on an Existing Plan

This is like the vanilla bean of invites. It's not quite as bland as vanilla, but it's just a hair above it without shooting for even white chocolate. It's pretty self-explanatory. One of the major things that terrifies me about asking somebody to hang out is the chance that they'll say no and be weirded out that I offered in the first place. Firstly, this has never happened, which should probably silence my irrational phobia. But of course it does no such thing. Inviting somebody along to an existing plan is like a pressure-free way to gauge the situation and get a feel for their thoughts on a potential friendship. It's pretty easy to tell from this if somebody is only being nice to you to get an employee discount or if they'd actually enjoy spending time with you outside Nordstrom. The real plot twist here? You don't even actually have to have an existing plan; just make it up. "Hey, a group of us were going to go see that new Diane Keaton movie on Friday. Wanna join? No biggie if not! Just thought I'd ask." Easy as that! Now you just have to cast that "group" you referenced. . . .

Plan Something Low-Maintenance

So you've graduated from the invite to the tag-along, and you're ready to get balls-deep into the real shit. Now, let's not all get ahead of ourselves and start whittling monogrammed wooden plaques and brushing up on our friendship bracelet techniques—although, if that's your instinctual reaction, I'm not going to judge you; I'm just going to ask for a bracelet in return. The early stages of a friendship can be just as awkward as the early stages of a romantic relationship. I go out of my way to prevent any uncomfortable situations, just as I do if I am dating somebody. I would never go on a first date to a candlelit dinner overlooking Malibu, partly because romantic gestures like that give me hives and cold sweats, but also because that forces us to rely 100 percent on our conversation without any activity to lean on for support. Same goes with friendships. Plan a group beach day, attend a school event, get ready for a dance together, get a round of drinks after work, agree to carpool together to a birthday party, plan to watch the premiere of *The Bachelor* together. Scheduling to hang out around a shared interest or a convenient occasion has the potential for serious bonding, but it also doesn't put too much pressure on it to happen. If you become the next Snooki and JWoww, score. If you fizzle and fade like Paris and Nicole, well, that's the simple life.

chapter 11

"you can't sit with us" is no longer a funny graphic t-shirt

I was picked last for every PE game of kickball I didn't weasel my way out of with a fake period. When we were left to form our own groups for class projects, I was never sought after. I brushed it off with humor, as I've always done in situations I feel uncomfortable in. No matter how self-aware we are, we don't want our shortcomings to be common knowledge. When it came to lack of athleticism, it was impossible not to notice. Please don't pity me for this or blame any of my classmates. It wasn't their fault that I have zero hand-eye coordination and bruise like a peach. I was and still am well aware that I wouldn't have brought too much to the table if an early pick had been wasted on me. Still, it never felt great. But I could deal with it, because it was based on very obvious facts. What I couldn't deal with was being excluded for no apparent reason. It's something we all go through, no matter how blessed we were in the gene pool. It starts young and fairly innocent. Someone won't share a toy, or a kid on the playground will tell us to dig a hole somewhere else. When we're that little, we don't read too much into it. We bounce back quickly, mostly because when we're that size, the sandbox really does fit us all. Until we reach an age where we form our own preferences and opinions on friends, our circles are pretty much determined by which parents our own parents will tolerate for playdates. Who we hang out with depends much more on convenience and proximity than our actual similarities or interests.

I grew up in a house way up in the hills. Our neighbors consisted of a wealthy older couple who always bought out my magazine drives, a handsome gay couple who both bared a striking resemblance to a Disney prince, a liberal lesbian politician, and my dad's ex-girlfriend. It was like a less wholesome and way more granola version of Stars Hollow. Being an only child, to me these neighbors were far less exciting, especially when the gay couple moved to Australia to open their own hair salon. Thankfully, farther down the hill lived the Johnson family. They had been friends with my parents for as long as I can remember, and by default their two sons became my best friends. Gabe was my age and he was my first love. As the story goes, I had that little boy wrapped around my finger. I don't recall any specific examples, but I don't doubt it. Gabe had an older brother, Adam, who I think was about three years older than us. Between the two of them, I was a spoiled, spoiled princess. When we got to kindergarten, Gabe opted for the more traditional K–5 route, while my parents enrolled me in the hippie-dippie "learning community" version. We drifted apart naturally, as most kids do at that age. Our days were now filled with geography in his case and felt sculpting in mine. We stopped playing wizards and witches in his backyard. I'd say that our elementary romance ended because of a transmission of "cooties," but in reality I never believed in that shit. Plus I was all over Brad and his underbite. As Gabe and I grew apart, I grew closer and closer to the girl who lived at the bottom of the hill. Her name was Mia.

Mia, her sister, Ruby, and I played together in the park across from their house. Our friendship stayed mostly contained to our encounters on the slide or the swings until Mia and I both began our first day of kindergarten in Tim's class. I feel like I need to clarify that Tim was our teacher. In this weird alternative learning thing, we referred to all our teachers by their first name. I really don't have a ton of memories of becoming friends with Mia and Ruby. For as long as I can remember, our moms have been best friends and they've always been more like my sisters. I think a large part of that has to do with how our school was set up. We had the same teacher for every course (except PE) and we stayed with the same group of ten kids all six years. It was a multi-age program, which basically meant that every year we'd always be with our grade (a whopping ten kids), but we'd alternate with filling the other ten or so seats with the grade above us or the grade below us. So while Mia and I had friends both younger and older than us, we, along with our friend Zoey, stayed together all through elementary school.

When middle school rolled around, there was quite the debate over where we'd all end up. With such a liberal elementary experience, most parents were hell-bent on continuing a nontraditional route. Mia and I toured a school thirty minutes away, and while we both loved the idea of the middle school version of where we just came from, our parents did not love the idea of that commute. So instead we enrolled in White Hill Middle School, the least granola, most stereotypical middle school in our district. Out of our very small fifth-grade class, an even smaller number joined us there. It was an adjustment, to say the least. I had spent my entire academic life in the same classroom with the same three teachers and the same dozen classmates. I had never received a grade, never taken a standardized test, never opened a textbook, was taught to refer to all my teachers by their first names, and for the life of me could not name how many stars were on the American flag or what they represented or what each state's capital was. We had spent the last six years in this bubble of inclusion and creative energy. Suddenly it popped and it threw me for a loop. The changes started right off the bat. A few weeks before classes started, a pamphlet was sent to our house. It outlined my schedule for the "semester," what teachers I had, what "periods" their classes were, what "room numbers" they'd be located in, and what "courses" I'd be taking. I called Mia up landline-style. We decoded these foreign packets and quickly realized that we didn't have a single class together. I panicked. I begged my mom to fix it or to call somebody who could fix it. I couldn't even comprehend being plopped into this massive pond without Mia by my side. Obviously my mom couldn't do anything about it. Mia and I were already deemed the alternative learning "freaks" before the first day.

I swallowed my instinctual terror and vowed to maintain an optimistic attitude about middle school. So, in the last week of August, I packed my purple JanSport covered in political pins and patches and threw on my thigh-high rainbow toe socks, a pair of platform flip-flops, a sparkly red dress, a leather trench coat lined with pink cheetah-print fur, and finally my signature piece, an inconspicuous and slightly eerie Princess Diana replica tiara. I probably should have just worn a "Pick on Me, I'm Not Normal" sign to save myself the pit stains, but let's move on. As I'm sure you can assume, my getup did not go unnoticed by my new classmates. I naively took their wide-eyed stares as looks of admiration and sheer envy of my lewk. It only took a few minutes into homeroom for me to assess my classmates and realize just how much I stuck out. I don't know if I immediately registered that as a negative thing, but I don't think there was any way I took it as a good way to start the year, either. To complete the American school movie stereotype, our seating assignments were up for grabs. Mrs. Wells's only instruction to limit the chaos was that each section of desks must consist of three boys and three girls. I immediately looked to Michael, the only one from my elementary school in this sixth-grade classroom. All the girls in denim miniskirts and Etnies sat at one table with all the guys in Heelys. All the girls in low-rise skinny jeans sat with the guys with sagging jeans, and all the girls in soccer shorts sat with the guys in track pants. I sat with Michael, with his long, curly hair and rolly backpack; another boy with long hair named Brandon (who would later attempt to bomb the music classroom with a homemade Molotov cocktail); Cody, whose resemblance to Ryan Atwood spanned both looks and delinquent demeanor; some other girl who I'm forgetting; and finally, the most important member of our table group: a girl with lime-green braces, a frizzy low ponytail tucked behind her ears, and a multicolored Lucky Brand hoodie covered in butterflies, zipped all the way up to her neck. Her name was Sydney.

To this day, when Sydney and I tell the story of our friendship, we attribute it to us bonding over the fact that we were the two ugliest girls in Mrs. Wells's sixth-grade class. We were both completely aware of it. We also say this without fishing for any sort of affirmations or skepticism at our ugly duckling stages. We're both pretty fucking glad they happened; otherwise we'd be just as dull and devoid of personality as the kids who were always pretty. Ugly builds character. Ugly kids have to work twice as hard for people to like them. We had to be twice as smart (in Sydney's case) or twice as funny (in my case). So while some of our classmates peaked before their sweet sixteens, Sydney and I constantly remind each other that we in fact were the lucky ones. Plus, as far as we're concerned, we grew out of that stage. The realization is summed up by seventeen-year-old Sydney: "At this rate I'll be a fucking supermodel by the time I'm thirty." Beyond our backward, shallow way of becoming friends, it turned out that Sydney and I had way more in common than just our unfortunate appearances. We were both bookworms, had an embarrassingly unwavering love of show tunes, and spent all our free moments discussing how much better life would have been if we hadn't been born muggles. By our first recess bell, Sydney and I had already bonded over clementines and Capri Sun. We were also excited to introduce each other to our elementary school friends at lunch. When Mrs. Wells excused us, Sydney and I ventured toward the blacktop to merge our circles together into one big happy loser family. We met up with Sydney's friend Jamie, who happened to be with Mia, whom she had befriended in their home-room. I looked for our friend Zoey, but she had played club soccer that summer. She traded in her hippie-kid freak status for a pair of Soffe shorts and an Adidas bag with her team name on it. I don't really re-member a lot about my falling-out with Zoey, but I do remember that it wasn't mutual. I remember crying on the bus and being really sad and asking my mom if she could ask Zoey's mom to convince her to be friends with me again. Whatever memories I blocked out from that left some scars, because even into high school I couldn't shake the feeling of betrayal.

It didn't take long before Mia followed suit. I mean, I don't blame her. I can't sit here and say that if I had looked like she did at that age I wouldn't have swooped up that popularity on a silver platter. Mia was (and still is, I might add) drop-dead gorgeous. If Facebook existed back then, she would have been on one of those fake news articles that says, like, "World's most beautiful girl—and SHOCKER she's only 12!" In addition to being way too pretty to be in middle school, Mia was also incredibly good at anything she tried. Soccer? Great—wanna join the club? Music? Oh, yeah, lemme just learn guitar and write songs and sing them at open-mic nights. She was a preteen manic pixie dream girl, and I was the best friend's body double. Before anyone gets the wrong idea or I get a screaming phone call from Mia, let me state that she didn't ditch me or exclude me. I was still invited to every birthday party, every Friday night sleepover, and everything in between. But for the first time since we befriended each other in our neighborhood park, I didn't feel like I belonged. I sat next to her as we blew out our candles on our joint birthday cake, but I still felt like an outsider. I wondered how much of the reason we remained so close was because of our obligation to our mothers. I wondered if Mia wished I was athletic and popular like her or if she was happy she didn't have to share the spotlight. I wondered if she liked her more "normal" friends better than me. I wondered if she was ashamed of our upbringing when she stopped wearing tie-dye and pants with bells on them and started wearing eyeliner and PacSun jeans. Before long I retired my tiara (mostly because the principal had called my parents and said it was a distraction to the other students) and started wearing white peds socks with low-top Converse sneakers and bootcut jeans with velour hoodies. While I am not upset at all at this style change, there's still a part of me that feels a pang of sadness knowing it came from that desire to fit in. I was so terrified of losing Mia to the middle school social scene that I molded myself into that image. As far as I know, Mia had no intentions of ghosting me as a friend. Reflecting on it now, I realize that I was the only one building up and perpetuating that worry.

Middle school turned into high school. Our friend groups expanded, and Mia and my interests in after-school activities changed. I kept up with theater and dance, while Mia continued music and started photography. We made new friends in different classes, and our weekly group sleepovers were rain checked and rain checked again. My instinctual reaction was to feel jaded and abandoned when I saw Mia laughing with new classmates and flirting with guys I didn't know the pro-con lists of. All the while, I was doing the same thing. She wasn't leaving me behind, and I wasn't leaving her behind. We were growing up—maybe not side by side as we had in the past, but we were still doing it together. So instead of associating that change and growth with exclusion, I let it happen. I let myself grow too. We've known each other for over twenty years, and Mia, Ruby, and I still consider each other sisters more than friends. They're among the few people who have ever seen me fully break down, and they're still the ones who I can count on for absolutely anything. Though we reference our younger years with ears reddened by embarrassment and pleas to silence the anecdotes recounted at our own personal expense, I think we're grateful not only that we had that space to grow up to be such different women but that we did it judgment-free. Except for my darkening transition lenses and some of Mia's ex-boyfriends . . . those we will never live down.

In addition to school, I faced cliques in summer camp, but that's nothing to really write home about (pun intended). When it comes to things that honor seniority or involve reputation or repertoire, a hierarchy is pretty much unavoidable. There will always be somebody with more experience who is more comfortable than you are. We all endure that freshman first-day-of-school feeling whenever we enter a situation in which we're the new kid. While I don't think this happens any less as you get older, I will say that I think you care a little less—or at least I like to think I'm caring a little less. But who knows, that might be bullshit. I've accepted the fact that a little bit of Regina George exists in everybody. Because there aren't enough buses in the world to solve that problem, I've compiled what I think to be the most helpful and constructive advice when it comes to cliques.

Let's start with the simple truth that **sometimes it's just in your head**. I know sometimes it's not, but hear me out. At least for me, I know I'm one to build things up in my head and let them snowball pretty far out of control. I tend to read a little too much into things, and if I indulge that, it won't be long before I've come to the conclusion that the person or people in question hate me. I find myself projecting those fears when I'm in the early stages of a friendship. When I'm going through a big life change, I begin to worry about the longevity in every relationship around me. So how do you figure out if you're being shut out or if it is all in your head? Well, it takes some blind trust, patience, and a little perspective. I know, probably not what you wanted to hear. Let's say you wait it out for a while and you discover you had not blown things out of proportion and your inklings were correct. Even with that as the outcome, your ability to control and silence that negative and neurotic voice in your head is far more valuable than a spot in any coveted clique.

It's easy to retreat into a corner when you feel like you're being pushed there. If we start to feel like we're being left behind, we do our best to become the least offensive versions of ourselves. We hope that if we don't make a peep, nobody will notice that we tagged along. Most of us could stand to be a bit more assertive when it comes to the course of our own lives, so **make the first move.** The easiest way to be left behind is by letting it happen. I'm not saying to start crying and screaming but rather bite the bullet before it gets to that point. So much of the drama I experienced growing up boiled down to an epic game of he said, she said. Even adults will tell you how much communication plays a part in their issues to this day. If you feel animosity coming from a friend, there is a huge chance that it stems from a major misunderstanding. And maybe it's not even that! Maybe it goes back to this fear being all in your head, and just by reaching out and spending some time together you'll come to that conclusion. On the flip side, asking someone straight up what their deal is is without fail the quickest, easiest, and most straightforward way to get your answer.

Let's say both those options or suggestions completely don't apply to your situation, because, honestly, they won't always. Sometimes people grow up to be worse people than when they started. I'm sure Hitler and Stalin were cute babies, but, shit, look what they became. **There isn't always a reason behind why people do the things they do.** As hard as that is to accept in daily life, it's even harder when you're a pawn in the game and you get crushed wizards chess style. As painful and confusing as it is, take solace in the fact that it happens to everyone. Seriously, everyone. Norah Jones wouldn't have the career she does today if socializing was easy, and therapists wouldn't keep the chaise longue furniture industry afloat. I know being told that what you're going through is normal doesn't make it feel any less shitty, but at least humor me and let me try to force some fake adult enlightenment on you.

First of all, **friendships should be mutual.** If somebody doesn't want to be your friend, why on earth do *you* want to be *their* friend? If you are the only one invested in this, not only are they going to treat you like a moldy everything bagel, you're going to *feel* like a moldy everything bagel.

Stand up for yourself. You are an active participant in your life, and you are entitled to remind people of that. I am all for setting a better example than what was done to you and being the bigger person. I think that's great. But I also think sometimes Becky needs to be called what she is—a bitch.

Don't squeeze if you don't fit. I won't go so far as to say that socializing is easy, because that would be a downright lie. But the right relationships should be easy.

Finding your people is like piecing together a jigsaw puzzle. Sure, there are some pieces you could soak in Kool-Aid and let get all soggy and squish them together so they kind of fit even though it makes the sky look like it has the chicken pox. But why go through all that effort when there's a piece that fits perfectly? We're quick to accept our current reality as our lot in life and we learn to settle without even realizing we're doing so. So know what you're worth, what you deserve, and rest assured it's out there. Don't settle for anything less, because **being surrounded by the wrong people is far lonelier than being alone.**

growing
up(ward)

KARMA'S A BIGGER BITCH THAN I COULD EVER BE. AND I CAN BE A MASSIVE BITCH.

chapter 12

the first time i got drunk

The first time I ever tried alcohol I was twelve. My best friend Sydney and I were feeling rebellious at my family's Christmas party, and we snuck a teacup filled with spiked eggnog into the bathroom. Oh, we also snuck in the six-year-old girl we were responsible for watching over. Meghan Rienks, role model since 1993. We locked the door behind us, all three of our bodies crammed over the toilet, and began to drink. Do I need to clarify that it was just me and Sydney participating? Like, if you read that and assumed that we were passing the booze to a first grader, then I think I really need to evaluate how my character comes across. The teacup couldn't have held more than four ounces, but Sydney and I barely made it through half before we agreed we were already "drunk." We flushed the rest down the toilet. Let the record state that we were nowhere near inebriated. I'm pretty sure I had felt stronger effects from a shot of NyQuil and my eucalyptus humidifier. But I mean, I was twelve. If I had decided I was drunk from three table-spoons of a slightly spiked holiday beverage, so be it. We spent the rest of the night AIM-ing our crushes and misspelling words in our away messages. We thought we were the fucking shit.

The next time I drank alcohol was about two years later. It was the summer I turned fourteen and I was spending it on a mother-daughter vacation in Mount Shasta with my mom, her best friend, and her two daughters, Ruby and Mia.

Her older daughter, Ruby, was the responsible one of our trio. She was sixteen at the time. She had a boyfriend and was in a band and she was way too cool for her little sister, Mia, and me. Naturally, Mia and I wanted to spend every second with Ruby. Usually we were pretty good at latching onto her and piggybacking on her social plans, but this year she had brought her boyfriend on the vacation. While that fact did not deter us—if anything, it made us more determined—their combined effort to escape us was ultimately successful. Ruby's absence, paired with our mothers' laissez-faire attitudes, meant that Mia and I were left to entertain ourselves. I could lie and say we spent the first hour playing an innocent game of go fish, but in reality, the second we realized we had been left to our own devices, we made a beeline for the ample alcohol stash our mothers had packed. Being two fourteen-year-olds without cable or access to MTV, our knowledge of alcohol was pretty slim. So, as if we were selecting books from the Scholastic fair, we based our picks entirely on which bottles had the most enticing packaging. We both agreed that the pretty white bottle decorated with oranges and flowers seemed like the best bet and was the closest thing to tasting like a Slurpee. We unscrewed the cap and swigged a sizable gulp of triple sec. We were then met by the immediate burn and regret one has when they drink a sweet liquor straight, and we reached for the closest thing to mask the taste: a jar of Betty Crocker vanilla frosting. With teenage taste buds about as sophisticated as Buddy the elf's, we found this unlikely pairing to be quite palatable. Before long we were scraping Betty's nooks and crannies. I don't think we even began to feel the effects of the alcohol before we felt the effects of the pounds of sugar and high-fructose corn syrup we had just ingested. We barely made it to the campsite showers before Mia and I felt the repercussions of our rebellion by way of the murky white liquid that burned far more coming up than it did going down.

I spent the next two years of my life standing strong against alcohol, drugs, and any other related rebellion. No, I did not find Jesus. I found the Jonas Brothers, and they had found Jesus. Naturally, I upped my morals to up my chances in joining Nicholas in holy matrimony. This is a slight exaggeration, but honestly not by much. My freshman year of high school I became close with this girl named Kaitlin and her sister, Juliana. And yes, this is the same girl from the "Toxic Friendships" chapter.

I don't know the origin of it, but at that time both Kaitlin and Juliana were really, really against drinking and drugs. It was refreshing, in a high school full of kids experimenting, to have friends whose interests spanned more than fuzzy memories of house parties. We spent our weekends making bad music video parodies and quoting Johnny Depp movies. It was innocent and fun and it lasted for a good two years. Which was just about as long as Kaitlin and I stayed friends.

I can still remember the expression of sheer excitement when I told my friends Emma and Sydney that I wanted to get drunk. They had made me swear months before that when I grew out of my "phase" they could be the first ones to get me drunk. I obliged and held up that promise. Emma enlisted her boyfriend to buy us bottles, and I told him to pick the fruitiest vodka he could get his underaged hands on. Thinking back on it, it's honestly laughable how big of a deal it was to us at that age. Texting in T9 under our desks about what he had picked out and how he was going to get it to us and where we were going to drink it, we put more thought into this plan than I had into my entire high school career. We were going to have a sleepover at Sydney's house and we'd ask her parents if we could sleep in the guesthouse for a "change of pace." They agreed because, honestly, looking at Sydney and me, I'm pretty sure they thought we could stand to rebel a little more. So that Friday night Emma arrived at Sydney's with her sleepover bag packed with the standard supplies as well as a fifth of watermelon Smirnoff wrapped in a pair of summer camp sweatpants. For some reason the seclusion of the guesthouse didn't seem safe enough, so we went the extra mile and locked ourselves in the bathroom and proceeded to drink while sitting in the shower. We took it slow, both their eyes on me with excitement and nerves as I took my first sip, to which I reminded them this wasn't my first taste, just the first time I'd (actually) be intoxicated. I'm sure I was only about three swigs in before I started to feel the warmth in my fingertips and easy laughter escaping my lips. And that was it. Three sixteen-year-old girls sitting in a shower, giggling, drinking, and feeling far cooler than we looked.

In less than a year I had gone from the antithesis of a party girl to the party queen herself. It started off pretty gradual, a couple of shots before the school dance, a low-key after-party, the occasional "My parents are out of town; let's have six people over" kind of thing. But we got older and our parents assumed with age came wisdom and common sense. We were allotted freer rein and we just got sloppier and sloppier. I'm generalizing here; this mostly applies to me. I felt like the best version of myself when I was drunk, the person I always had wanted to be. No longer was my confidence a ruse; I actually felt it. I felt cool and, for once, I didn't second-guess everything I said and did. If I was drunk, the thought of conversation didn't make my palms sweat. Flirting with a boy didn't seem so panic inducing, and not giving a fuck was so much simpler. I thrived on being the center of attention for something other than being ridiculed for a bad grade. I was never going to be the smartest girl in class, or the prettiest, but suddenly none of that mattered. It didn't matter that only the year before I was not worth a first kiss or a second glance. Now I was crazy and reckless and fun. I was a hot fucking mess, but I didn't care. For once in my life, I felt like I knew who I was. I had an identity, and she was fucking cool.

I was that girl your parents were terrified of you becoming, so they locked you in your room until your eighteenth birthday. I'd make out with a thirty-year-old dude to get us into a hookah lounge. I'd be the first to suggest body shots and I'd be the first to offer myself up as the body. I loved the reactions of the guys at my promiscuous behavior and I loved the jealous looks of the girls. That validation and false confidence was like a high. The more I drank, the more I liked the girl I became. Despite the amount of alcohol I had consumed in my short yet potent drinking life, I had no idea how to drink. Up until my twenties, I had never gotten drunk without blacking out, or at least browning out. I was a total lightweight. I could easily get comfortably inebriated from two to three shots, but I never stopped there. While it didn't take much to get me drunk, I could handle a lot more alcohol. I held it like some NASA-grade impenetrable tank. I rarely got visibly sloppy. Even in a blacked-out belligerent state, I could seem dead sober, thus raising no objections from my friends. I didn't fall or stumble or pass out with my shoes on. I was the last one standing and I was the first one awake the next morning. I had finally become the best at something; it's just not the thing you really want to be best at.

Party girl Meghan took a (much-needed) ten-month hiatus due to mono. I could hardly stay awake past nine, let alone climb on top of a table to sing Miley Cyrus. By the time second semester of my senior year rolled around, I was newly single, free of academic responsibilities (or at least the ones that would affect my postgraduation education), and ready to reclaim my title. If you thought I had had no inhibitions before, subtract a long-term relationship and factor in the vengeful freedom of singleness. You'll have a whole new kind of beast. Let it be said that my ex-boyfriend was not controlling or overbearing by any means. With the rest of the guys, he egged us girls on to make out. He had no issues with my perpetually half-naked nature, probably because a lot of that time the circumstances favored him. Thankfully, I was blacked out for most of this period. It's not something I'd love to share, but for the sake of the story, I'll give you three highlights (retold to me) to paint a picture:

1. My underwear was found in a VCR player and posted on Facebook for me to claim ownership of, which I did.

2. I crawled into bed butt naked with my best friend. When she asked where I had been, I told her a freshman was fingering me while I played Bubble Trouble.

3. I tried to convince my friend Austin to make out with me after prom while his date (and girlfriend) sat next to him. I proceeded to tell him that I didn't think she was that cool, anyway.

I'm not proud of some of the stupid shit I did, but that's just the learning curve of teenage rebellion. There's a part of me that really wants to skip over this next thing, but I don't think you'd understand my future relationship with alcohol without it. So here it is.

In the spring of senior year, my friend Claire threw a house party. I had originally gone with my two best friends, Sydney and Jake. Early in the night they went home to study, and I assured them I was fine to crash there, as I had done so many times before. Without the social comfort of my best friends, I compensated for my awkwardness with more alcohol. Honestly, I hardly remember them leaving. As the night went on, it just got fuzzier and fuzzier. At some point I'm sure I deemed none of the boys make-out material, so I tapped out, settling into the extra bed in my friend's room. I don't know how long I was out for, but at some point I began to realize that one of my male classmates had slipped into bed with me, half-naked, his hands and lips all over me. I was wasted. That was a fact. I didn't know how much I had drunk or what time it was, but I knew I didn't want this. I don't know if I said no. I don't know if the reason I don't remember how far he got before he passed out is because it wasn't too far or if it was because my brain chose to spare me from replaying that night more than I already do right now. The last thing I remember was the rustling of sheets. My friend Claire was in the bed next to us the whole time.

I woke up the next morning to Sydney and Jake at the foot of the bed. They had returned to the house to reclaim me after they hadn't heard from me all night. I blinked away the sleep, and before the tears could even come, they were silently peeling the covers off me, collecting my belongings, and guiding me to the car. We never really talked about it. We didn't have to. They knew. It was written all over my face. The guy told people we hooked up, and I didn't correct him. Part of me wanted so badly for that to be the truth. I tried to rewrite that night in hopes of ditching that weight I felt in the pit of my stomach. I told myself that I was asking for it, that this was just another stupid thing I'd done while drunk. I'd made out with my fair share of embarrassing guys, but this was different. I flinched anytime anyone tapped me on the shoulder, and I fought to swallow bile every time I passed the guy in the hallway. I couldn't deal with it. For a long time I didn't. It took me four years to relinquish the entirety of the blame onto him. I was too drunk to consent and that's all that matters. To which you'll probably wonder why I felt the need to include this story in this section. If I don't assume any guilt for what happened, why group it here? Because, at seventeen years old, I refused to be a victim of a sexual assault. I couldn't erase it, so instead I vowed to be that promiscuous, wild child of a girl who was "all for" whatever had happened that night.

By the time I began my freshman year of college, I had officially succeeded in becoming that girl. Any constraints or limitations I may have had in high school, such as parents and curfews, were eliminated with college. I moved 449.9 miles away from home and I had never been more terrified. When it became abundantly clear that my parents weren't going to pick up and let me bail on the whole "higher education" thing, I made the most out of a terrible situation. If you have never been to Riverside, California, congratulations. If you love Riverside, California, you're lying—or your idea of a good time is chugging Four Lokos in 106-degree weather. I fell into line with the latter.

There's not really much to explain involving drinking in the next few years. I was a pretty typical college sorority girl. Did we party more than some other people? Probably. Did we party less than others? I mean, yeah, considering Riverside was the meth capital of the world. I light-weight "dated" a guy who turned out to be a drug addict—I thought he was just stupid—and we lived next to a drug cartel. Seriously, it could have been a lot worse. I'll spare you the pretty standard stories. To pay tribute to the rest of my (short-lived) college career, I'll highlight some of my finest moments. Please note that I don't say this to glamorize underage drinking, or losing control, but rather to hopefully make you feel better about your alcohol-driven embarrassments.

1. I wore a Twister mat to an ABC (anything but clothes) party. Because I was drunk when I made the costume, I thought duct-taping it to my body was a stellar idea. At four a.m., when I finally got home and decided I no longer wanted to be in said costume, I woke up my sleeping roommate (who I had met less than a week prior) and made her cut it off my body. I'm also pretty sure I did a naked shimmy, which I don't think she appreciated.

2. The day after Halloween (which was a Tuesday), I woke up fully clothed (which wasn't saying a lot, as I was an "office ho" and was wearing a bandage skirt, a blazer, and black bra) with nine-teen tally marks on my stomach, the result of a drink-off I insti-gated with fraternity pledges. Allegedly, I won. I also fell down a flight of concrete stairs.

3. At the time of the Jewish frat's annual "Jew-monji" party (*l'chaim*), I was dating an upperclassman who lived at the frat house. I had spent the night there like I spent most nights, but this time my morning walk hit a new level of shame. I had worn a cheetah-print scarf as a top and a matching strip of fabric as a skirt. In our drunken disrobing, my skirt ripped and I was left with

nothing but a left sandal and my scarf/top thing. As I began to ask him to borrow a pair of basketball shorts, he excitedly offered me something with much more of a . . . statement: a pair of white booty shorts that had his fraternity letters printed on the butt—"So everyone knows where you spent the night," he explained. At that time, it was the most romantic gesture anyone had ever made to me. I arrived at the dorm dining hall clad in my cheetah tube top, the groupie booty shorts, and my left sandal in hand, only to realize I had lost my keys as well. The saddest part was nobody looked twice.

4. At a campus concert festival—accurately titled "Heat," because Riverside thrived at a solid 109 degrees—I attended a pregame at the frat of the guy I was "dating" at the time. (Essentially, I just made out with him a lot in hopes he'd ask me to be his date to their formal in Vegas. Which he did. But then he uninvited me the night of, when I was less than enthused that he had offered our room as the "drug zone"—convenient, because he was bringing all the drugs. I know, I'm SUPER uptight.) I feared that security at the concert would be too tight for me to sneak sips of his drink once we were inside, so I decided to drink enough at the pregame to "last me all night." I must have had at least ten shots at the frat house before somehow convincing him to buy me two Four Lokos, which I downed in a matter of seconds. By the time we arrived back on campus, I was too drunk to walk. With the boys' arms casually wrapped around my waist, we attempted to get me in without drawing attention to my (incredibly obvious) underage inebriation. We were doing pretty well (I was told) until I dropped my student ID. As the gentlemanly police officer bent down to pick it up, I vomited in his face. I'm really not sure how we still got in, but we did. A rapper performed. I have no memory of it. I also have no memory of rolling into a ditch, hiding in the bushes, getting kicked out of the concert, being carried to my

room, falling asleep with my clothes on, sleeping through the fire alarm, or punching my roommate in the face when she insisted I evacuate with the rest of the building. I woke up the next morning in a pool of my own vomit and a very angry roommate.

I'd like to take this time to formally apologize (again) to my roommate Ava. Ava, you were way too good to me. I didn't deserve you.

You're probably expecting me to have this earth-shattering story or revelation that completely changed the way I looked at alcohol. But the truth is, the only reason I cut back on partying my sophomore year was because my college "best friends" decided to exile me and I didn't have anyone to hang out with. I was underage, so drinking alone wasn't really an option. It's not that I was anti-drinking; it was that my former friends were anti-Meghan. I went out occasionally with a few girls who still acknowledged my presence, and of course I went to house parties back in my hometown, but I didn't drink nearly as often or as much as I had before. That false confidence of my drunk persona had been completely shattered. I constantly felt like I was walking on eggshells, holding on to people who wanted nothing more than to see me fall. I dropped out of college and moved to LA a few months later, and I found myself in a somewhat similar situation.

Over the next two years I slowly lost touch with the girl I used to be. As hard as I tried to hold on to the friends I'd made in LA, it became abundantly clear that I was the only one invested. I threw myself into work and auditions and absolutely anything to distract me from the fact that I was basically completely alone in the city. I had no intention of cleaning up my act. Honestly, I would have killed to get trashed at some party full of twentysomething Vine stars. But it's pretty hard to get invited to parties when the friendliest person you interact with is the cashier at Target.

As somebody who suffers from generalized social anxiety, I viewed alcohol as a crutch to compensate for my nerves. I'm not going to lie and say that it doesn't work, because it does. Alcohol makes you more comfortable and at ease, and there's really nothing wrong with that unless there is. I believe lots of people can maintain a healthy relationship with alcohol. I am just not one of those people. In my mid-twenties, most of my peers spend their Monday nights watching *The Bachelor* and drinking wine, their Thursdays at happy hour, and their weekends at bottomless brunch. And they're fine; I'm not. Would events and parties be easier with a drink in my hand? Yeah! But it's a temporary Band-Aid to a bigger psychological problem. Instead of using alcohol to cope with my insecurities and anxiety, I go to therapy. And I'm saving myself quite the hangover—maybe an emotional one, but at least I'm not barfing. Who knows, maybe down the road my stomach will be able to handle it and my therapy will have paid off and I can learn how to enjoy a glass of wine. Just don't let me be one of those Etsy "It's wine o'clock" kitschy people.

While my party girl days are behind me, I still look back on that era with a mix of nostalgia, embarrassment, and a longing to have done it a little better. If I could go back in time to the night Sydney, Emma, and I sat on the shower floor with the bottle of Smirnoff, I wouldn't pass on the shot or pledge sobriety for life. That desire to experiment is natural. I'm not going to tell you not to drink. That's not realistic. Instead, here's the advice you're more likely to take.

1. Drink smarter, not harder. Be strategic with your alcohol consumption rather than just going fucking ham. A shot has the highest percentage of alcohol and it's also the smallest amount of liquid and the thing you can drink the quickest. A beer has a lower percentage of alcohol and it's going to take you a while to drink. So if your friends are drinking beer and you're pounding shots, you're only going to be able to keep that up until everything comes back up. I mean vomit. Take it from a girl who exclusively drank shots: Save them for birthdays, spring breaks in Mexico, and weddings of people you hate. Mixed drinks will not only (hopefully) have something in them that'll hydrate you, they also come with teeny-tiny straws that take forever to drink out of. Actually, don't use those. Save the turtles! Plus, if you have a drink in your hand, it prevents you from doing a two-handed fist pump (always a bad idea) and it gives you an automatic out if some creep starts pressuring you to participate in an ice luge shot.

2. Mixed drinks are great. Mixing your alcohol is not. Beer before liquor, never sicker; liquor before beer, in the clear. That's the phrase, and it doesn't just roll off the tongue—it's also true. Choose a drink and stick to it all night. If you're too noncommittal for that, at least stick to the same alcohol or in the same color family. Which brings me to:

3. Find your signature. Drink, that is. Find a drink that doesn't taste like nail polish remover, one you can confidently order at a bar and that you're familiar enough with that you can gauge the outcome of your night based on your consumption.

4. SpongeBob needs water and you do too. Alternate between one alcoholic beverage and one glass of water through the night. Booze is a diuretic, and the hangover you'll experience the next morning is mostly due to the dehydration from the alcohol. HYDRATE AS IT HAPPENS! Not only is it going to make your morning much more pleasant, it's also going to keep you from drinking too fast. It takes twenty minutes for a drink to hit your system, so sip on some water before you decide you need the next one.

5. Work on your tolerance. I have no idea why we think we sound cool as fuck when we brag about how much alcohol we can drink or how much it takes us to get drunk. Like, okay, congratulations, you had to ingest three bottles' worth of white wine to get a buzz and I'm over here four sips deep and pretty tipsy? Who is winning here?!?! I get it—the more you drink, the more of a tolerance you build up. But I mean, it's like getting antibiotics: you don't want your body to get too used to them and build up a tolerance. That's how the Black Death happened, right? (I don't know; I went to alternative learning.) Now, if you're drinking a lot, no shade. I mean, have you read this chapter? Naturally, in doing so, your tolerance will increase and it'll take you more and more to feel the buzz. To prevent building a tolerance so high it requires stomach pumping, take breaks or "dry spells" from drinking whenever it's taking you *a lot* to get drunk. This was our shit in college. If we didn't drink for two weeks before winter formal, not only would we not look bloated for the first time since orientation, we'd also need way less to feel it. (Also, if you stop wearing makeup and only wear laundry day clothes the week before, when you show up to the event looking fucking amazing, you'll look *even better*, because everyone was so used to seeing you look like a troll all week. You're welcome.)

6. Don't get cross faded. The first time I did, I hooked up with a freshman . . . when I was a senior. The second time, I woke up in the bed of a guy I had never met before, fourteen miles away from where I lived. Nothing good comes out of getting cross faded, trust me. Weed + booze = bad. On the other hand, I actually know a ton of people who can handle this fine. Maybe I'm just jealous.

7. Everclear is not your friend. It sounds like a winter-fresh mint, right? WRONG. I honestly have no idea what Everclear even is, but I drank it (do as I say, not as I do) and the rest of the night is a mystery to me. On the bright(ish) side, my friend also hard-core blacked out, so neither of us could blackmail the other on the embarrassing shit we did. Ignorance really can be bliss. Also absinthe—stay away from that shit.

8. Watch your drink. Watch it like a goddamn mother of a newborn. Do not let that shit leave your sight. Date rape drugs are a real thing, not just a plot twist in a *Law & Order: SVU* episode. One of the first nights of my freshman year I was roofied. One second I was at a house party dancing with some guy, and the next I was waking up in my dorm room. I had no clue what had happened and I was too embarrassed (I shouldn't have been) to ask anyone. I didn't find out, but you can be sure as shit I never left my drink unattended there again. You wouldn't take candy from a stranger as a kid, so why the hell are you taking "tequila" from a guy who's wearing three polos and cargo shorts?

Only take drinks made by people you trust, and watch them like the stingy guac guy at Chipotle. Or, better yet, be the self-sufficient boss-ass bitch that you are and make your own drinks! Not only will it guarantee that you'll be drinking your favorite drink all night, but it's *highly unlikely* that you're gonna slip some ketamine in your own cocktail. Unless you do, in which case I'd suggest maybe working on a more robust schedule of extracurriculars, because that just seems a little extreme. Take up knitting.

9. Drunchie. This is how twenty-four-hour Mexican restaurants stay in business. I have no shame in saying that my favorite part of going out was, hands down, stopping at the drive-through on the ride back. We'd be getting ready to go out and in the middle of applying winged eyeliner I'd already be thinking about what I was going to drunkenly snack on when I got home. I am a firm believer in this process. In combination with a substantial meal prior to drinking (seriously, do it, otherwise you will get chlamydia and die—not really; you'll just get really sick), finishing your night with a midnight snack isn't just satisfying, I'm pretty convinced it helps the hangover the next morning. I'm not going to lie to you and pretend my high school drunchies weren't entire Baskin-Robbins sheet cakes and microwaved quesadillas, and my college ones weren't Carl's Jr. fries and questionably lukewarm chicken wings. None of the above was even worth it, because chances are I was too drunk to remember or enjoy ingesting them. Save your P.F. Chang's leftovers and the expensive ice cream for when you're coherent enough to enjoy it. Drunchies are the time to clean out your fridge—the ends of bread, stale cereal, and your least favorite yogurt flavors.

I hope this chapter taught you something, or enlightened you, or at least didn't make you regret buying this book for anyone under twenty-one. I could say something inspirational and all-encompassing here, but I just admitted that I slept in a pile of my own vomit, so I've got some more self-reflecting to do before I start spewing motivational quotes. I'll just leave you again with the image of somebody extracting my lacy pink Victoria's Secret thong from a VCR player. You're welcome. Also, please tell me you know what a VCR player is.

chapter 13

10 ways to trick people into thinking you have your shit together

You know those people you see at the airport who aren't struggling to pull their laptop out of their bag, and despite that they're wearing a sun hat, they don't have hat hair? They lift their luggage into the overhead compartment with no struggle or forced help from the Dennis Quaid dad type behind them. You just look at them with envy and realize that, while you can vote and buy a lottery ticket and do various "adult" things, you are just a big fat fibber. *That* person is an adult. You are a giant kid with responsibilities. I am also not sure why this is so aviation-specific.

I don't have my shit together by any means. I have a cavity that is starting to resemble the Grand Canyon and I haven't gotten my roots done in months. Sometimes I eat popcorn for dinner and my gas tank is literally never full. To the outside world I've got this whole "adulting" thing mastered. In reality the only thing I've mastered is the illusion that I have any idea what I'm doing. It's like science. Except not at all.

1. Braid your hair.

This probably sounds like the dumbest thing you've ever heard, right? WRONG! I have said much dumber things. (One time I asked my mom, "When is the Fourth of July?") Seriously, though, have you ever looked at someone with a meticulously braided updo and thought to yourself, *They look like somebody who evades their taxes and skips leg day.* NO! You think, *I bet she pays her phone bill on time and reads books for fun.* Also, just washing it counts too.

2. Do your nails.

We humans are judgy creatures. As much as I would like to say that the first thing I notice about someone is their dazzling personality or their radiating aura, the reality is I'm looking at your fingernails. Actually I'm not, but for argument's sake, let's say I am. Are your cuticles trimmed? Are your nails filed and clean? Are they perfectly glossy and chip-free? If they are, I have now automatically assumed that you're great at time management, get your hair trimmed regularly, and don't spend an unhealthy amount of money online shopping. And I'm not the only person who sees it this way. As Abraham Lincoln famously once said, "In the end, it's not the years in your life that count. It's the polish on your fingernails." Okay, I'm lying. Lincoln didn't say that, but it's probably just because he had bigger problems to worry about. If you're Abraham Lincoln, you can pass on this one.

3. Use reusable grocery bags.

Not only are you saving the earth with this one, but now you no longer have to envy those moms at Whole Foods who delicately place produce in their wicker totes as they side-eye your choice of plastic bags. As though you were standing at the register, screaming, *"The world is on fire and I don't believe in global warming!"*

With this one simple shopping accessory you've now created the illusion that all your recipes come from Pinterest and Gwyneth Paltrow's Goop. In reality, the only thing you buy from the grocery store is toilet paper and ranch dressing to dip your Domino's pizza in. Also recycle—not because it makes you look like you have your shit together, but because you're not a fucking garbage human.

4. Buy a bed frame.

This only really applies when you invite people over to where you live, but I cannot stress the importance of it enough. If your mattress is just chillin' on the floor, I am automatically going to assume that you've never washed your sheets, that Nickelback is your favorite band, and that you consider Olive Garden a romantic first date. If you have a bed frame and maybe even a dresser (whoa, dream big), I'm already forgetting how boring you are. I'm halfway to picking out our future babies' names. Or at least halfway undressed.

5. Expand your vocabulary.

I wouldn't necessarily suggest investing in a word-a-day calendar unless you want to come across as more pretentious than Holden Caulfield. Or like when Joey gets the "V" volume of the encyclopedia on *Friends*. Occasionally use words like "anomaly," "brusque," "dichotomy," and "euphemism." You may notice that I listed those alphabetically, because that's how they came up when I googled "words that make you sound smart." Hey, I'm working on this one too.

6. Pimp out your bag.

Mary Poppins invented having your shit together. She was the OG of together shit. I'm not suggesting you need a tote bag that possesses magical powers. Just don't leave the house without a Tide to Go pen and some breath mints. You can thank me later.

7. Read one piece of news a day.

It cannot have anything to do with the following: J.Lo's abs, a cat meme, or anything close to resembling a ranking of Mary-Kate and Ashley's movies in order of greatness (number one is *Billboard Dad*, duh). While I wish I could sit here and tell you that I drink my morning tea while actively absorbing the latest world news on CNN, I don't. My morning ritual involves watching Ina Garten gush over good olive oil and counting how many times she says Jeffrey's name. I'm a realist. I don't expect you to be riveted by this evening's forecast. Instead of giving up entirely, scan the *New York Times* home page for one story that requires minimal effort to understand. Memorize it and bring it up in conversation. Just hope nobody else read the same one, because chances are you have no real insight on it. Hey, fake it till you make it, right?

8. Use a daily planner.

Now, if you actually *use* the planner, you're beyond just creating the illusion that your life is organized; you're actually getting your shit together! But let's take this one step at a time. Having a planner strategically pop out of your Everlane bag gives the signal to people around you that you meal prep, attend spin classes thrice weekly, and always know when you're going to run out of organic almond milk.

9. Wash your car.

Or leave it outside in the rain. Or drive past a Jonas Brothers concert and let the tears of their adoring fans (I will be one of them) wash the dirt and grime off your mom's Toyota Camry, which you've been passing off as your own since you got your permit. There is nothing sexier than a clean car (or a car at all; my standards are low). I don't care if you bought your car on Craigslist or if it cost more than getting your master's degree. It should come clean like a Hilary Duff song.

10. If all else fails, lie.

Reference the yoga retreat you went on where you took a vow of silence for three days and consumed nothing but wheatgrass and clay. Talk about how life changing the documentary about paper you just watched was. Just don't say it blatantly, because nothing says "Hey, I don't have my shit together" like saying "Hey, I have my shit together."

chapter 14

confidence and insecurities

I hate to break it to you, but no Instagram filter is going to make you look like Karlie Kloss—and that's okay. It took me twenty-five years to realize that I will never be 100 percent confident in every aspect of my life. It also took me twenty-six years to realize that that's *normal*. In all my years of faking it, I've actually come to the conclusion that *pretending* to feel great about yourself is the quickest way to actually feel it.

If you go to my Instagram account any day of the week, you're bound to see an aesthetically pleasing feed (if I do say so myself). More likely than not it's composed of palm trees, baked goods, and selfies. Now, when you see somebody flood their own timeline with pictures of themselves, it's natural to assume that they like their appearance. How surprised would you be to learn that although there are over 400 videos of me and over 2,500 Instagram pictures of me on the internet, the truth of the matter is that I am not totally confident in my looks.

I grew up in a time before smartphones. My childhood was documented on film cameras, and we communicated solely on landlines (a blow to my already nonexistent dating life). Despite the lack of instant gratification and anonymity that social media offers, I was not immune to comparing myself to others. For the first few years of my life, I was confident, because I was, like, five and blissfully unaware of anything but Barbies. The first memory I have of wishing I had something belonging to somebody else was in fourth grade. We did the play *Annie* and I was cast as Duffy, the "biggest" of the orphans. My friend Nikki got cast as Molly. Not only did she have a solo, but she was described as tiny and cute, fitting for the petite and adorable Nikki. I remember this aching feeling in the pit of my stomach as I watched the older kids coddle her and gush over how small she was. In that moment I decided that I hated my height. I hated how big my feet were, and I hated that I had to wear a bra before the rest of my classmates. I wanted to be small and cute like Nikki.

The day of my fifth-grade graduation, my mom asked me if I was sure that I wanted to wear a bikini on the class trip to the beach because "a one-piece might be more flattering." This comment came about two weeks after I came home from school crying because a boy in my class called me fat. To which my mom's response was that I was going to go through a growth spurt and I wouldn't be chunky forever. I couldn't tell you what my favorite color was at that age, or what I got for Christmas that year, but that exact moment is still burned into my brain twelve years later. As I got ready for the beach, I stared at the one-piece bathing suit my mom laid out on my bed. Before I could second-guess myself, I grabbed the Hawaiian-print bikini from my drawer, tossed it into my backpack, and left those fat comments with the one-piece. I spent the day doing cartwheels in the sand, showing off my swimming skills, and eating Popsicles until my lips turned blue. I have no memories of sucking my stomach in or hiding my body underneath a towel—not because I willed those thoughts out of my head, but because I've willed myself to forget them since.

Middle school was fresh and new and I was ready to leave all my insecurities behind. I was so sick and tired of feeling secondary to my friends, and jealousy green was just not a good color for me. On the first day of sixth grade, I packed my pink messenger bag, threw on a tiara, and let my parents drop me off right in front of the school. I walked into that place like I owned it. I spoke up in class, I cracked jokes, I poked fun at myself, and I made friends. Inside I was screaming with pure terror, but on the outside I embodied that confidence I always wished I had. As we played the standard getting-to-know-you and icebreaker games, we were asked to anonymously compliment our classmates. As I read the sheets of paper in my lap, it was overwhelmingly flooded with words like "confident," "funny," and "unique." I was floored. My ruse had worked! From that moment on, I realized I could just fake that confidence, and that false reality rang true in the minds of others. Also, let's be real, "unique" was an insult, but what the hell did I know.

Here's the thing nobody will admit: we're *all* faking it. Not a single person on this earth is happy with themselves 100 percent of the time. It's just not possible. As you envy the most popular girl in school and her effortless ability to be "cool," I guarantee that under all of that her knees are shaking. I promise you that even supermodels who get told on a daily basis how enchantingly beautiful they are can spew off a list of their own flaws at the drop of a hat. This idea that you would be happier if you had something that somebody else has, or looked a certain way like somebody else does, is total bullshit. You could look at the prettiest person in the world and you'd never be able to comprehend how they could dislike what they see in the mirror. You are the only person who lives in your mind and in your skin. You spend hundreds of thousands of hours with yourself until the day you die. You can be your own harshest critic or your own biggest fan. It's your call.

Girls are programmed to be great at faking it (dirty joke implied). With the help of push-up bras, *Sex and the City* marathons, and lip liner, we can get away with pretty much anything. The secret is in the silence and the unwavering conviction. I spent the rest of middle school surrounded by the mystic allure that I was brimming with self-assuredness. The trick was that I never dropped the act. I was confident presenting in class. I was confident performing in school plays. I was confident flirting with boys, and I was confident dancing alone. I lived that lie until slowly but surely that lie got smaller, and it got quieter, and I forgot that I was lying. I got so used to pretending that it became instinct. I no longer felt that I was creating a facade. I just got so used to living in that reality that it *became* my reality. But here's the kicker: I wasn't confident. I just thought I was, and that's the next best thing.

I'm not advising you to wear a tiara to work (if you do, please send me a picture), but I *am* asking you to just take one human-sized step in that direction.

5 steps to being more confident

1. Stop shit-talking yourself. And stop letting your friends shit-talk themselves. Remember that scene in *Mean Girls* where they're standing in front of a mirror, picking out their flaws? How uncomfortable is it when you hear somebody talk about how much they hate their thighs when you'd legitimately body snatch for them? Really annoying, right? So don't be that person. I think we all see ourselves differently; the person you see in the mirror isn't necessarily the same person that the rest of the world sees. It's like colors: the blue I know might be different from the blue in your mind, but each of those realities only exist for ourselves. Who does it help when you say that you hate your arms or how you wish you had a thigh gap? What do those statements accomplish other than tearing down yourself and anyone in the vicinity of those remarks? We all want what we don't have, the grass is always greener on the other side, and everybody's butt looks better to us than it does to them.

2. Stop normalizing the routine of complaining about things you have no intention of changing. I'm not going to sit here and tell you to love your "flaws" when I got a nose job. I mean, it turned out I needed one medically, but you best believe that I sauntered into Dr.

Vartanian's office because I decided the days of my nose being compared to a butt crack were over. If you can't live with something, then by all means make a change! It's your life; you're the only one who has to live it. I don't preach much, but I do stand behind the belief that the only right way to live is to live for yourself. If you don't hate it enough to change it, then you need to change the narrative. If it's something you're going to live with, you have to learn how to neutralize your feelings toward it.

3. Stop waiting for the moment confidence "kicks in." There is this misconception that once you reach a certain goal or milestone, your unwavering confidence will automatically kick in and suddenly you'll start to feel amazing about yourself. I hate to break it to you, but that, my friends, is a myth. Putting blame on life events and relinquishing the power of your own happiness to external variables is a never-ending cycle. There will always be something or somebody to wait for. No relationship, dress size, job title, bank account, or number on a scale will ever be enough. The only thing you need to change is your mindset. If you're living your life for tomorrows, you're wasting all of your todays.

4. Create a routine that makes you feel like Beyoncé. I'm not kidding. Find a song that would be your entrance music in a teen movie. For me that song is "Boss-Ass Bitch." You're more than welcome to steal my song, because I'm pretty sure it's impossible not to feel like a boss-ass bitch as you scream the lyrics and pop your (nonexistent, in my case) ass. Have a go-to outfit that you feel really great in—something that's not only physically comfortable but that makes you feel like *you*. Same goes for your hair/makeup look. Hammer down one specific look that makes you want to take ten thousand Snapchats with the puppy dog filter. Have this routine in your back pocket for spontaneous dates, job interviews, and random moments of self-doubt.

5. Draw the line. If you're spending forty-five minutes scrolling through pictures of heavily Photoshopped Victoria's Secret models, close your laptop and walk away. Know your triggers and avoid them like UTIs. Participating in an activity that you know is bringing you down is like sprinkling salt on a paper cut. Dumb. Like, really, really dumb. And you don't want to be dumb.

So fake it until you make it. Toss your hair in a sassy Ariana Grande ponytail, throw your shoulders back, strap on some heels, and walk like Tyra Banks is watching.

Confidence isn't about what you look like. Confidence is a mindset, an illusion, and completely and utterly attainable.

chapter 15

self-love

Let me get this out of the way: I am not against self-love. I don't think we should all be self-loathing, self-pitying, and detrimentally introspective beings. But I also don't sip that motivational Kool-Aid. Before you shank me in my chakras with your sage, let me explain.

You've probably caught on that I've been a pretty insecure person for as long as I can remember. I'm not proud of that fact, but it is what it is. I don't know if I believe that my deep-rooted confidence issues were something I was born with or the result of how I was brought up, but—whatever the reason—the issue is still there. My struggles with self-esteem have nothing to do with the world around me and everything to do with myself. Maybe you're reading this and wondering what on earth I had to be insecure about, or maybe you can count enough reasons to rival Veruca Salt's Christmas list. Regardless of whether you think my insecurities are well deserved, I cannot deny their existence.

There are just some things I don't like about myself no matter how hard I try to like them. I hate my front teeth. They're too big and they protrude far past my bottom ones. I hate my arms; I have stubborn eczema all over them and no matter the season I'd rather be in sleeves. I hate my feet. They're flat, ugly, and each is about as wide as my shoulders. I hate those things about myself. I can't change the size of my feet, according to my doctor my eczema is about as under control as it'll ever be, and the only fix for my teeth would be adult braces or tuition-priced porcelain veneers. I am never going to love those things about myself. I am not going to wake up one day and rub my hands across my bumpy, reptilian skin and light up with joy. As I struggle to squeeze my foot into the largest size the Nordstrom sale has to offer, I will not be beaming with excitement as I notice they make my feet resemble cross-country skis. I am not going to love every single part of myself all the time. And that's okay.

One of my major gripes with the concept of self-love is the unrealistic expectations that are involved. We're instructed to love our flaws. I don't know about you, but I'm not the biggest fan of my large pores. I could honestly do without them. Does my dislike and disdain for a part of myself make me a vain and horribly self-indulgent person? No. Does it make me human? Yes. I don't expect you to transform your darkest feelings about yourself into positive mantras. That's not realistic.

Don't expect to love yourself and your life 100 percent of the time. Or even 75 percent of the time. I think some days you're gonna feel your look more than others. Some days you'll look in the mirror and wish you saw someone else staring back. That doesn't make you a superficial person. Instead of pounding the concept over everyone's head that they should be so jazzed about their insecurities, how about we start treating our "flaws" more like high-maintenance poodles that sometimes need a bit more attention? You don't need to find your blackheads beautiful. Negative thoughts are a part of life, they're temporary, and they're not crippling. Instructing someone to not just accept but *love* their flaws is daunting. You don't need to love them, you need to live with them. I think setting the bar too high doesn't always inspire; rather, it turns people off from it as something unachievable. Maybe if my role models had opened up about their own insecurities and how it's perfectly normal and attainable to coexist with them, I'd have been a little less obsessive.

Sometimes self-love takes form in acceptance, sometimes it takes form in neutrality, and sometimes it takes form in change. If I had been told that I needed to love my life regardless of the circumstances, I would never be where I am today. If I had not let myself hate college, I wouldn't have thrown myself into work, moved to Los Angeles, and ultimately made my dreams a reality. If I had thought I needed to love my life, I would have remained at school, denied my misery, and embarked on a mundane and unfulfilled life. That desire to change and grow led me through a series of choices I made to ultimately value myself more than ever. It was self-preservation, and once I made it out the other side, it looked a lot like self-love.

You are the only person in your skin (I hope), and you are the only person inside your mind, body, and soul. You are numero uno. You are the head honcho. You are the captain of your own ship and you are the Celine Dion of your Vegas. You are the only one whose opinion of yourself matters. So do what makes you happy. Will dyeing your hair hot pink make you happy? Then go for it. I don't care what society says about how "shallow" it is to change your appearance; if it makes you happy, that's all that matters. While to some people getting plastic surgery might seem like the ultimate display of insecurity, for me it was quite the opposite. Getting a nose job was my proclamation that I was taking my happiness into my own hands. I was making a decision to do something that I knew would boost my confidence, make me feel better about myself, and finally put that repulsion to rest. I spent nearly my whole life hating my nose. If ultimate self-love were entirely attainable for me, I would never have gotten my rhinoplasty and I would have saved a hefty chunk of change. I don't think self-love is bullshit and I don't even think it's necessarily impossible. I think it's important for us to value and treasure ourselves, but I also believe there is no right way to do that. I believe that some days you might love yourself more than others, and if you are truly unhappy with something in your life, you have every right to change it.

chapter 16

dealing with failure

I am great at failing. I fail all the time. I pretty much majored in failing. Not literally, because if that really was a major, I'm pretty sure I would have walked away with a much better GPA. I got fired from a job at a frozen yogurt shop because I couldn't make a medium sundae. I also ditched work to go to a party, but I was already on thin ice (cream). If anyone inquired why I no longer served them waffle cones, I blamed the rigors of my schedule (lol) conflicting with my schoolwork (lol). The big thing about failure is that nobody wants to admit to it. It's like picking your nose: everybody pretends they don't go digging for gold in their car during traffic, but they're just lying.

Yeah, it sucks to fail. It feels fucking terrible, and I'm not going to dispute that. But, sadly, it's not going anywhere: failure is an unavoidable obstacle in life. You don't grow out of failing, you learn to fail better or just differently. The things we struggled with or that tanked us in our younger years, we learn from—and we use that to avoid making those mistakes again. But with age and maturity comes a whole new wave of obstacles and life events for us to fail at. It's not about trying to eliminate failure from our lives; that's just unrealistic. It's about learning how to deal with our failures in a way that helps us grow and also doesn't make us complete emotional wrecks all the time. (But you are certainly allowed to be an emotional wreck *some* of the time, or at least that's what I tell myself in order to feel okay about the fact that my car has seen more tears than a showing of *P.S. I Love You*.) In my long-term committed relationship with failure, I've learned a few things. Without further ado, my takeaways:

5 steps to a foolproof failure

Step 1: Let it happen. Not to be confused with "Adele Dazeem's" "Let It Go." More like what they teach you in a trust fall: Just let it happen. I mean, if you're driving a car and you start to drift into oncoming traffic, yeah, merge your ass back into your own lane. But if you're in the middle of a math test you didn't study for, and it's too late to fake illness, don't bust out the waterworks and attempt to dish blame on everybody else. If you don't take ownership of your responsibilities, and the second something goes wrong you start to play the blame game, you never learn how to prevent those mistakes. Sometimes you just need to fall on your ass before you can pick yourself back up. This also goes for watching somebody else fail. If we coddle our friends and our partners in attempts to shield them from any mistakes or misfortune, they live their lives in this bubble. And when that bubble inevitably bursts, it'll be so overwhelming, they won't know how to deal with it. Sometimes we need to be wrong. Sometimes we need to try our best and have that still not be good enough. There is nothing more motivating than building something from the ground up, making diamonds out of coal, and making yourself proud. If failure hits you head-on, take it with grace and inspiration. If you need to cry, I highly recommend showers and cars. Avoid bathroom stalls—so cliché.

Step 2: Sit in it. Or wallow in it, depending on the severity and your level of dramatics. This is a common theme in most of the advice I dish out: Allow a certain amount of time to let yourself feel whatever you're feeling. I strongly believe that in order to fully understand and move past something, you need to give your feelings their due and let them run their course. However big or small your failure was, your automatic reaction is justified: your feelings are valid because you feel them. The chances are low that whatever happened will be detrimental to all aspects of your life from this point on, but in that moment it's going to feel like the end of the world. That's okay. Feel whatever you're feeling, because shutting that away and ignoring it isn't doing anybody any good. It's crippling and it's immobilizing. Feel it for a moment or a day or a weekend, or the length of time it takes you to drive to Target for some retail therapy.

Step 3: Accept responsibility, but don't assume defeat. I think this step is the hardest. We have a hard time owning up to our mistakes. It is just a fact that nobody wants to be at fault, especially when it affects other people. We tend to naturally come up with excuses and blame the circumstances and situations that led to our failures. These hopefully take some if not all of the blame off us. I, for one, blame nonexistent traffic and street construction for tardiness when in reality I couldn't pick out what shoes to wear. Those common white lies we tell can be completely harmless, but that habit can bleed into much bigger things. We point fingers left and right at people who we think are at fault because our ego and our sense of pride cannot take the embarrassment and self-loathing that come with failure that's all our own. I'm not saying you should accept the full weight of the blame for a class or group project you guys tanked; just own up to your part in the debacle. That said, you also need to be careful about not taking responsibility too far or letting it eat away at you. There's a difference in accepting that you're the one at fault for something and letting that guilt and shame weigh you down. I really used to struggle with this and, honestly, sometimes I still do. When I know I've done something wrong or made a grave mistake, my instinctive reaction is to completely shut down. What's really helped me get better at this is the realization that a tail-between-the-legs moment is just so unproductive. The time I've spent beating myself up about whatever does nothing but drag me down further. If I continue to be down about it, I'm walking away from the situation more insecure, unsure, and timid than I was when I was in it. If I'm so terrified about making a mistake that I'm looking over my shoulder—or, worse, I just remove myself from those situations or deny myself those opportunities—I've let this single failure define my work ethic and damage my self-confidence. Find the aspects of the failure that were by your hand, accept that fact, and . . .

Step 4: Learn from it. This takes time. I honestly think I'm finally learning from failures that are fifteen years old. I'm not kidding. I also believe that this is an ongoing process rather than just a step. There are the seemingly obvious lessons that come pretty quickly, but as we get older and our perception of the world and ourselves widens, I think there's room to learn more lessons from those same mistakes. It's not about figuring everything out as fast as you can but more about just being open to whatever realizations come from it, no matter how long they take. More than just recognizing the lessons to be learned, it's about applying them. There are the obvious ways to implement said lessons—something as simple as setting your alarm an hour earlier or signing up for an Excel class. Those are the immediate and pro-active ways to ensure that you'll never make the same mistake again. Then there are the less obvious lessons to be learned, and those take time and a lot of self-reflection. Sometimes those lessons take multiple failures before they really start to sink in and spark a change. We're ever-changing, ever-evolving creatures, and there is no timeline or ex-piration date on our growth. We just have to be open to it.

Step 5: Make better mistakes, because you're still going to make them. The only time you really fail is when you make the same mistake twice. Fail better. You probably won't fail less often, because as we get older, we have more opportunities to fail. As a kid I assumed that being "grown up" knighted you with some sort of all-knowing godlike power and knowledge. But the older I get, I'm no closer to this undefinable "grown-up" stage in my life. It's like when you're a freshman in high school and the seniors seem so big, but when you become a senior you wonder why you never got as big as they were. We have this idea of what it's going to feel like, to one day be the thing we're looking up at. I don't think there's anything wrong with that. When we're growing up, holding our superiors and elders to an untouchable standard gives us role models and qualities to aspire to. It holds us accountable and makes us want to fill those big shoes. As we get older, we begin to realize everybody is just making it up as they go along. Now it's comforting to know everybody is just as lost as I am; as a kid it was comforting to feel like somebody had all the answers. I wanted so desperately to achieve that level of adulthood, and that made me fail better. It made me reach high for things that made me fall further, but it kept me climbing in the trees and not staying there on the ground.

I still fuck up all the time. Like, *all* the time. I run out of gas, I lose my wallet, I say something dumb in front of somebody important, and I neglect to go to the dentist until I need a root canal. I do all kinds of stupid shit, and I do it all the time. That's just life. All I can do is try to make the shit I do a little less stupid, hopefully, sometimes.

You're going to fail. I know that's probably not comforting or what you want to hear, but it's the truth. I do hope you find some comfort in the fact that everyone does fail. Some people wear their failures with pride, and others tuck them far away so nobody can see. The people we put on pedestals are imperfect creatures. We all are. We're human and we're flawed and we're one and the same. So fail. Fail hard, fail often, and fail again, because that means you're trying. It means you're taking risks and you're growing. Trust that if you fall, you'll stand back up and try again.

chapter 17

and you thought trolls lived under bridges

There's no denying that this surge in technology has defined our generation and the generations to come. While most baby boomers were skeptical about its sustainability and longevity, the proof is here. There are college classes and courses and majors that not only didn't apply to prior generations, they didn't even exist. The digital age has rewritten how products are marketed, how we interact socially, how relationships are built, how information is generated, how we ingest our news, how we share our memories, how we order our food, how we get around, and how we get through virtually all our day-to-day activities. Some may be wistful for a simpler time when meet-cutes weren't a rarity and libraries were analog. While I can agree that my generation could stand to gain some perspective off a phone screen, I wouldn't be where I am today without the internet. I also most certainly would not have gotten into college. Or have spelled anything right in this book.

Now, as Uncle Ben said, with great power comes great responsibility. (Not the Uncle Ben who's ready to make rice. The Uncle Ben from *Spider-Man*.) But here's the issue: we're all guinea pigs. Not literally, unless it's taken me so long to write this book that now rodents have opposable thumbs and a fifth-grade reading level. We're the pioneers and test dummies of this technological age. With any great advancement, there's a learning curve. Remember the first iPhone? Kinks need to be ironed out and bugs need to be spotted and fixed. And that doesn't just apply to the hardware of technology. We've ended up in completely uncharted waters with the new responsibility it puts on us morally. Every individual has been handed more power at their fingertips than any dictator in history ever had.

Now, because all of this is so new, there are no rules. There's no standard or common knowledge on how one should act digitally. We're the ones teaching our parents how to tweet, Snapchat, and start calling the number sign a hashtag. Suddenly it's teenagers with the utmost knowledge and information. Back in the day, the biggest fear adults had for their children was whatever debauchery they could get up to on a family landline. If your kids were under your roof, you had a pretty good idea of what they could be up to. But now those options and those fears are endless. I think we all need a crash course on how to internet—not like how to compose something funny and relatable in 160 characters or less, but more along the lines of how to engage and take part in the digital age without being a terrible human headed straight for hell. If the pen is mightier than the sword, then the iPhone is a goddamn bomb.

The Dos and Don'ts of Navigating the Digital Age Without Being an Asshole

DO like your friends' pictures. Regardless of what it's of. Their morning latte? Like. Their basic flat lay? Like. A blurry drunken selfie? Like. I don't care if you don't actually like the picture of their office holiday party; it is your duty as a friend to double tap and do your part in the quest for double digits. The only exception to this rule is an unsightly #tbt in which you are featured. I would never expect you to double tap your own lime-green braces and gauchos.

DON'T let unsavvy adults stalk your crush on IG on your phone. Do not trust anyone over the age of forty to know how to zoom on Instagram without accidentally liking. Is this offensive? Probably. Is it true? Yes. Do you want to explain to your crush why you were stalking fifty-nine weeks back to a picture of him shirtless at a family reunion at Lake Michigan? No. Or explain to your ex–best friend or your best friend's ex or your ex's new lover why you liked a picture of them from the seventh grade? No. Unless you're doing it on purpose, in which case I'd like to offer you some vinegar for that salt. There are two options here to prevent all of that.

(a) You could just not stalk that deep, but I'm not familiar with that kind of restraint.

Or (b) screenshot whatever pictures or posts you want to show around. Now, instead of giving the control of your social media to someone who still refers to an iPhone as a tablet, you've given them a picture that they can zoom in on and triple tap on endlessly. Problem solved. Just make sure the picture isn't sandwiched between your nudes. Don't say I didn't warn you.

DO pull a Hannah Montana (or, I guess, more like a Miley Stewart). I'm not expecting you to lead the double life of a part-time pop star (though, if given the option, I totally wouldn't turn it down). What I mean is: Take inspiration from the alias. Relatable and reference-free, this translates to the simple suggestion of keeping your real last name off your social media profiles. This probably seems ridiculous and unnecessary to you, but let me explain. In a college recruiting assembly at my high school, the counselors informed us that one of the things colleges did in researching prospective students was the same thing we did to research them: Google search. We were shocked. We were under the naive impression that the admissions office would see only the materials we gave them. Less than twenty-four hours later, every senior had changed their last name on Facebook to their middle name, and other more creative (weird) folks chose totally different names altogether. Most of us had intended the swap to be temporary, but as we got into the real world of job applications and background searches, the comfort of knowing the recruiter at a marketing firm couldn't tie us back to a status from 2009 about our love of DJ Pauly D was something we just couldn't give up.

DON'T subtweet. This one I really just don't get, and not in a high-and-mighty, holier-than-thou kind of way. Mostly just because I'm super-confrontational, and I could never see a passive-aggressive subtweet supplying the same feeling as a direct verbal confrontation. I'm totally not advising that as an alternative, by the way. But come on, subtweeting is not only the slimiest form of perpetuating drama, it blows things way out of proportion and invites public opinion. If something pisses you off enough to subtweet about it, it's worth hashing out in person. If that's not doable, then save that shit to drafts and move along.

DO keep your profile PC. I get it. You turned twenty-one, you drink, you're cool, you hang out with D-list celebrities' sisters. That's awesome. I'm totally stoked for you.

Does that mean I want to see pictures of you doing lines of coke off dirty pool tables? I'd really rather not. I struggle with thinking that everybody's social media account should be private, and then knowing that, if that were true, I'd no longer have a job. Plus stalking the guys my friends date would be WAY harder. Obviously, I understand the public profile when you're building your brand, and I think there are two ways to go about it. If you're selling woven baskets and tiny spoons on Etsy, make accounts solely for your profession. Not only does this create a work-life balance by separating the two, it also keeps you from being a social pariah because you clog everyone's feed with rusting cutlery. Now, if your brand is you, that's a different story. In that case the content you post not only reflects your interests, it's how you're perceived professionally. It's up to you to determine what your brand is, what you want to be known for, and what your potential business partners see. If you're hesitating on uploading something because you're doing something illegal? Not worth it.

DON'T be that asshole hiding behind a screen (unless you're being stalked in a Best Buy, in which case go for the sixty-inchers). One of my favorite things about the internet is that it gives a voice to the voiceless. There is that ambiguity and anonymity of it that can be really positive. It's like a virtual masquerade ball where we all get dressed up and act like the person we've always wanted the courage to be. And while that can breed confidence and allies and open up a world in which you find like-minded people, it doesn't always end up that way. I mean, if it did, catfish would just be the lunch special. Honestly, in my early years as an internet kid, it really did come from a pure and genuine place. But as the years have gone by, the culture and community seem far less based on acceptance and far more based in negativity and cruelty. Apparently, being anonymous means that you've been given this free pass to be a completely terrible person. You can say atrocious things that you'd never in a million years dream of saying to somebody in person. We're under this impression that freedom of speech essentially translates into saying whatever the fuck you want, and who cares who it hurts, because I certainly don't, even though I've got a Bible verse in my bio saying to love thy neighbor. The justification of these terrible lapses in (or lack of) manners is the self-proclaimed entitlement to one's own opinion. Which I personally think is fucking insane. Yes, you can have an opinion on things, sure. You can even have an opinion on people, especially if those people are hurting you, or are hurting other people, or have a last name that rhymes with Hump. But except for the last one, why? Like, honestly, why do people care? I'm actually baffled by the fact that so much of the world has *so* much free time that they're legitimately dissecting and critiquing other people and their lives. I don't know what they lecture about in school these days, but back in my Manor Elementary years, it seemed that every day ended with Mr. Tim telling us that if we had nothing nice to say, then we should say nothing at all. I'm not sure when this precept petered out, but I think it's time we reintroduce it. There is a special place in hell reserved for internet trolls, and I bet you the Wi-Fi sucks there. Think what you want, but I really believe that what goes around comes around. Fifteen years from now, when Becky is sitting alone in the apartment she is about to be evicted from and is wondering why she's still single, I hope she finally realizes that those long nights of spamming Disney Channel stars with death threats put her where she is today. Don't be like Becky.

DO live a life that looks good without a lens. Don't get me wrong, I am *all* about the aesthetic *cough* @meghanrienks *cough* . . . While I will not confirm or deny that I made my boyfriend repaint my (already white) walls five different shades of white until I found one that fit my Instagram theme, I do in fact have boundaries. It's easy to get caught up in curating your life to look good in a tiny square box, and I'm all for documenting milestones.

I'm stoked that so much of my life is encapsulated in memories and photographs and videos. But if I'm being honest, I have no visual record of most of my greatest memories. I'm too happy and caught up in a moment to ruin it with a camera flash or a second take. Make a conscious decision to put your phone on time-out and look around and pursue a life that you're happy with, even if nobody else sees it. We're seeking this validation of our life and our choices when in reality the only approval we need is our own.

DO take everything with a grain of salt, like WebMD, Wikipedia, and all those Facebook ads claiming a rare tropical fruit is the secret to Adriana Lima's physique. I'm a self-proclaimed skeptic, and that's probably why my email has never gotten hacked. I'm fairly certain I don't have a distant cousin who's a king in Ireland who left me $3 million in his will but it requires my Social Security number and bank routing information. Moral of the story: Don't believe everything you hear or read on the internet. While this directly applies to facts and statistics, it also applies to just general interactions on social media. Trolls don't just live under bridges; they lurk on your favorite platforms and they can say terribly derogatory things. And while your automatic reaction may go from hurt to considering the degree of truth in their words, it's important not to lose sight of the fact that you're letting somebody else's small-minded opinion become your reality. Opinions aren't facts, and facts aren't opinions. Don't sign your life away to a junk mail lottery win, and remember that Wikipedia accepts community edits.

DO remember the internet is forever. I wish this weren't true. In a perfect world there would be no evidence of my affair with raccoon eyeliner or really any pictures of me from ages twelve to fifteen. Or more like twelve to twenty-two. I mean, if you google me, I'm pretty sure one of the first images that pop up is from high school at a hookah bar. Also bear in mind I didn't even post that picture; I was tagged in a private picture. I untagged myself, and I *still* can't escape it. Once anyone has sent something into cyberspace, you can't ever get it back. You can delete things and wipe your hard drive and erase as much as you possibly can, but nothing is guaranteed. If you even have a shred of hesitation, follow your gut. Because if you don't, that shit will follow you forever.

chapter 18

a comprehensive step-by-step program on how to give zero fucks

Step 1: Look for fucks to give.
Step 2: Realize you cannot find any.
Step 3: Move on.

Okay, I know it's harder than it sounds—but, really, there is no trick, because it is that simple. The truth of the matter is that, deep down, everybody cares about what people think. It's human instinct to be aware of other people and their points of view and perceptions. This isn't inherently bad. It promotes empathy and understanding and a healthier sense of self. But it can also be incredibly hindering and un-productive if you manifest it in an unbalanced way. Should you care what your friends think about how your boyfriend treats you? Yeah. Should you care what your teacher thinks about your schoolwork? Yeah. Should you care what a random lady in the international food aisle thinks about your choice in salsa? No. There are times when other people's opinions are not only welcome, they're also important to you. But at the same time you're entitled to not give a fucking shit about what other people think.

More times than not, you're probably stressing out over something that nobody is paying attention to anyway. For some reason we're all under the impression that everyone is just as concerned with our shit as we are. Hate to break it to you, but that's not true. While you're freaking out about how awkward your voice sounds on the phone, that lady on the bus sitting next to you is busy worrying whether she turned her straightener off before she left the house. That "look" you're pretty sure some girl is giving you as you laugh-snort? She's probably just sneaky farting. But let's say she is sending you a judgmental glare: Why do you care? What is she to you? Does she have power over you? Does she know your Social Security number? Not unless you fell for that inheritance scam.

You cannot control how other people treat you, but you can control how it affects you. If somebody is so incredibly caught up in worrying about and judging your every move, that's their problem. It's also their prerogative. Just because they've decided you're the star of their life movie doesn't mean you need to watch it. I know I shit on Pinterest inspirational quotes all the time, but I actually really like this one. It's a real quote, not one from a blogger in Arkansas. The saying goes, "Those who mind don't matter, and those who matter don't mind." The people who know you best in your life are the only people whose opinions matter, and sometimes even those opinions don't matter. If we lived our lives trying to please and appease everybody around us, random aquaintances and friends alike, I'm pretty sure we'd all internally combust.

I'm aware this isn't an easy feat. You can't just turn off that insecure part of your brain. As you get older, that part of your brain tends to slowly silence itself or at least turn off push notifications. And while it's awesome that you (sort of) grow out of it, I really wish I had made the conscious effort to care a little less about what people thought about me a little sooner in life. I was completely terrified to raise my hand in class for fear of saying something stupid. Guess what? I've said about a million stupid things in my life, and I'll say a million more. We're attempting to avoid the unavoidable by portraying an image that we cannot uphold for eternity. It's like how the shyest and quietest girls from high school go to college, shave their heads, tat up their bodies, and join the Peace Corps. People always talk about some massive life event that inspired them to "find themselves" and become somebody they always wanted to be. But why can't that start now? At the end of it, your opinion of yourself is the only one that matters. That one person who makes you feel this big? I promise you that, four years down the road, you won't remember their name. You'll remember how you felt when they rolled their eyes at your presentation and how you thought about that moment for months, and then you'll feel so silly. I swear, I could have learned Mandarin in the time I spent worrying about what these people I hardly knew thought about me. So fake it. Pretend that you don't have a damn care in the world. Shut those feelings of insecurity and self-doubt in a tiny box, then pretend they don't exist. Imagine that you don't give a single fuck, and one day you'll realize you've stopped pretending—and still there is not a fuck to be found.

You can be the finest peach in the world, and still somebody is going to call you fuzzy. Wouldn't you rather be like Cher and wear a face mask to do errands? Or wear pajamas to a movie and do whatever the fuck makes you happy? The second you stop second-guessing yourself is the first second you really get to be yourself. Go do it. If you get some side-eyes and snide remarks, just know they're probably just jealous. They're far too concerned with how they look to have any fun. Those people are 100 percent the type who pretend they don't poop. I don't trust them for a second.

how to deal with crappy people

The Purge! Kidding, that's not real. It would also be illegal. I also reference this movie far too often for someone who's never seen it. I'm a big phony, which is a great lead-in to the content of this chapter: crappy people. Not that I'm identifying as a crappy person, but I do have my fair share of experiences in dealing with them. Some people are just going to suck, and not in a good way. That's just how it is. Ideally we'd be living in a conflict-free world full of free health care and free refills on french fries, but we aren't. While we can be wistful and wish and hope that the terrible people we encounter will see the error of their ways, it's really a waste of time and energy, which could be much better spent in more useful ways, like learning the fox-trot or memorizing lyrics from *Hamilton*. Those crappy people aren't going anywhere (except hell). We might as well deal with them in a way that doesn't make us gray before we've stocked up on Diane Keaton turtlenecks.

Cut them out if you can. At this point in my life, I have a zero-tolerance policy for shitty people. I wasted way too much of my young adult life surrounded by arbitrarily crappy people. I don't have any more time to waste, and you shouldn't, either. I could go into the whole "Life is short" blah blah bullshit that closes every Cameron Diaz movie, but you get the gist. If you can, cut them out. I wish I had implemented this so much sooner in my own life, but for some reason I was under the impression that it wasn't an option. Which is why I'm telling you now: it *is* an option! Utilize it.

Except when it's not an option. Like when the crappy person in your life is a coworker. In those cases, **don't engage them** (and definitely don't get engaged to them). We all know those douchebags who never grew out of childhood drama and pride themselves on being assholes.

Those kinds of shitty people thrive on attention. Their atrocious actions are purely done in hopes of a reaction, so don't give them that satisfaction. Some people just like to stir the pot to get a rise out of people, and they also lead sad, sexless lives. They need to make, like, a vast collection of parking tickets and get ignored. Now, if they're hurting somebody, that's obviously a whole different story. But in most cases the only things they're really hurting are themselves and any chance of being respectable. Have fun in the bad place, Adam.

In some instances, neither of the two prior suggestions can be followed. Sometimes you have to work closely or spend extended amounts of time with somebody who just sucks. In that case, **take them for what they're worth.** Sans a few (Hitler, Donald Trump, my mother), I truly don't believe that many people are inherently evil to their core. I mean, even Sean Spicer has a dog. Not that it makes him any less of a garbage, idiotic excuse of a person, but it's certainly a *slightly* redeeming quality. I don't think we're required to find the good in the people we dislike, but I do think it's important to humanize them. Even Mojo JoJo. And Voldemort. Most of the time, terrible people lash out as a way to express and project their own issues. Does that make it any better? Personally, I don't think so. I think you're entitled to dislike people whatever their situation. It's unrealistic to expect somebody to be so selfless and understanding that they tolerate bad behavior with open arms. That's sweet, but that's bullshit. You don't need to be friends with your enemies, but you don't need to take part in an epic feud. If you have to coexist with somebody you can't stand, just let them serve their purpose. Let them play the part that they've been given and expect nothing more. Set your expectations low, and when they don't even meet those, set them lower. And who knows? Maybe one day things will change. Turns out even Miranda Priestly has a heart.

Regardless, always (try) to **be the bigger person.** Unless your feud is with Shaq, in which case I'd accept his vertical advantage. Bad joke; what's new? Despite my early growth spurt, as a kid I really struggled with this one. I've always been pretty confrontational, and it took a while for me to learn how to pick my battles. There is this innate frustration I feel when somebody does something idiotic, malicious, or just overall vile. In my mind it becomes my civic duty to make this person understand their actions and make things right. In some cases, yes, it's necessary to intervene when you witness an injustice. But when that injustice is a game of he said, she said behind-your-back gossip, it's better to just walk away and not participate. Stooping down to their level of pettiness does nothing but make you look just as bad. But you know what makes you look great? Letting them run their mouth on and on with no engagement on your end. Not only does it highlight their true colors perfectly, it also portrays you in a way more mature and flattering light. Translation? You look way better. You go, Glen Coco.

Finally, find solace in that **karma's a bigger bitch than I could ever be.** Know that I don't say this lightly. I can be a massive bitch, so this means a lot coming from me. Like, a lot. Just let life run its natural course and trust that those terrible people will get what they deserve in the end. Any revenge or attempts to "get even" will pale in comparison to what karma will do. And I'd never want to rob you of experiencing the feeling you get when you stumble upon a photo of your middle school bully with a receding hairline, Crocs with socks, and a beyond-unfortunate pair of khakis. Nothing compares to that feeling. If I could bottle that feeling and sell it, I'd be a fucking millionaire.

And if all else fails? Just remember that Harry Potter survived the Dursleys, Malfoy, Snape, Professor Quirrell, (the memory of) Tom Riddle, a basilisk, Wormtail, a multitude of dragons, Death Eaters, Umbridge, seven Horcruxes, Voldemort himself, and a whole load of other shit. Suck it up, your Squib is showing.

chapter 19

depression

Oh, you know, just another uplifting, fun, carefree, and lighthearted chapter! Ha. Okay, there's no smooth way to transition into this, so I'm not even going to try. I, like a large part of the world's population, deal with depression. Unlike a large part of the world's population, I told millions of people on the internet. To say that I hate talking about my depression probably seems counterintuitive, since I uploaded a You-Tube video talking about it. But if you've seen it, you might notice that I don't really say much. Despite the response praising my authenticity, the content itself is pretty general and abstract. This was an intentional choice on my part. I've never been a big "feelings" person, and I'm even less inclined to talk about my feelings with strangers. So why on earth did I upload that video? Truthfully, because I couldn't *not*. My channel was a documentary of my life, and what I was going through was a part of my life. I just didn't expect other people to define it as my *entire* life.

I hate that my struggles with mental illness have become something I'm known for. Don't get me wrong, I don't regret uploading that video by any means. Nor do I resent the attention it has gotten, because that reach implies relatability. It means other people are finding it and identifying with it and, hopefully, feeling a little less alone. What I *do* hate is that it's treated like an aberration. That it's such a shock that someone you'd never expect suffers from something like depression. I just wish that it wasn't a big deal. I wish that I wasn't "brave" for talking about it. I just wish other people would talk about it.

I don't want to be the poster child for depression, because I'm not that. Depression doesn't look like any one person. It's not a choice or a phase or anything up for debate. It's something that some of us have to live with all our lives. I, for one, am sick of talking about it as if that's all there is to me. I am more than an ongoing battle with this mental illness. I hope that, in telling you my story, you'll find me a little less special. I hope that, by being more honest than I ever have been on this subject, it inspires you to be a little more honest too.

I've been called sensitive and dramatic my whole life. I don't deny either, but as an adult I'm able to understand more of where that comes from. I was raised in a really unhappy home by two people who didn't love each other and made sure I knew that. And before you go all "Wah wah wah, another millennial pinning their problems on their parents. How typical," that's not what I'm doing. In the nature-versus-nurture debate, I believe that we all have the ability to grow up in spite of both. Some aspects of how I was brought up, or what I was told to believe or value, have stuck with me, both good and bad. But who I am as an adult was a conscious decision on my part, and it's something that I work on every day. As a kid, I was a sponge soaking up the environment in which I lived, and that environment bred a deeply insecure little girl who was desperate for any love and attention she could get. From a really young age I remember worrying about my appearance and how people perceived me. I remember having a hard time in school and having my mom tell me I just wasn't trying hard enough. I remember having a teacher suspect that I might have attention deficit hyperactivity disorder. My parents wouldn't even consider it. I just needed to try harder. I remember feeling like a disappointment, and I was ashamed that my hardest wasn't good enough. This mentality of feeling inadequate and somewhat of a burden continued as I got older, leaving me just really insecure.

These issues with self-worth and confidence persisted as I grew up, but because I didn't know any different, I didn't think anything of it. Later on, I'd find out that this manifested itself into social and general anxiety, but that's another chapter. It wasn't until my sophomore year of college that I hit a low point that I didn't even know was possible. This was my first battle with something classified as "situational depression." Situational depression is a "short-term" form of depression that occurs following a traumatic incident in your life. For me, that traumatic incident was the bullying I endured from my two roommates and sorority sisters. It's also referred to as "adjustment disorder" and has a three-month window of expected upset. But I accepted this diagnosis, because it meant that this darkness was temporary. It meant that there was a solution. I'd move out of that apartment, get my own place, and get over it within a few months. When I look back on it now, I realize there were so many red flags and signs that the damage they inflicted on my psyche was far more than anybody thought, but we never talked about it like that. There was a problem at hand that needed to be solved, and that was it. My parents came to Riverside to help me move into a new apartment, which would solve the problem. There was no conversation about what would happen next, because once I got out of the situation, it would all get better. What do you know? It didn't.

My instinctive reaction was to blame myself for not being forthcoming with everything that had happened—to fault myself for not being as candid and as open about what I was feeling. On the other hand, when you're in such a broken state, it's unnerving. I just felt embarrassed. I was mad at myself for not feeling better. I felt as if I had wasted my parents' time moving me out, since that didn't fix how I felt. I mean, obviously it was a necessary step. I can't even imagine what consequences staying there would have had on me. I wanted so badly to feel good again. I wanted to believe that happiness was a choice, so

I tried as hard as I could to be happy. I threw myself into work in LA, even staying out later in the city by myself, shopping, getting coffee, and befriending the people I met on set. I'd accept friendship in any form just to feel a little less lonely. I'd wake up early and fill my day with errands and things to do that got me out of the house. I was petrified of being alone. If I was alone, I didn't have to pretend to be okay. There was nobody I had to fool and nobody to hold me accountable. There is nothing more terrifying than being scared of yourself.

Without the blessing of my friends or my family back home, I dropped out of college that spring. I felt like I was disappointing everybody, but staying just wasn't an option for me. I really did try to move on. For the first time in my life, I made serious headway in contending with my social anxiety. I put myself into social situations despite the terror that would usually ensue. At that time, the depression was so bad, I was ready to try anything to get back to feeling somewhat normal. I went to all my classes, I struck up conversations with anybody I came across, and I went above and beyond to try to foster new relationships that would ease this feeling of worthlessness. I participated more in my sorority's events than I ever had before. I tried so hard to feel like I belonged somewhere and wasn't completely broken on the inside. It was too hard. It was too hard to be okay with the fact that everybody knew what had happened and they all chose to ignore it. It was too hard to have gone through the shit that they put me through and know that nobody there had my back. I was as alone as I felt, and I couldn't do it anymore. My parents begged me to at least finish the year and then take the summer to think about it. They asked what I would do for the remainder of my Riverside lease. Would I just wallow aimlessly in my apartment? They reminded me that if I dropped out, I was 100 percent on my own. If I made that choice, they would not support it emotionally or financially. They asked me what on earth I was planning to do with my life without a college education. They bet me that I would go back: "Just give it a few months; you'll see." Dropping out of school without the support of anybody in my life may have been the scariest thing I've ever done. But it was also the first time I valued myself more than the opinions of the people around me.

My lease in Riverside wasn't up until the start of summer, and with all my friends back home still in school until June, I decided to bide my time in Southern California until then. I spent nearly every day driving from Riverside to LA, taking whatever work I could get to help myself financially.

I moved to LA in the fall. I was doing okay, not great. But okay was the best I had felt in a year. My expectations were low, which set me up pretty well. I truly believed that if I wanted to be fine, I would be fine. Without realizing it, I figured out my triggers and how to cope with them. I felt important and useful if I was busy, so I kept busy. If I was by myself for extended periods of time, I felt panicked. I found myself hyperventilating and overwhelmed with feelings of great upset I couldn't shake. So I surrounded myself with any friends I could get. And when I got screwed over again and again, I would turn my camera on, smile, and pretend the audience I was talking to was right in my room. I don't think I was running away from my problems or ignoring them. I don't think that putting on a happy face when you feel like shit is lying or unhealthy. I think if you want to feel better, you will do anything in your power to, and that is anything but weak. Did this desperation for normalcy result in some pretty shitty circumstances? Yeah. Did I befriend some people I shouldn't have, do some things to fit in I don't entirely stand by, and say things or put forth an image I don't necessarily wholeheartedly agree with? Yeah. But I don't regret the intentions behind my actions. I was living in spite of how I felt—not out of denial, but out of resilience and sheer determination.

After a while I began to realize that I was never going to feel "normal" again. I began to accept my current state as my new normal. I'd rather settle for this person I had become than strive toward an unreachable goal. Deep down, I knew the depression wasn't situational.

It had been more than a year since Riverside, and I wasn't "adjusting to change." *I* had changed. It wasn't a three-month window of me "getting over it"; it wasn't ending. So I continued to cope, unaware that my bouts of inexplicable hollowness and hysterical episodes of sheer panic indicated anything that might require attention. It wasn't an ideal situation, obviously, but it was what I had, and that was okay with me.

Then my best friend Sydney moved to LA for a summer internship, and I was nothing short of ecstatic. Having her around made me feel whole and like I was home again.

Sydney takes care of me in ways I don't know how to take care of myself. She'll say she took the internship in LA for the experience, but I think she also took it for me. Without ever addressing it, I think Sydney could sense the change in me. If she couldn't be there for me year-round, she'd spend the summer collecting people for me who could. In that one summer I was more social and adventurous than I had ever been since moving to Southern California. Sydney was like my security blanket. I felt better about myself when she was around. I got out of my own head, and in doing so I was able to let people in.

When Sydney headed back to school at the end of summer, our goodbyes were easier than I expected they'd be. While nobody could ever replace her, she left me in LA better than she had found me. We had all celebrated my twenty-first birthday together in Vegas, and my new legality opened a whole new pool of social prospects. I had even started dating a guy earlier that summer. I felt like I had a grasp on where my life was headed, and I actually felt like I had a say in it. I was happy. Really, really happy. The kind of happy where the thought that it might be too good to be true doesn't even cross your mind. Or at least it didn't cross *my* mind.

One specific day in October sticks out as the day it all came crashing down. I'm sure it happened slowly, but it felt like it hit me all at once. I must have woken up at five or six a.m. I hadn't been sleeping well for the previous week, and that day was no exception. As I lay there in bed next to my boyfriend of the past three months, I felt smothered by this feeling of darkness. My chest felt tight and constricted, and the ache in my body felt like it would pull me straight through the floor. I had tried to shake this feeling all week. I thought if I didn't validate it, maybe it would just go away. But it felt like I had left my body, and an unprepared understudy had taken my place. My boyfriend and I had made plans to go to brunch, but I begged him to cancel and let me sleep in. He refused, so I begrudgingly dragged myself out of bed, threw on sunglasses and shoes, wore my slept-in pajamas, and ignored his disapproving look as we walked toward the café. He didn't ask me what was wrong. He'd asked that question earlier that week, and my answer of "I don't know; I'm just feeling really down" was not sufficient in his eyes, so he didn't ask me again. I couldn't have spoken more than five words at brunch. It was all I could do not to burst into tears at the restaurant. I could feel the room getting smaller and smaller. The music was building, and every sound of every knife against a plate seemed to be amplified. I thought I was going to shatter into a million pieces. Staring at my uneaten food, I said the first thought that came to my mind: "I think I need to go home to my parents' house for a while." I could feel his eyes digging into me, but I refused to look up. "With me, you mean?" he asked, his fists white from clutching his cutlery. I whispered, "Alone." As the word left my mouth, his fists hit the table with a BANG! He stood up, knocking his chair over in the now-silent restaurant. All eyes were on us as he stormed out, leaving me fighting tears and fumbling in my wallet for cash. He spent the walk back to the apartment apologizing, stroking my hair, and saying he was sorry for getting upset. I just needed to understand that he loved me so much that the thought of me wanting to spend time away from him made him sad. He forgave my lapse in judgment, and he knew I didn't mean it. When we got back inside, I grabbed my laptop and settled back into bed. I positioned my body so his eyes couldn't see the screen as I began to type in a same-day flight search for San Francisco. I didn't even make it past the Google results before he slammed my laptop shut. This was when I lost it. The tears I had been fighting back streamed down my face as I collapsed into hysterics. He cradled me, cooing soft words and kissing my head. Through the tears, I managed to spit out the words I was running away from for so long: "I think I'm depressed." As soon as I said it, I regretted it. His once warm and consoling demeanor turned back to the angry, white-fisted guy at brunch. "You're not depressed," he said to me, his voice cold and piercing. "You have nothing to be depressed about. You don't know what it's like to be depressed. *I* know what it's like to be depressed. *I* have faced actual shit in my life. You have no fucking idea what that even means, Meghan." He went on like this as I lay facing the wall, my shoulders shuddering with sobs. At some point he left. Instead of feeling a sense of relief, I felt more scared than before. The thought of being alone terrified me. What scared me even more were the thoughts I had. I had never before been so afraid of what I might do, so I booked myself a one-way flight that night, and I texted my family that I was coming home.

I spent the first two days ignoring my boyfriend's calls and evading questions from my parents. I took Benadryl to fall asleep. If I wasn't sleeping, I was crying. I didn't know how to explain what was happening, because I didn't know. I couldn't bring myself to tell my parents why I had come home. I was embarrassed and ashamed to admit that I was scared of what I would do if I was left alone. At some point my mom told me she thought this might be due to a thyroid imbalance, so she made an appointment for me to get blood work done. I nodded in agreement, it could be a thyroid problem. Google says it can mess with your emotions, so that must be it. I really *wanted* that to be it. I couldn't figure out how I had gotten to where I was, and I wanted there to be a reason and a solution. The doctor's office called. They had time to go over my lab results if we came in later that afternoon. I remember sitting in the waiting room in a pair of my high school sweatpants and the same flannel shirt I had worn all week. I had my glasses on and my unkempt hair was thrown into a haphazard ponytail. I looked about as terrible as I felt. I can't imagine what other people thought when they saw us: my mom casually leafing through an old *Oprah* magazine and me curled up in a ball, staring blankly ahead. When my doctor called us into her office, she did a quick once-over of my current state and began scanning her clipboard. She told me everything had come back normal. I was still in the anemic range, but that was old news. My thyroid was fine and my levels were in the clear. My face fell. My mom's brow furrowed. She questioned the doctor about what exactly they had tested. We were probably the only two people she had ever come across who were so visibly distraught by a clean bill of health. She asked what we were hoping to find. Before I could put it into words, my mom told her that I was "feeling down." She seemed to think it was a side effect of a multitude of curable and treatable things. "I'll be right back," the doctor said as she slipped out of the room. She reappeared with a new clipboard and pen, which she handed to me with a sympathetic smile. I looked down at the questionnaire in my hand. The title read "Mental Health Assessment." My eyes welled up with tears just reading those three words. "Because you're over eighteen and a legal adult, I have to ask you: Would you like your mother to stay in the room, or would you rather fill this out alone?" the doctor said to me. My mom crossed her arms. "I'd rather be alone if that's okay," I said to the floor. She nodded, ushered my mom out, and shut the door behind her.

It was the first time I didn't cheat on a test, though I did downplay it. Reading on paper some of the thoughts I was having made them seem scarier and more worrisome than they sounded in my head. In a way, it should have made me feel less crazy. If nobody else ever thought or felt these things, then they wouldn't be on this test. But at the same time it made me feel completely crazy. The things I thought were normal to feel were nothing of the sort. I answered almost everything honestly, and before I could scribble out or change my answers, the door opened and the doctor came to collect it. She told me that she'd read it over and would be back in a minute to discuss the results. As I sat there on the crinkly paper on the examination table, I tried to steady my breathing and compose myself. If the results were bad, I would pretend I misread the questions. She came back a minute later and sat next to me. She told me that I had scored a level of severe clinical depression that required them to suggest I look into an outpatient mental health facility. I opened my mouth but nothing came out. I curled my legs up onto the bed and sobbed. The hysterics dwindled down to manageable cries, and I lifted my head from my legs as she asked me, "Do you want me to tell your mom?" I nodded, and she was gone. When she returned, she was accompanied by my mother. My mom asked what other tests they could run and what other, bigger issues could be causing this. Was the birth control I was on recalled? Had they checked my hormonal levels and anything else that could cause this? The doctor assured her that they had but agreed to run more tests. My mom looked at me with an expression of pity and said, "Don't worry, we're going to figure out what's actually wrong." It was supposed to be comforting, I think, but all it did was make me feel guilty. I knew the results would all come back normal and I'd have nothing to blame this feeling on other than myself.

I never checked into a facility. That wasn't even a discussion. I went off my birth control and any medications I was on that might possibly have something to do with my "emotional issues." My mom asked if my boyfriend had caused this. I told her no but that he wasn't helping, either. We agreed I should break up with him. She asked about work in LA: Was my team causing this? I told her no, but they weren't helping, either. We agreed I should get new representation. Then I booked my flight back to LA.

My boyfriend and I broke up. I took a break from social media for about two weeks. When it came time for me to upload a video, I couldn't fake it. I couldn't get on camera and pretend to be bubbly and happy and talk about things as trivial as my favorite sweatshirt. I knew that people would see right through it, and the shitstorm of hateful comments would just kick me even further down. So I turned on my camera and said the only thing on my mind for the past month: "I'm depressed." I posted it, closed my laptop, turned my phone off, and slipped into a NyQuil-induced slumber.

The feedback I woke up to was insane. My inbox on every platform was filled with so much love and support from people I knew and people I didn't. My high school friends were calling me around the clock, Facetiming me between their classes, and collectively ensuring that I felt their long-distance love twenty-four hours a day. I was getting emails and Facebook messages from people I knew all over saying that they had been through what I had. They'd end it with their phone number and an open invitation for friendship. All these people I knew and interacted with had struggled with this in various forms, and for the first time since that doctor read my test results, my diagnosis didn't feel as unusual as it did before.

It's been a process, to say the least. You cannot battle depression alone. As solitary as the illness feels, it's something you can't keep to yourself. You need a support system of friends and professionals, people to check in on you and hold you accountable for how you treat yourself. There is a misconception that asking for help means that you're weak, but I think asking for help is the strongest thing you can do. I used to feel defeated because I couldn't choose happiness no matter how hard I tried. I put so much pressure and blame on myself for my depression when in reality it's something so much bigger than me. With professional help I learned about the chemicals that are released in your brain that cause happiness, how some people are born with an imbalance from the start, and others fluctuate throughout their whole lives. That was out of my control. I can't control everything, but I control what I can. I set myself up for success, putting myself in the best possible position to be happy. That means therapy, psychiatrist appointments, staying on top of medications, filling my schedule with work, getting enough sleep, eating the right foods, staying organized, and surrounding myself with people who make me want to be a better person. Some days are better than others, but that's how it goes. The bad days might be bad weeks or bad months, but as long as you treat them as the outliers and not the norm, you are moving through it. When things get really dark, I try to find happiness in the little things, like morning coffee, or a funny meme. If you add enough of them together, they make a big thing.

I'm never going to be "recovered" or "healed" from my depression, and that's okay. No matter where I am or what I'm doing, my depression is always there. Sometimes she's dormant, hiding away to let me bask in the sunshine; other times she rears her ugly head and engulfs me for months at a time. I can't prepare for the bad times, or anticipate the good times. The only things I can rely on are my support system and my treatment plan. I don't know if I'd still be here without therapy. I won't ever be able to get rid of my depression, but as you put in the work, you learn how to cope with it in healthier ways. There's a light at the end of the tunnel. There's another tunnel after that, and that one has a light too.

chapter 20

anxiety

I think I've dealt with anxiety my whole life; I just didn't always know what it was. I've touched on the fact that I was a really insecure kid who overcompensated by projecting an over-the-top image of confidence. Which I don't necessarily see as a bad thing. I mean, it would have been ideal if I actually felt those feelings. I think the attempt was a step in the right direction. I'm bringing this fact back up because it has a lot to do with my history with anxiety.

Growing up is hard. We sit through health classes that discuss hormones and the changes our bodies go through physically. In some cases they touch on the emotional changes that also occur, but a lot of the time they don't. All I was told was that my teenage hormones were blowing all my feelings and reactions way out of proportion. I was reassured that I would grow out of it, and that was that. Now, there is much truth in this. Hormones can cause your body to do crazy things, like grow boobs, a mustache, or both. I am not discounting a scientific fact. The problem I have is that at that age we're basically told to be patient and "ride it out" without any follow-up or actual conversation about what we're feeling. If we run a fever, our parents are quick to schedule a check-in with our pediatrician just to be safe. When it comes to mental health, we lump the symptoms and side effects together with the emotional roller coaster of puberty and growing up instead of validating those feelings and taking time to figure out whether they're caused by this change in hormones or if they are the result of a permanent condition.

I grew up hearing that these invisible "hormones" were the root of all my problems, and I believed that. I blindly assumed that I was going through a phase and that these feelings did not deserve attention because they were temporary. Which, when you think about it, is kind of a shitty way to live: just letting yourself be okay with being unhappy. As if we're paying our dues until we're grown-ups, at which point we've finally earned happiness. I never found it comforting when people told me that life didn't get good until college. They'd say it as if that was supposed to take the pressure off. I shouldn't waste my energy, because this was just the dress rehearsal for my life. I listened to them because I didn't know any better, and my feelings were given no credibility by the adults around me. Therefore, I didn't give them credibility, either; I swept all those thoughts and feelings I had under the carpet, and I just ignored them. Some of them went away, and others stuck around. The ones that stayed, I normalized. I got used to them, and I thought either everybody else did, too, or I was completely crazy.

I'm now only just starting to recognize aspects of my adolescence that might not have been as normal as I assumed; although normalcy is somewhat of a spectrum, you get what I mean. My whole life I was classified as an extrovert. I was outgoing, chatty, loud, and a total ham. I was in theater and I told anybody who would listen about my dreams of being an actress. I was so confused that, despite all that, I spent most of my day feeling inexplicably terrified. I was fine when I was with my friends, but if I had to do anything alone, I completely shut down. The thought of getting called on in class brought me to tears. If I knew it was coming, I would plan out exactly what I would say and repeat it in a loop over and over in my head, agonizing over how it would sound out loud. My palms were constantly sweaty, my stomach was permanently in knots, and my voice shook like a shake weight. I loved performing and acting in plays, but I was completely petrified the whole way through. I made excuse after excuse for why I couldn't participate in PE. If my best friend was home sick from school, I'd fake illness. If my only friend in math class had to miss it for a doctor's appointment, I'd ditch. It sounds so dramatic in writing, but I honestly don't know how to convey the feeling of being so anxious, you're actually afraid your heart might stop. I had no idea what anxiety was at the time. I associated a fear of public speaking with being shy. Because I wasn't shy, that did not apply to me. There wasn't one "fear" I was facing, and I'm not sure if you could even classify it as a fear at all. It's not that I was afraid of something. I was paralyzed by everything.

Mental health wasn't something that was discussed in depth at school. We had those flyers posted on the walls telling us that if we knew someone was planning on harming themselves or somebody else, we should call 911. The only exposure I had to talking about mental health as more than "suicide prevention" was reruns of the original UK series *Skins* that I LimeWired to my family desktop. Even then my knowledge was limited at best. I had no concept of anxiety as a disorder, just as a word. I don't necessarily believe in labels wholeheartedly. But in this situation, if I had stumbled upon a description of what it meant to have "anxiety," I might have stopped thinking I was just broken. I might have started getting help.

Without intending to, I found an outlet in writing. Every social interaction I was so terrified of in person was 10,000 times easier online. I could think about what I wanted to say, type it, and erase it a hundred times before anyone could even see it. I could write down everything I wanted to, and the words looked so much more beautiful on paper or on the screen than they did collecting dust inside my brain. I would write stories (fanfic) about mystical lands (Hogwarts) and the people of these worlds (the golden trio). I could finally just let go and be myself. I never saw this timid, shaking, stammering girl as a facet of my personality or even closely related. It felt like *Invasion of the Body Snatchers*. The real Meghan was the one who laughed so hard she snorted, lip-synched to Ashlee Simpson songs, and quoted *The Producers*. The version of myself I identified with the most was when I was surrounded by my few close friends. When I was out of that safe place, it felt as if somebody else had taken over my body entirely. I did everything I could to avoid leaving my comfort zone at any cost. This is also why I personally benefited so much from the technology boom at this time. I started keeping an online journal, and I'd write about anything and everything I was feeling. Just getting those words out started to make me feel a little lighter. I still dreaded the social demands of Monday mornings, but I at least had this nightly escape.

My junior year, I found a new coping mechanism. His name was Captain Morgan.

Being drunk made the jittery and uneasy parts of me disappear, leaving me with the boisterous and uninhibited person I pretended to be. Suddenly, I was in control. I was not a slave to these emotions I knew were useless. I could shut them up or drown them with liquor. When I was drunk, my comfort zone was no longer limited to a handful of people. I could talk to whoever and say whatever without a care in the world. Everything was easier. The social interactions I had so desperately dreaded became a breeze, and it was invigorating. In my mind I had unlocked the key to being the best version of myself. It just also happened to be the drunkest version of myself. I won't go too much more into detail about my relationship with alcohol, as it has its own chapter. I bring it up again here because it does play an important role in my journey with anxiety. As I still remained ignorant about what I was struggling with mentally, instead of suffering in silence, I had found an intoxicating (literally) solution. Or so I thought.

The social demands and obligations of high school were nothing compared to those of college. The comfort zone I rarely strayed from was now four hundred miles away. I had none of my best friends as buffers.

I didn't have my bed, my little blue bedroom, or the backyard where I used to pretend I was making potions, imagining I was at Hogwarts, grinding up acorns with dirt and grass and calling it an "elixir." I was as far out of my element as I could be, and I hated it. Before I knew it, it was September and I was in River-fucking-side, California. "Miserable" doesn't even begin to describe how I felt. I was that girl moving into the dorms in full-blown hysterics. My parents patted me on the shoulder and told me it would all be fine. I curled up into the fetal position on the twin XL mattress in my dorm and cried. And then cried some more. At some point my sobs turned into shallow breaths, and I began hyperventilating until I passed out. I woke up with a searing migraine and what I assumed to be my new roommate looking at me, wondering what the fuck she had gotten herself into. Same, girl. Same. At this time I didn't know what a panic attack was. I had cried myself to the point of passing out before, and I popped Excedrin for migraines like Hugh Hefner popped Viagra. While this "episode" may seem alarming, it wasn't my first.

On paper, college should have caused me a hundred times more anxiety than high school did, but it didn't. While it checked off every box on my no-go and will-send-me-into-Colin-Creevey-like-petrification list, it also allowed me a lifestyle in which I could silence that stress. And by "lifestyle," I mean going out five to seven days a week, living solely on dining hall tater tots, Diet Coke, questionable pho, and blue raspberry Svedka. Or the whipped cream flavor. Who am I kidding? I'd drink anything I was handed.

I wasn't growing out of my anxiety at all. If anything, it was getting worse; I was just now in an environment that favored my coping mechanism. The effects it had on me were not unique; I think a lot of people feel the same way, even if it's not to the same degree. I was essentially self-medicating for an underlying issue I didn't know I had, and that can be a very slippery slope.

Everything came crashing down sophomore year. The satellite safety zone I had found with two of my sorority sisters imploded. I started having regular panic attacks, anywhere between one and six a day. It was crippling. Those irrational fears I had of not being liked were no longer irrational and no longer fears. They were real and they were happening. I tried as hard as I could to push through those feelings, but it was so overwhelming. I felt completely broken and I didn't know what to do. I tried to just continue on as if nothing had happened, but it was like rubbing my stomach and patting my head at the same time. I felt so disconnected from myself but somehow, at the same time, beyond hyperaware of my every atom and molecule. I felt completely and utterly out of control and so painfully alone. I slept in my closet for two months—though I don't know if I really slept at all.

After Thanksgiving break, I moved into my own one-bedroom apartment in Riverside. When my parents visited, they pointed out the changes in me. I was fidgety, my eyes darted all over the place, I wasn't sleeping, I was making list after list, and I was neurotic to the point of obsessive. I would later find out through therapy that I was displaying obsessive-compulsive tendencies. It was a desperate attempt on my part to feel a sense of control when I had none. I had no clue what was going on with me. I just thought I was as broken as I felt.

In everyone's mind, my problems could be traced back to the bullying and those girls from Riverside. Once I was removed from that situation, everything after that should have been better. Part of me naively believed that as well. I thought the whole out-of-sight-and-out-of-mind thing would come into effect, but it did nothing of the sort. I can only relate it to a mistreated dog that gets rescued and adopted. In theory, once it's out of the house where it was abused and mistreated, the dog would just respond to the new, better, happier, more loving place. But instead the dog retains the same tendencies and demeanor from the unhealthy environment. Time can heal wounds, but there are some things that really stick with you. Those alarming red flags in regard to my mental state and general well-being went unnoticed by my friends in LA because those indications were all they knew of me. There was no previous Meghan to compare them to. Then my best friend Sydney moved in with me for a summer, and she witnessed a particularly bad panic attack.

It was a seemingly typical evening. Sydney and I were catching up on chores and doing laundry. After putting my clothes in the dryer, I fell asleep on the couch watching *Sex and the City* reruns. The next thing I knew, I was being shaken out of a deep sleep. I opened my eyes to find Sydney kneeling beside me and the apartment filled with smoke.

She ran toward the bathroom, which seemed to be where the smoke was the thickest. She shouted that the door was slightly warm to the touch but nowhere near hot as she gingerly opened it. Upon doing so, a wave of smoke poured out, and flames could be seen from what used to be the washer-dryer unit. Up until that point the smoke alarm had been dead silent, but now, with the door open, it rang through the apartment complex. This all happened in a matter of seconds. Suddenly, Sydney was back by my side, grabbing our coats and our phones, ushering me outside as she dialed 911. I don't know if I was still asleep or in shock, but my memories of this skip around. We sat on the pavement as the fire department rushed in to put out the flames. I don't know how long we sat there in silence, Sydney's arms wrapped around me, stroking my hair as I stared blankly ahead. She put her arm around my waist to help me stand up as the fire chief approached us. She held my hand as he explained that our apartment complex had installed our laundry unit without following proper protocol. In doing so, there was debris trapped in the ventilation system, which had caused the fire. Sydney nodded, asked all the right questions, and answered all the fire chief's questions, all without ever letting go of my hand. He said they had removed the unit for disposal in the morning but they'd need another forty-five minutes to ventilate our apartment before we could go back inside. She thanked him and we returned to our previous spot on the curb. At the time I felt eerily numb, which I now understand to be shock. Forty-five minutes later the fire department packed up and left. With Sydney's arm wrapped around my waist to steady me, we began to make our way to the apartment. As we rounded the corner, we saw what used to be our washer-dryer unit. Or at least what was left of it. It was covered in soot and ash, melted, deformed, and emitting a foul smell reminiscent of burning hair, but one hundred times worse. I didn't even bother to peer inside. It would only make matters worse to see what this fiery beast had done to my bedding, underwear, and sweatshirts. I wasn't sure what I was expecting to see once we got inside the apartment, but whatever I had thought, the reality was so much worse. The walls were stained with smoke, some were streaked with soot, the carpets were about ten shades darker than they had been that morning, and the number of footprints left by the firemen's boots looked less like a crime scene and more like a line dance. The door to the laundry unit had been turned to ash, the linoleum floor had melted and warped, and the walls were burned from the baseboard to the ceiling. It was so bad in some places that it created holes in the drywall. The once-white ceiling was now the color of burnt marshmallows. Despite the machine they had used to circulate fresh air, it still smelled and tasted like we were inside a doused campfire. We wove our way through the rest of the apartment. We were met with the same discoloration of the carpet and the walls, as well as a thick coating of ash on every surface and object in sight. We cracked the door open to the bedroom. I stood there staring at the bare bed and the stained walls, and it all hit me. Tears flooded from my eyes as I collapsed onto the naked mattress and curled into a ball as my body was racked by hysterical sobs. Sydney silently lay down next to me and softly traced my spine with her fingers. When my cries turned into convulsions and my breath began to escape me, she flipped off the light switches. She softly coached my breathing and reassured me that everything was going to be okay. I don't know how long it lasted. When my heartbeat started to return to normal, she held a glass of water to my lips. She made me take tiny sips until my breathing evened out. I must have fallen asleep soon after that, because the next thing I remember, it was morning. Over coffee and *Barefoot Contessa*, Sydney asked me how often I was getting panic attacks. I didn't know what to say. I wasn't even really sure what a panic attack was. I had heard the term before but only in the abstract way people dance around discussing mental disorders. I had assumed I would know if I had a panic attack. I thought it would be like getting a bloody nose: something I didn't consciously go out of my way to get, but an obvious fact when it occurred. When I answered her question, I mustered the biggest smile and chalked it up to a long and stressful night.

Sydney definitely didn't believe me, but she didn't push the matter. Instead she leaned over to give me a hug. After a few minutes I told her she'd be late for work if she didn't let go, but she just held on tighter.

It wasn't until I started seeing a professional to help with my longtime battle with ADHD that the conversation about my anxiety even came up. Together we've been able to identify it as a partial source of my anxiety. I learned that while my general and social anxiety did not stem from any one specific thing or event, my frustration with myself and concern with others' perception of me were partially tied to the fact that I was so deeply insecure about my intellect. I had always felt like the funny friend, as in the whole "Dance, monkey, dance" thing. From the time I was eleven or twelve I was already labeled a ditzy blonde and an airhead, and I really believed that. I struggled so hard in school to follow what was happening. Even in casual conversations, I would try as hard as I could to stay focused and listen, but it was physically impossible. It made me come across like a self-absorbed and disinterested bitch. I knew that. I struggled to hold up my half of a conversation or, even worse, explain something. I could hear how circular my sentences were and how many times I said "like" to buy myself more time to get my mind back on track. A large part of my fear surrounding social interactions was due to this insecurity; I just didn't know it was a result of my ADHD.

Anxiety fucking sucks. I want to say that it's gotten better; it hasn't, but it's gotten different. I go to therapy, and through that I've been able to unpack more of where my anxiety comes from and now have tools to talk myself through it. I've accepted that I'm going to battle anxiety for the rest of my life. I have also accepted that this fact doesn't make me special; it makes me human. Anxiety disorders affect a massive percentage of the world's population. No matter how alone I may feel, by straight-up mathematical evidence I am not alone. #Science. Or, I guess, #Math in this case.

a comprehensive paint-by-numbers, step-by-step how-to on dealing with depression and anxiety from a completely unqualified twenty-something with no medical degree, let alone any college degree

Tell Somebody

It could be your best friend, a family member, or anybody you trust. It doesn't really matter who you tell, just that you do it. I wish I could promise that the second you say it out loud you'll feel a weight off your shoulders, but that's not always the case.

Sometimes the person you tell won't understand, believe you, or take your statements seriously—which, I can say from personal experience, is pretty disheartening. But that doesn't mean you should stop trying. Tell somebody else. Tell them repeatedly. Reiterate that you're not okay and that you're not okay staying not okay. Eventually someone will listen, or you can do what I do and pay somebody to listen.

Talk to a Professional

This step is obligatory.

Something I've learned from being in my twenties is that everybody is kind of fucked-up. Everybody is going through shit, dealing with shit, and working on their shit. I think that's probably always been the case, but at least, when I got to this age, people started talking about it more freely than before. Being able to have candid conversations with my friends about our psychiatrists and why going to Target on a weekend afternoon is a nonnegotiable never-going-to-happen thing, is cathartic and comforting. But it's not the same as seeking help from a medical professional. I cannot stress the importance of that enough. So much of the time we try to check our own emotions and discredit them; we think, *Other people have it worse*, or we could personally get lower than where we're at right now. That's essentially like saying, "People have terminal cancer, so I'm not going to the hospital for my broken arm because it could be worse" or "I cut my finger, but I'll just wait until it's infected and requires amputation." The best time to get help is BEFORE you hit rock bottom. Would you rather fall twenty stories or two stories? I mean, (d) none of the above, but you get the gist. A common misconception is that therapy and psychiatric help are expensive. Which they can be. But so are school, rent, and food—all necessary and justified survival expenses. We spend money to be educated and have roofs over our heads and food to eat, so we can grow up, get a good job, start a family, and live happily into old age. If we disregard our mental well-being, all of that money we have put into those other aspects of our lives and our futures will be rendered completely useless. It's a necessary, vital expense and investment in your future. When it comes to this professional help, there are so many different options and all different price points. There are in-person therapists and psychiatrists who work in private practices, and there are therapists employed by schools. There is group therapy and there are support groups—some cost money, others are free of charge or are covered by insurance. There are video sessions, phone sessions, and even apps you can download on your phone to help you get through the day. There is literally no excuse for thinking that professional help is not an option for you. It's like dating: it might take a while to find the right fit, but there is help out there for everyone. It took me trying a handful of therapists and psychiatrists before I found the right ones for me, but it's worth it.

Find Your Triggers

If you're unfamiliar, triggers are basically anything that causes, provokes, or progresses a feeling, in my case anxiety and depression. I've always likened it to having an allergy. For example, if I were allergic to nuts and I went balls-deep into a vat of Costco lightly salted fancy mixed nuts, I could be assured that my throat would swell up and I would go into anaphylactic shock. So I wouldn't do that. Another way to describe it would be that somebody who gets terrible motion sickness should avoid roller coasters and whale-watching boat tours. Enough explaining? Okay, cool. At least for me, the discussion of my own triggers came up pretty early on in treatment. I'd assume that's true in most cases (hopefully), because the whole point of working on yourself is to apply it to your daily life. You're not just ignoring it all until you're forced to discuss it weekly or biweekly. In the case of my own social anxiety, I had a way easier time deciphering my specific triggers than I did with my general anxiety. Automatically, I was able to rattle off a list of social situations that made me uncomfortable, but even those were pretty much blanket statements. It's easy to say that social interactions make me anxious, but it's way harder to pinpoint what exactly makes me uncomfortable within those interactions. So, Meghan, how *do* I find my triggers? Great question, thank you *so* much for asking. Truthfully, it's trial and error. I'm a huge list maker, and at some point I found myself keeping a list on my phone of things that triggered my anxiety and depression. Keeping a record of them might sound weird or pointless, but I really felt in control. I was able to put my feelings into words rather than letting them just stew as feelings. Plus there is nothing more rewarding than being able to delete something off that list. Granted, I'll probably add another thing later, but that's beside the point.

ways i cope with my social anxiety

1. Push (but not too hard).

How terrible is it that I wanted to make a sharting joke here? Sorry, gross, moving on. Anxiety is something I am going to live with for my whole life. With that in mind, my goal is to constantly strive to not just live with my anxiety but live in *spite* of my anxiety. In order to do that, I have to push myself to do things I am not entirely thrilled about or comfortable doing. Stepping outside my comfort zone is the only way I can begin to expand that. It was daunting at first. It seemed pretty pointless, as I saw no real drastic changes in myself. You don't walk 10,000 miles overnight. But if you take intentional and steady strides, one day you will turn around and need to squint to see how far you've come. It can be really frustrating at times, especially if you push yourself too far. Instead of propelling yourself forward, you stumble three steps back. Low points are difficult but not debilitating, and they make those high points feel like you're Usain Bolt (or whoever is the new fastest person in the world when you're reading this).

2. Know your limits.

This isn't to detract from the inspirational as fuck paragraph I just wrote above. It's more like that paragraph's cynical yet starkly realistic cousin. There are some things that just aren't going to happen for me right now, and that's okay. They may be things I've tried multiple times but they all ended terribly. They might be things that I wouldn't do even if it was my last day on earth. They might not always remain such deal breakers or hard lines, but for the time being, they are. That's okay. There is nothing wrong with knowing your limits and standing by them. It doesn't make you a party pooper or a wimp; it makes you self-aware and strong. If anybody tells you differently, I will shank them. Or at least @ them.

3. Find alternatives for FOMO.

I don't know if I should be proud of my nonexistent FOMO, but I totally am. This is largely due to the fact that instead of just forgoing all social activities, I've found alternatives that are far less terrifying and are actually—dare I say it?—ENJOYABLE! And by "alternatives" I just mean I force people to hang out with me at my house. We don't have to leave the couch, and I don't have to put on pants. This also works on a grander scale: dinner parties, brunches, and at-home game nights too! Believe it or not, people are actually looking to have low-key sober fun sometimes, and the options are slim. You're not a regular mom; you're a cool mom.

4. Work the (buddy) system.

Sometimes anxiety-inducing situations are unavoidable. At some point your friend will throw a rambunctious party at a bar, you'll need something at Target that is store-pickup only, or your work will make a satellite group bonding event mandatory. There are just some things you cannot get out of no matter how hard you try. (Believe me, I've tried.) In these cases I rely on the buddy system. Whether that means getting a +1 and bribing a friend to accompany me, or just planning ahead with someone I know who will be there as well, that built-in comfort of having someone with me is calming. You can also be candid and clue them in that you're feeling anxious about the situation.

5. The internet.

Use it. Love it. Live it. Not only will you be able to interact with fellow humans on days you need to recharge, you'll also find a truckload of very helpful information and techniques about coping with anxiety. Let it be said that online interactions cannot substitute for real-life interactions in their entirety. Think of the internet as your training wheels or your Olympic camp. Use it to build your confidence before you venture into the real world. Or at least use it to avoid customer service phone calls.

6. Set small goals with bigger rewards.

Because incentive, duh. For me this could be something as simple as grocery shopping alone or braving the crowds at Coachella (which I am zero for two right now, so that one is more hypothetical). If I'm able to successfully do something that usually would terrify me, I'm so fucking proud of myself. I'll play some happy Kelly Clarkson songs in my car and I'll treat myself to some new throw pillows. (My life is exciting, I swear.) Being able to give myself a pat on the back for accomplishing something that used to seem impossible not only reinforces wanting to keep up this streak, it also reminds me that I am making progress.

how i cope with general anxiety

1. Create a safe space.

For me, this means making my home happier than Disneyland. I think it's important for everyone to have a place where they can feel a sense of comfort and peace. This means completely different things to different people. It could be supersoft blankets and muted colors or even just being surrounded by familiar things that bring you joy. Whatever it is, make your space a reflection of that sense of calm.

2. Have a routine.

The frustrating thing about general anxiety is that in most cases it isn't brought on by anything specific that you can avoid. There is usually zero logic behind our anxious thoughts, but that lack of rationality doesn't stop them. One thing I have been able to notice in myself is that my anxiety tends to get worse when I'm confronted with sponta-neity and sudden change. If I have ample time to mentally prepare for something, I can almost guarantee I will feel far less stressed-out than I would if something is sprung on me at the last minute. Although some aspects of my day-to-day life are out of my control, I at least structure what I can. For me, that means waking up with ample time to get ready and drink my morning coffee in front of the TV with the latest episode of *Barefoot Contessa* on as I scroll through baking blogs, pinning cookie recipes. Even if that morning time is the only part of my day that brings me a sense of peace, I can always look forward to the next morning.

3. Sleep better.

If I could go back in time and shake some sense into my whining pre-school self when I was throwing a tantrum about bedtime, I would. I vastly underestimated how important sleep was to a healthy mindset. I always assumed that the only real side effect of not sleeping was just, you know, being sleepy. But in reality a lack of sleep or a restless night of sleep doesn't just leave you feeling groggy in the morning; it can leave you feeling tense, irritable, and extra-anxious. The kicker here is that insomnia is closely tied to mental disorders in general. While those of us with those challenges need sleep for our mental well-being, it's also harder to fall and stay asleep. I 100,000 percent struggle with this, and while I am by no means perfect at taking my own advice, I do make the effort. First, I need an hour of zero work—minimal brainpower—to "cool down," if you will. My brain is like a horny teenager: it needs time to simmer down. I might spend this hour reading, or Facetiming my best friend, or watching *The Great British Bake Off*. Next, I make myself a cup of tea. Usually a Sleepytime or a "calming" blend—which might be a placebo effect, but who cares. Into that tea I add a few drops of CBD oil, which (for those of you who live where it's legal) is A GODDAMN GAME CHANGER. Do your research if you're not well-read on it, but from my experience it's like herbal Valium. The next crucial step for me is getting into bed early. I have never been one of those people who fall asleep the second their head hits the pillow. Once horizontal, it's going to take me another solid hour or more to actually fall asleep, so I'd better get the process started early. Knowing that I'm not going to get enough sleep is another source of anxiety for me. Instead of waiting until "bedtime" to crawl into bed, expecting to pass out right there, if I give myself a cushion of time to actually get tired and fall asleep, I find that I'm less worried about falling asleep, so it's easier *to* fall asleep. Also, invest in a weighted blanket. Best $100 I ever spent. There's a whole scientific reason why it works, but who cares why. It just works.

4. Get a security blanket.

I don't actually carry a blanket Chuckie Finster–style with me everywhere I go, but I'm not above traveling with my weighted blanket. As somebody with a very addictive personality, I struggled to find something comforting I could do that wasn't destructive. As a teenager I used to pull out my eyebrow hairs and eyelashes. When I stopped that, I began to chew the inside of my cheek until I'd have a mouth full of blood blisters and welts. Cute, I know.

These days, in particularly bad moments of discomfort or anxiety, I'll fiddle with the rings on my fingers. Some hold sentimental value, but in general just the act of busying my hands and holding on to something tangible is grounding.

I've developed other little idiosyncrasies, like rubbing the tips of my fingers together or intertwining my toes together. But I think having a physical object you can hold not only prevents you from adopting a habit that may turn harmful, it also offers a comfort outside the confines of your own body. It's something that grounds you to the world outside your racing mind.

Things I Say to Myself to Make Me Feel Better When I Feel Like I Could Actually Die from Things I Can't Actually Die from, Like Listening to a Voice Mail

You are not going to die. A man walked on the moon.

David Blaine is still alive.

This will pass.

chapter 21

finding your own family

I never wanted to write this chapter, and I didn't intend to. The event that this chapter leads up to was one of the hardest things I've ever gone through. It was earth-shattering and it broke me. It was the first time I resented my own success, the first time I truly wished that nobody knew who I was. It was something so painful and personal to deal with in my everyday life, and suddenly I couldn't escape it anywhere. My mentions were filled with questions, my comments were flooded, and every time someone brought up my family in person, I almost lost it. I don't want to talk about this, because it still really hurts. But I think it's always going to hurt. I'm done keeping this in, letting people speculate and create their own versions of the truth. I'm sick of people asking about it, and I'm so sick of lying. For the first and last time, I am telling the whole story. I am setting the record straight, and then I am done. I am really, really done.

I didn't grow up in a happy home. I don't remember a time when my parents were happy. Maybe their wedding pictures. My mom was seventeen years younger than my dad, and when I was born she was the age I am now. Which is terrifying to think about, as I am not even close to being equipped for motherhood. Neither was she. I was their first and last kid together, which was both a blessing and a curse: a curse because I had nobody to endure childhood with, and a blessing because nobody else had to endure it. I think a large part of the reason I turned out okay was because it was just me. If I had had siblings or someone to talk to about it, I probably wouldn't have been able to justify so many things as normal. I mean, it affected me at the time, but I also had less to overcome, because I didn't know I had something to overcome. I thought most moms hated cuddling with their kids because it made them feel smothered. I assumed all moms wrote notes critiquing their kids' performance in school plays for them to review once they got home. I presumed all dads worked seven days a week. I thought if your parents fought, it was your duty as a kid to be a pawn in their drama. I got used to the sounds of incessant screaming and doors slamming, as well as one of them grabbing me out of bed and buckling me in the back seat as they drove away. For a while I tried to make them get along. I felt guilty, because so much of what they fought over were things that had to do with me. I tried to make them kiss like in the movies. I remember being, like, six years old and having a pile of change I had saved up from couch cushions and sidewalks. I offered it to them, asking that, in return, they kiss. On a good day they'd laugh and force a one-armed hug. Most times they just changed the subject. Eventually I gave up.

As I got older, the feeling that I was a burden got stronger and stronger. My mom worked from home, which meant she was around more, but she was mostly in her office and not available. My dad wasn't around a lot. He left for work before I was up in the morning and didn't get home until late at night. I loved every moment I got to spend with my dad. They came few and far between, but when they happened, I was the happiest kid in the world. My mom used to say that I was his little princess, but she didn't seem to say it with pride or love. I think she detested the fact that I loved him so much, and she constantly reminded me that he was not a good father. She said he loved his job more than he loved us, and no matter what, I was never going to be his first priority. She would bring up my half brother with an eyebrow raised, as if she was reminding me that my dad might walk out on us. My dad and an ex-girlfriend had a kid when they were teenagers. Despite that my brother and my dad made amends over the years, my mom liked to remind me of his past. I tried not to listen to her. It was hard when she'd remind me Christmas morning that my dad had nothing to do with the presents. She'd sign only her name, so I could be assured he had no part in it. Over the course of my life, I've kept a box of everything my dad has ever given me. Some things were just pens from his office, some cards, a cloth doll. One year he bought me a Bratz motorcycle and I loved it—not because of what it was, but because he gave it to me, and that meant my mom was wrong. At the end of the day, I knew my dad loved me. I also knew he loved his job, but I just chose not to participate in that competition. I wasn't sure I wanted to know the answer.

By the time I was in middle school, I was spending more time hanging around my friends' houses than my own. My friends' parents always invited me to stay for dinner. They'd ask, "Your parents are okay with that?" I'd say that they were and that they had a meeting that night. Which sometimes was true. Other times it just sounded better than admitting that we rarely had family dinners. If I was lucky and I begged enough for a sit-down dinner, it wouldn't happen until nine or ten p.m. Truthfully, I think my parents didn't mind if I ate elsewhere. My dad wasn't home anyway, and this way I was out of my mom's hair.

Despite this, I think my spending time at friends' houses also made my mom feel threatened. She'd dissect a story I told about what we did that day, and she'd twist it into me, saying that I liked these other parents more than my own. She'd lash out and call me ungrateful, say how she worked more than these other mothers, and she had bigger things to worry about than they did. I loved "frivolous" things, like clothes and the arts, whereas she valued things that required her to use her brain, and she thought that I didn't use mine enough. She told me that

I was selling myself short—I was smarter than the grades I got, and if I actually put in the effort, I'd realize that. But I *was* putting in effort. It felt like nothing I did was ever good enough for her. If I did something well, it was ignored; however, if even the smallest thing was not to her liking, it was the end of the damn world. All I wanted was validation and praise and for her just to notice how badly I wanted to make her proud. But most often I would get the words "That's it?" or "Is that all?" I brought it up one day. I told her it felt defeating, that I thought maybe if she could point out my successes as often as my shortcomings, maybe it would give me greater incentive. She patted me on the shoulder and said something like, "Oh, sweetie, I just know you're more capable than this. I'm not impressed with it because I expect better than this." I pretended she meant it as a compliment.

My mom would never be considered a "warm" person. As a kid I used to screen her calls, hoping she'd leave a voice mail in which she said she loved me. By the time I graduated high school, I think I had accumulated about three. Truth be told, both my parents have always been confrontational. That's probably why their fights were always a tug-of-war over getting the last word. If they weren't fighting, they were talking about a previous fight or what the other person did wrong, why they hated them, and how vile they were. With a household of three, I became the audience. I probably asked them not to bring me into it about ten times each day. Eventually, I could just recite it by memory: "I love Mom/Dad and it makes me feel uncomfortable when you talk bad about my mom/dad in front of me. I don't think it's healthy for me to hear about this. Maybe you should talk to a friend instead?" Every time I said it to my dad, he shut up and apologized. "You're right, Meggy," he'd say with genuine remorse. My mom said she'd stop after she said just one last thing. "Don't marry young. Don't marry someone broke," I remember her telling me. "Don't end up like I did." To which I'd nod, trying really hard to tell myself she didn't regret the choice she made in having me.

The tumultuous relationship between my mom and me settled down my senior year. I was sick with mono for almost the entire school year; it sentenced me to house arrest. With her working from home, it forced us to be around each other almost 24/7. I used to think her yelling eased up because of how ill I was, but in hindsight I think it may have been because this was the most control she'd ever had over me. By summer I was given a clean bill of health, just in time to get ready for college. I've said it before, but it deserves restating: I did not want to go to college. Period. I settled on UCR not because it was the best school I got into (lol); no, I chose it purely based on its proximity to Los Angeles, the city I intended to live in once I inevitably dropped out of school. By the time August rolled around, I had no idea how I had gotten to freshman orientation. I knew the second I stepped on campus that this wasn't the school for me. My assumptions were confirmed when members of my orientation group made loud comments about me. Boys were spitting gross sexual remarks, and the girls were laughing along, all the while refusing to call me anything but Malibu Barbie. I quietly reminded them that they all lived closer to Malibu than I did. "I'm from NorCal," I said. I should have thrown in a "hella" or a "hyphy"; maybe then they would have dropped it. I remember texting my mom about all of this in all caps, ending with the definitive: "THERE IS LITERALLY ZERO CHANCE IN HELL YOU'RE LEAVING ME HERE." She was across campus at the "parents'" orientation, where she was having a similar experience—not the creepy remarks, just her utter disdain for the school I had haphazardly chosen. But I had already committed to UCR, and enrollment for all the other schools had started, so I really had no other choice. I was stuck, at least for now.

When it all went downhill sophomore year, my parents were the first people I told. They tried to reason with me, asking if I had in fact done anything wrong to deserve this exile from my friends. My mom suggested making more of an effort, as she thought I was stubborn to a fault. I insisted that I was trying as hard as I could, but my efforts seemed to go unnoticed. I called my parents every day in hysterics, pleading with them to let me drop out, but they refused. I had been crashing on the couch in another friend's apartment, but with the school year just beginning, it wasn't really a permanent solution. After Thanksgiving break my parents and I agreed on a compromise: I would move out of the shared apartment and into my own, I'd stay in school, and I would be fine. They came down to Riverside to help pack my room up. Despite my pleas with my mom not to stir the pot, she couldn't resist. She made passive-aggressive snaps at my roommates' parents who were visiting for the weekend, and aggressive-aggressive comments at the girls. I begged her to just be the bigger person, but that wasn't in her wheelhouse. When she started greeting them with "Oh, look, the bitches are back," I excused myself to focus on unpacking at the new apartment. I like to think that this was her way of expressing maternal instinct, but in reality I suspect she just thrived on the drama. I lasted in Riverside for the remainder of the school year, but I lasted at UCR for only a quarter of that. Undeterred by the protests of my parents, I dropped out of school. I was nineteen, I was financially independent, and they knew they couldn't stop me. Despite their objections, they helped me move to LA, something I will be eternally grateful for. They didn't like it, they didn't support it, but they still helped unpack my boxes and build my furniture.

While I was going through the roughest part of college, I had gotten into the habit of talking to my mom and dad multiple times a day. As I began to acclimate to LA and make new friends, I called them less and less. I realized that so much of our communication was initiated on my end, but I was okay with it. My schedule had filled up tremendously, and now I didn't have time to keep them updated on every aspect of my life. We still talked on the phone once or twice a week, and I cut down my visits home to just Thanksgiving and Christmas. I loved going back to Marin for the holidays. My friends were all on college break, and we'd plan weeks in advance for everything we wanted to do in the short amount of time we were all home at the same time. While most of my friends' schedules were filled with family time, mine wasn't. I didn't let much get to me in regard to my parents; I had given up being disappointed long before that. If I came home to visit for a weekend, I might see my parents for dinner only once. If I asked them if we could spend the day together or hang out, their schedules were already full. I rationalized the first few times as flukes, but as it became clear that this was just how it was, I finally said something. It was Christmas break and I had asked my mom if she wanted to watch a movie with me that night. She was going hiking all day with her friend, a Friday tradition they'd established when I was a kid. It was something she didn't reschedule, even if it meant missing something important of mine. She begrudgingly agreed that if she had time that night, she might be able to "watch an episode of something." We watched an episode of *Gilmore Girls* and then her phone buzzed. Her friends were all going out together, and as she made moves to meet them, I asked if she could stay. I wanted to spend time with her. She let out an exasperated sigh and said, "Fine, Meg. What do you want to do?" I offered a smile and said I just wanted to stay in together. She spent the remainder of the night agitated and looking at the clock. I tried to ignore it. The next morning was a Saturday, and I made my way into the kitchen to make tea. I called to her and asked if she might want to do something together that day. Before I could even suggest ideas on what that could be, she cut me off and reminded me that her life didn't stop when I got home, and that she couldn't just drop everything and hang out with me. You could hear a pin drop. Then she continued to do her crossword and eat her scrambled eggs. I just stood there in the kitchen frozen, tears streaming down my face. I tried to tell myself that she didn't mean anything by it. Later that week I woke on Christmas Day to an empty house and not a note in sight. When my parents came through the door with the guests from out of town who they were entertaining, I asked where they had gone. My mom looked at me in surprise. "Oh! We forgot you were here!" She laughed, ushering everybody inside. "We all went out for brunch," she said, smiling. Merry Christmas?

I'd been completely financially independent by the time I was nineteen, and by about twenty-one I was living pretty comfortably. I felt so lucky to be making a living off something that used to be a hobby, but by no means was it easy work. Sure, it wasn't brain surgery, but it also wasn't a cakewalk. Suddenly, I was getting professional opportunities I never thought possible. While many of these opportunities had no monetary value, some did offer compensation. Money is not something I like to talk about. There's this odd idea out there that it's okay to ask "influencers" how much money they make, because to internet trolls, it's not a real job. On this point, my mom would agree with them. She seemed to bring up my bank account balance at any opportunity she could. We'd be at dinner with her friends and their kids, and my mom would do that gasp you do when you've got great gossip you forgot to spill. She'd grab the arm of the friend across from her and say something like, "You'll never believe how much money Meghan made from a hair tutorial!" I'd try to cut her off, but she'd howl with laughter as she heckled my job. She'd shake her head in disbelief, saying she couldn't fathom how something so unimportant and frivolous was better compensated than her job as a psychologist, which "actually made a difference for people." When our extended family would come to town, some of them would drunkenly comment about how I didn't deserve the success I had. My mom just sat there, never once defending me. She even managed to shit-talk me, my profession, and the entire industry surrounding it to my boyfriend, Mats. It was the second time she met him. (The first was when he dropped a package off at my apartment. She invited him in for tequila and proceeded to show him embarrassing home movies of me, heckling the whole time.) At the time, we weren't dating; he was my manager's assistant. I had a work event to attend, and I brought my mom as my plus one. Mats congratulated her on raising such a talented girl—his words, not mine—and he said how impressed he was with my success in the space. My mother rolled her eyes and said, "I feel like anyone could have done it."

From the start of my YouTube career, my parents both expressed their opinions on my channel. They said I was "feeding into capitalist America" even when my content was things like advice and humor. My mom chose to focus on the "consumerism" I was perpetuating. I guess you could say it made me develop a thick skin quicker than most, as I was facing "h8rz" both online and at home. Compared to my mom, my dad has always been my cheerleader. Even in high school, when I'd work my ass off for a mediocre grade in stats, he'd scream and jump up and down in excitement and pride. He was the first person I'd call if I booked a role or landed a major campaign. He didn't always understand what it entailed, but he was always happy for me. I stopped telling my mom the exciting things that were happening because her responses would just put a damper on it. She would find out through my dad what projects were in the works, or else she'd see them when the content was live. Her responses came in the form of either a phone call or a text message, and I often sensed a change in her priorities, as if my work would translate into something for her. In fact, when I gave her gifts, her excitement in receiving them seemed to directly correspond to their price. When she came to visit me in LA, I remember her inquiring about how much each designer purse in my closet cost. When I wouldn't tell her, she'd look them up herself. She'd ask why I didn't give them to her, why I didn't spend that kind of money on her. I'd feel guilty, and promise to keep her requests in mind for Mother's Day. This feeling of guilt got worse and worse as time went on. I no longer got excited about the opportunities that came my way. Instead of basking in the pride of my hard work and accomplishments, I dreaded what that success meant. The better I did, the worse I would feel about it.

Even through all of this, my parents were still prominent features in my YouTube videos, and across my social platforms. Initially, when I first started in 2010, they both were strongly against ever being shown on camera. But as it became more widely accepted as a medium, they eased up on that. I didn't go out of my way to include them, but when it happened, I noticed a shift in their behavior. If the camera was on them, or even in their vicinity, they didn't fight. They plastered on smiles and put on a show. My mom would refresh the comments on my videos. If she found that the viewers found my dad far sweeter and her far bitchier, she wasn't happy. My audience had taken a liking to my dad and his excitement to be on camera. Somehow that felt like it was my fault. So I started to include my mom more in filming, and she started matching his level of excitement. It didn't feel genuine to me, but I didn't care. Filming carved out a part of the day when I was guaranteed not to be yelled at or become collateral damage in one of their battles. But more than that, the footage was something tangible for me to hold on to. It was like the voice mails of my mom saying she loved me. It was a sliver of time caught on tape when I could pretend this version of reality was true.

This is the part of the story where things began to break down. It was September, and my mother had come to visit LA for the weekend. This was the first time she had ever come to visit just for "fun," which probably should have been a red flag. Her agenda became clear on her second night. It was probably ten or eleven, and we had already said our good nights. She nonchalantly waltzed into my dark bedroom and plopped herself on my bed, startling me out of my half-asleep state. She said that she had something to tell me, but she didn't think she needed to say it. She said I surely already knew. I sat up and nodded. I did. I had been expecting this conversation my entire life. I just thought my parents would have the decency to sit down together to tell me they were getting divorced. She said it anyway. I think she liked how the word "divorce" sounded. She said it without emotion, waving her hands as if she were brushing off some useless gossip she had heard that day. She didn't even pause for breath before she began rattling off all the terrible things about my father and their relationship, including references to their sex life and how she wanted to explore new men; I found it all startling and grossly inappropriate. She spoke as if I were an old friend she was grabbing cosmos with, rather than her daughter. She went on about how she deserved more and how my dad had never been her soul mate. She had settled for him, and when they got pregnant with me, she thought it would get better. As soon as I was born, she realized it wasn't going to. She had always wanted to divorce him, but she had seen how much divorce affected her friend's kids in middle school, so she put it off. She had wanted to do it when I reached high school, but then I got sick and the timing was bad. Then she was going to do it when I went to college, but because I had such a hard time with bullying there, she didn't think I could handle it. When I dropped out of school, moved out to LA, and got settled, she was going to do it then. But then there was that whole "depression thing," she said. The bottom-line message: If they had not had me, she could have ended it sooner, and she would have not been so miserable for the past twenty-two years. She owed it to herself and her happiness to make this change. She said that *I* owed it to her. She had stayed with my father for my sake, and now that I was an adult, I needed to act like one and support her decision. She told me that in order to maintain her lifestyle she needed "somewhere between $250K and $500K" to get a condo. She said it was kind of for me, too, as I'd be spending the holidays there. She didn't ask for a loan or even ask for the money; it was said like a statement I had already agreed to. (Sometime later, she left me a long voice mail touching on a variety of topics, including that she wasn't after my money and saying that she was not a "moneygrubbing bitch.") I hadn't said a word this whole time and she didn't even seem to notice. She ended with the same "piece of advice" she always left me with: Don't marry young and don't marry broke. She smiled without a trace of sadness and said good night.

When I could hear the familiar laugh track of *Modern Family* coming from the living room, I texted Mats. I told him my parents were getting a divorce. I didn't offer an explanation. He called me and stayed on the line while I cried.

She didn't bring it up for the rest of her trip. My mother kept getting frustrated with me, because I was acting all "down" and was "not fun"—as if our prior conversation and her lack of empathy were things I had no right to be upset over. In a way, I was kind of relieved. Which is probably an odd thing to say, but it's true. For my entire life, I had felt obligated to tolerate all my mom's toxicity. I was supposed to love her unconditionally, when I never felt that in return. For the first time I didn't feel like I was reading too much into things or that it was all in my head. It was as though I had been waiting all this time, internalizing her criticism and resentment, until we reached this point. It wasn't about the divorce. My parents hated each other; there was no perfect family image to shatter. It was the fact that she put a voice to all those negative thoughts I tried to push out of my head. I wasn't crazy. I finally felt like I could be done with her.

My dad visited me the following week. I waited for him to bring up the divorce, but he never did. Not only did he not mention it, he acted like they were still together, referencing her schedule for the week, speaking in terms of "us" and "we," and going on as if nothing had changed at all. I set up dozens of opportunities for him to tell the truth, but he didn't take the bait. The week ended and he didn't say a damn thing.

For more than a month, Mats was the only person who knew. Bear in mind that we hadn't begun dating at this point, yet he was still the first person I told. Next I told a friend who had been staying with me. She noticed I seemed a little off and asked if anything was up, so I filled her in. Again I left out the gritty details, generalizing it as just a standard divorce. It was easier to tell people who didn't know me too well or didn't know my mother. They had fewer questions and required a much less detailed story. I put off telling my best friend Sydney for nearly two months. The second I told her, it would be real. It would no longer be something I refused to think about. It would be something I would be forced to explain. She called me one day in November, asking what days I was going to be home for Thanksgiving. I answered the call while I was at the Coffee Bean & Tea Leaf. "Oh, my parents are getting divorced and my mom has officially turned into Dina fucking Lohan." As I said it, I made eye contact with an extremely uncomfortable-looking barista. "Swedish Berries?" he asked timidly. I was unfazed. "That's me," I said as he handed it to me, and I made my way toward the door. "Have a . . . um . . . Have a good day!" he stammered after me. You too, buddy. You too.

I pulled away for a while. I dodged their calls, until finally I just asked them to give me space. I assured them I would come to them when I was ready to talk. I was startled at how liberating this distance was. I felt lighter. I no longer vested my self-worth in the hands of people who I felt I couldn't trust with it. I was excited about succeeding again, and I didn't have that constant worry of what strings were attached, or that I didn't deserve it. I wasn't sure where my relationship with my mother would go; I needed that time and separation to figure it out. I didn't speak to them again until Christmas Day. I had been staying at my friend's parents' house for the holidays, and I sent both my parents an email asking if we could meet up for coffee later that week. I said I wanted to get the whole truth and the full story. The only way I felt like that would happen is if we all were able to sit together and talk about it. They declined.

With an afternoon free, I made plans with one of my best friends, Sierra. Sierra was my oldest childhood friend. You'd be hard-pressed to find a baby photo of one of us without the other. Our parents had all been friends before we came along, and when I was born, a six-month-old Sierra was at the hospital to meet me. We had always considered each other sisters, which was ironic, because she then told me that my mother was dating her dad.

At this point I thought myself unshockable, but apparently, I was wrong. That night of December 25 was the last time I talked to my mother. She had sent me a slew of texts that sent me spiraling, so I called her. I asked Sydney to stay in the room for moral support, and frankly, I needed someone else to hear the version of my mom that she reserved almost exclusively for me. That call was the nail in the coffin. I watched Sydney's eyes widen as she heard how my mother talked to me, refused to take responsibility, and continued to villainize me and my dad and deflect the blame onto us. The conversation veered into territory that was just inappropriate and cruel, and that shouldn't have been shared with me. It was another "light switch" moment for me. The kind of moment where someone shows you their hand and the proof is right there. I was done. And I told her that.

After I hung up, Sydney and I just sat there quietly for a while. I knew she was waiting for me to make the first move. She knew me well enough not to hug me or touch me, because I would burst into tears. She handed me a pillow and asked if I wanted to scream into it. I said yes. I screamed. Then I started laughing. Hysterically. This was becoming a habit of mine in times of crisis, and I couldn't hold it in. I couldn't stop laughing, and soon Syd was laughing with me. We laughed because it was better than crying. Our fit of hysterics halted when my phone vibrated with a new text from my mom. After that call I didn't know what I expected her to write, but I hardly made it two lines in before the tears came. I kept reading. For the first time since all of this started, I didn't respond with an eye roll or laughter. This time I broke down. Sydney grabbed the phone to read it, and her eyes filled with tears too. She dropped the phone on the bed and put her arms around me. She didn't say anything. We were both crying too hard to form words, and there was really nothing to say.

The rest of my trip to Marin was spent being honest with my friends about my home life, and trying to get some answers for myself. After some digging, I found out my parents weren't officially divorced, but they hadn't been together for almost two years (which translates to roughly eight trips back home, where they kept up the facade). Also, it turns out that my mom and Sierra's dad actually had had an affair when we were kids. That came out in passing over brunch, and my friends and I were equally shocked—me, at the news; them, at the fact that I didn't know. Surprise, surprise, I didn't. I shouldn't have been taken aback. Being in the dark was a common occurrence in my life. When I was thirteen or fourteen my mom nonchalantly told me she had had cancer a few years before. The next day at school I asked my friends if they had known; they did. I spent a chunk of elementary school wondering why I had visited her at the hospital, why other moms packed my lunches, why teachers looked at me with pity, and why my classmates seemed to treat me like a charity case.

I went back to LA at the end of the week. I emailed my dad when I landed. I told him that it was shitty for him to choose hatred over love on Christmas of all days, but I would get past that when I got some honesty. When he finally responded, I left the email unread in my inbox for three days. When I finally opened it, it wasn't much, but it resembled an apology, and I accepted it. I responded a few days later, telling him that I wanted a fresh start—how I felt that I hardly knew him and so much of what I knew was memories tainted by my mom. He said he'd like that too. Sometimes it's really good, like when he sends a text telling me how he has watched every episode of *Freakish*, albeit a few months late. It was good when Mats and I came to Marin and had dinner with him. He drew a sign that said "welcome home, meggy" and pinned it on the doorway. It was great to watch Mats and my dad meet and get along and pretty much cut me out of the conversation. It made me smile to get a text from him that night, saying that he loved Mats and loved how much Mats loved me even more. Then sometimes it's not so great, like when he chooses to work on a Saturday rather than see me on my last day in town. That stuff hurts, but it's like the hurt you know is coming. The kind that makes you feel stupid for thinking you were in the clear. It took him days to even respond to my message about it and acknowledge how shitty that was. And, honestly, his "apology" was more frustrating than the act itself. He's not a bad guy, he's just a workaholic, and he can be a bit self-righteous. He's dedicated his life to social justice reform and being a father figure to countless kids who never had one. It just so happens that he sort of missed being that to his own daughter. A part of me still really resents him for leaving me alone with my mom. He knew how terrible and toxic she was, and he just left me there. Maybe he worked so much because he couldn't bear to be around my mom, or maybe my mom was right, and he valued his career more than his family. I try not to dwell on his motives, because at this point it's moot—it was what it was. I remind myself that I'm a grown-up. I am no longer a sad kid wishing her dad put her first. If I kept thinking like that little girl, I would always end up disappointed. Instead, I will accept whatever my dad wants to give and expect nothing more.

So where does that leave my mom? Well, for one thing, she began DM-ing my manager. Super appropriate, right? You know, bringing in somebody I work with professionally who has zero clue about all of this shit happening in my personal life. The contents boiled down to my mom saying that she was sure the quality of my work was slipping, and she gave the impression that without her, I was lost, unpredictable, and unstable. Naturally, this forced me to have an awkward and far more personal talk with my manager on the matter than I intended to. My mom then took to Twitter, sloppily sub-tweeting me and responding to my followers about our relationship. She sent me a birthday gift of some childhood toy that was supposed to spark some feeling of nostalgia in me, but I didn't even remember it. She was essentially text-stalking Sydney until Syd told her it made her really uncomfortable and that she would appreciate it if she stopped contacting her. Which she hasn't totally, but we'll take it.

When I moved in January 2017, I never publicly announced it online because I didn't want my mom to know. A few weeks later an orchid arrived: a housewarming gift from my mother. In the past three years I've received Christmas and birthday gifts, including (but not limited to) clothes (size XL), foods I'm allergic to, things I already have, blown-glass figurines, baby shoes, and gift cards for more money than she'd ever gifted me before. In every package she also includes a check to "cover the return if you see fit," but she also adds that "some of these are from local artisans, so just contact me directly if you don't want them." Sneaky. She throws in gifts for Mats as well: sweaters, socks, matching XL footie pajamas. For a while the most memorable mommy moment was when she sent me flowers on Mother's Day with the note "Are you thinking about me today?" *So fucking creepy.*

December 25, 2018, marked three years since I had spoken to my mom. Despite having blocked her number years ago, she still manages to leave me voice mails from random and unknown numbers. They're triggers for me, so I rarely listen to them. On a good day I can compare them to a badly written student film; on a bad day, they send me straight back to childhood with feelings of manipulation and gaslighting. One that particularly stood out to me was her downright insistence that we watch the *Gilmore Girls* revival together. I actually laughed out loud when I heard that. For two people who hadn't spoken in nearly a year at that point, she expected that we watch six hours of television together. My mother maintained the impression that she had done absolutely nothing wrong, and that I was just being a drama queen or "a brat" (basically my childhood nickname). So this insistence that we watch *Gilmore Girls* together was not a white flag or even a sad excuse for an apology: it was just something we must do. I still get a kick out of the delusion of that one.

But one rainy night in March 2017 is the biggest standout.

It was about nine o'clock on a Sunday, and I was cooking a late dinner for Mats and myself, when we heard a loud knock at the door. This was a rare occurrence, not only because I'm antisocial, but because we have a front gate with a doorbell. Most people, upon arrival, ring the doorbell outside the gate; they don't walk through the gate and bang directly on the door. To be fair, should the gate have been locked? Yes. Was it? No. Mats and I looked up at each other, wordlessly asking if the other was expecting someone, but clearly neither of us was. It was too late for mail, Jehovah's Witnesses, or Scientologists, and the only logical explanation I could settle on was that it had to be our neighbors. So while I continued to cook, Mats went downstairs to answer the door. I had turned the stove fan on, and combined with the sounds of turkey burgers sizzling, I couldn't hear who it ended up being at the door. As minutes passed I started to feel guilty: it was obviously our crazy neighbors and Mats was being roped into their drama. A few minutes later he came back up with this odd look on his face. "Um, your godmother is here?" he half stated, half asked. What the actual fuck. "What did she say her name was?" I asked him, holding my breath. "Karen," he replied. Again, what the actual fuck. Honestly, it would have been less alarming if it had been a random person claiming to be my godmother. No, it actually *was* my godmother. Who lives in Connecticut. Whom I hadn't spoken to in about seven years. Out of nowhere about a month prior, she texted me to let me know that she was going to be visiting family in LA and wanted to know if I was free to see her. She had to sign the text with her name; I didn't even have her phone number. Considering Karen was my mother's best friend and the woman she had spent the last few holidays with, naturally I ignored it. In hindsight I should have been on high alert when I first got it, considering there was only one person she would have gotten my number from. But she wasn't supposed to have my address.

"What do you want me to tell her?" Mats asked, adding, "She's pretty rude." I was fuming. "Tell. Her. I. Will. Text. Her," I said with restraint. I was fucking livid. Her more recent texts were fluffed with things like "I miss you girl" and "I want to have a relationship with you." When I first read those, I felt guilty that I was ignoring her. I wasn't really in a place to turn away family, and I had always liked

Karen. A part of me hoped it was an olive branch—an "I know your mother is crazy" branch—but I knew if that were the case, she would have said so. Here was the proof. My mom had clearly gotten to her. Mats went downstairs to deliver my message, and this time I could hear Karen snapping at him, asking him, "Who the hell are YOU?" as if she were the one looking out for me. They continued to exchange words until Mats came back upstairs, informing me that she refused to leave without seeing me. "She says she doesn't have your correct number." I rolled my eyes. "Tell her she has the right number; therefore, I have *her* number. I will fucking text her," I said. He nodded, went downstairs a final time, and repeated what I said. (The jury is still out on whether he said "fucking," but I like to think he did. Though, according to Mats: "I did not say 'fucking,' but I let my voice drip with contempt when I passed along the message.")

I heard the front door shut and lock, then heard Mats walking back upstairs. It took Karen another ten minutes to actually leave. Mats stood at our living room window, arms crossed, staring daggers down at the street until he was sure she had left.

"Did she get in an Uber?" I asked when he called out that she'd finally left.

"No, she drove. Dark silver car."

I nodded, noting the detail. I grabbed my phone to set a reminder to text Karen that next morning. I'd let her know that I had cut off communication with anyone who was still in my mother's circle. Therefore I wouldn't be seeing her, but I hoped she had a nice trip.

It was gloomy and pouring rain the next day, a rarity in Los Angeles. I spent the morning running errands and catching up on emails, and around eleven I texted Karen. She replied quickly, trying to press for information, but I left it at that. Then my phone rang. I assumed it was Karen and was ready to send her to voice mail, but I realized it was my dad. I picked up, ready to tell him about the weird events that had transpired the night prior, but before I could even start, he cut me off. "Jennifer is driving me INSANE!" he continued, explaining that my mother had skipped out on yet another mediation session and instead had gone to Lake Tahoe. I rolled my eyes. This was so very her.

"Who did she go with?" I asked, knowing that her friends in Marin were now few and far between.

"Your godmother, Karen," he replied.

Suddenly it clicked. I jumped up from the couch, took the stairs two at a time, threw the front door open, sprinted to the gate, locked it, secured the dead bolt on the front door, then raced to the back gate, locked it, and secured the dead bolt on the back door.

My dad continued like he didn't notice my panting. "She and Karen loaded up the car yesterday morning and drove down in the late afternoon."

Fucking shit. "Dad, they didn't go to Tahoe. Karen showed up here last night." I instinctively made my way around the apartment, turning all the lights off, erasing any signs that I might be home. Just as I started toward the curtains to shut them, the doorbell rang. I dropped to an army crawl. "I'm gonna have to call you back, Dad."

Thanks to modern technology and my paranoia, we got security cameras, so every time someone rings the doorbell, it taps into a live video feed. Let it also be known that when I say "doorbell," I don't mean the standard ring. It's a twelve-second jingle involving chimes and gongs in various octaves. My mother rang the doorbell nonstop for nearly an hour. Every time the last note of the bell chimed, it would start right back up again. The second she arrived, I texted Mats a picture from the security feed. He called me immediately with a "IS THAT YOUR MOTHER? WHAT THE FUCK?!?" I told him I was fine, even though I was curled in a ball and hiding in the kitchen in the dark, afraid to be anywhere close to the curtains I hadn't managed to close. He told me if she didn't leave within the next half hour, he'd come home from work. She didn't leave. By the time Mats arrived, she'd been at it for an hour and a half. At this point I think the doorbell jingle had gotten so deep into my psyche that I'd developed an eye twitch and a stutter. I had told Mats that I had locked both gates, and upon arrival his goal was to make it inside the apartment without letting my mother through the outer perimeter. He pulled into the driveway and she bolted from her perch outside our front gate and immediately started chasing his car. He parked, jumped out, and raced her to the back gate, ignoring her screams as he managed to unlock it, slip in, and relock it before she could push her way through. Now, here's where I'll let him take over to relate what happened while I just hid inside.

* * *

mats's account

Driving home, I tried to formulate a plan for when I got there. My goal was to avoid a direct confrontation. I figured Meghan's mom was either going to be standing at our gate or sitting in the passenger seat of Karen's car in front of our apartment. If I could swing my car into our driveway fast enough, I would be able to hustle into our apartment without having to argue with Jennifer in the middle of the driveway, instead being able to go back and forth with her from behind a door. I knew I had to be fast.

As I turned onto our street, I saw Meghan's mom standing at her gate. When she heard my car coming down the street, she instinctively turned and caught sight of me behind the wheel. Like a cornerback making a jump on a poorly thrown pass, she started moving toward the driveway to cut me off. Seeing this, I cut the turn a little too close, clipping the right-hand side of my bumper as I turned into the driveway. (You can send me a check for the repairs whenever, Jennifer.) As I screeched to a halt at the end of the driveway, Jennifer rounded the corner, speed walking with a purpose. "MATS!" she yelled. "I'm her mother and I have a right to talk to her!"

"Nope!" I jumped out of the car and didn't even bother to grab my bag. The stupidity of this didn't hit me until I was inside, because if Jennifer had been a little more patient, she would have realized I needed to get my bag eventually. Alas, her normal wiliness must have deserted her.

"MATS!"

"NOPE!"

I made it to the back gate and locked it behind me just as Jennifer came around the last corner. I jumped up the back stairs two at a time and ran through the apartment as I made my way to the front door. Jennifer was already waiting for me.

I opened the porthole in the front door. "You need to leave. She doesn't want to see you," I said firmly.

"She is my daughter and I have a right to talk to her."

"No, if she doesn't want to talk to you, then you don't have that right. You need to leave now."

"Let me talk to her."

"If you don't leave now, I'll have to call the police." And that was it. I shut the porthole and walked upstairs.

*   *   *

I called my attorney and let him know what was going on. He informed me that I needed to call the cops, regardless of whether I thought she was dangerous: she was trespassing, and having a 911 call on record would help in the process if I wanted to get a formal restraining order in the future. I'm pretty sure I made Mats call; he told the operator that it wasn't an emergency, and they said they'd have officers swing by when they were in the neighborhood. He thanked them and hung up. About forty-five minutes after Mats showed up, my mom and Karen finally left. A few hours after that the cops stopped by to take my statement. I gave them an abbreviated version of the past two days, along with our security camera footage and the make and model of the car they were driving. I assured them I felt safe inside my apartment and that I would call 911 if she showed up again. Thankfully she didn't.

My friends didn't leave me alone until my mother was confirmed to be back in Marin. They took shifts at my apartment, calling me when they got outside so I didn't have to hear that fucking doorbell again. It's the silver lining in all of this: when you realize how much you can be loved and taken care of by people who aren't obligated to do so. I swear I heard the doorbell in my head for *weeks*. Every time it rains I get paranoid, as if it's an omen that she's coming back.

Since then, she's bought a house with Sierra's dad, and officially divorced my dad. For some reason they insisted on mediation, which is designed for people who actually like each other and want to get it done quickly. But the process ended up being drawn out. My dad was buying my mom out of the house, and the value went up daily. The more time my mother stayed in the house, the more the house was worth, which meant she got more money out of the property settlement. The day their divorce was finalized, she texted my dad, "I'm sad :(" (I hope to God you're rolling your eyes as hard as I am.)

When my movie *The Honor List* was gearing to come out, the press asked me if any of it was inspired by my real life. I had written the story the script was based on, and while it was fiction, one plotline was based on what happened between my mom and Sierra's dad. I was pretty petrified for people to see it. I was nervous Sierra would think it was based on our relationship (it wasn't), but I was mostly nervous about what my mother would do once she saw it. She had been posting trailers to her Facebook page, writing over-the-top captions, keeping the public appearance up that we were closer than ever. My friends would send me screenshots with eye-rolling gifs, and I asked them to keep me updated once she posted about actually seeing the film. To my surprise, she told people that she saw the movie, and that she thought my character's mom reminded her of Sierra's mom. (Let me remind you that Sierra's mother did not cheat on Sierra's father with Sierra's best friend's father. That was my mother. And that was a plot in the movie.) She posted about it on Facebook, encouraging people to watch the film and saying how *proud* she was of her little girl. Eye fucking roll.

Truthfully, I don't feel like I "lost" my parents. To be frank, I didn't really have them to begin with. As I mentioned earlier, I was less like their kid and more like their weapon to be used against each other. I was a pawn. They would scream and shout, and get into each other's faces, with zero regard that their little girl was sitting right there. They'd argue about me, in front of me. Even if it had nothing to do with me, they'd rope me in, asking me whose side I was on. My mother would tell me how mean my dad was to her and how he didn't care about me or love me. So I hated my dad. My dad would tell me how mean my mother was to him, how mean she was to me, and that it was her fault he was never around. So I hated my mom.

There's a lot I didn't remember about my childhood. Initially, I blamed it on just having a shitty memory, but through therapy I've been able to see that it was a coping mechanism. My six-, seven-, and eight-year-old brain recognized trauma and blocked it out. My parents' relationship scared me. Any moment with them in the same room ended with doors slamming and floors shaking. They'd scream in each other's faces so loud I thought the windows would shatter. I remember crying, begging them to stop, and one of them would take notice and yell "NOW YOU'RE SCARING THE KID!" as a way of using me against the other. The physicality and intensity of my parents' fights wasn't normal. The "playful" nudges and prods from my mother during our interactions weren't normal, either. She used to tell me that I had a "hitting issue" and she was just responding to what I had started. I don't have any personal memories of my "issue"; I just took her word for it. Maybe it was true, maybe I mirrored the behavior I saw at home. All I know is that physicality never left our relationship, and it never really felt fun or playful to me.

The more time and separation I have from my upbringing, the clearer I'm able to see how toxic it was. There's this video I uploaded to Facebook where my mom is backing out of a parking spot, crashes, and yells, "SEE?!?!" At the time I thought it was hilarious until a friend of mine who had never met my mom pointed out how disconcerting it was—how even though I was already into my twenties in the video, the second she yells at me, my demeanor shifts, my voice changes, and before the camera cuts you can hear me ask, "Why is this my fault?" Watching it now just makes me sad. As "typical" of an interaction as it was, I still didn't understand the psychological impact that twenty-two years of such experiences had on me.

The older I get, the more I'm able to understand that, despite my best efforts, my childhood affects who I am today. There's a part of me that grew up in spite of my circumstances, but there's also a part of me that grew up *because* of my circumstances. It took years for me to admit that it got to me, and I don't know if I would have gotten there without therapy. My therapist once told me that "if it's hysterical, it's historical." If something sends me plummeting, it's because I've been there before. I've already paved the way. It's why any hint of a raised voice sends me into a panic attack. Why doors slamming and loud noises make me feel like I'm a scared and helpless third grader. Those triggers and underlying signs of trauma don't leave us. But they're a hell of a lot easier to manage once we unpack them. I have more than two decades' worth of rewiring to do, and it's been hard to acknowledge that. There's this ugly, judgmental side of me that feels like admitting that I've been damaged by them somehow means that they've won. Or that I'm letting down the eight-year-old version of me who so desperately tried to protect my mind from the trauma. I know none of that's true, but that ugly voice can be hard to quiet. I'm working on it.

Sometimes life just happens to us. We're not at the steering wheel; we're in a car seat in the back. There are times when we don't ask for what we're given. There are people who don't deserve you who will hurt you. It doesn't make you weak if it leaves you with scars and a few extra pieces of baggage. Nobody needs our endorsement to wreak havoc on our lives; they come uninvited and leave the place the worse for wear. We can't control everything—believe me, I've tried. People can hurt you without your permission. I used to believe that feeling that hurt was my fault. It wasn't. Just because I didn't invite it in, that doesn't mean it's not there.

I guess it's time for the moral of the story. My relationship with my parents has been one of the hardest things I've ever had to deal with, but I've learned a lot. Mats and I started dating at the very beginning of all of this, and he stuck by my side the whole way through. He did it without even acknowledging that there was any other option. He made me stop believing that I was unlovable. I learned that if it's not loving, it's not love. I used to think I never wanted to get married or have kids—and you probably think that going through all of this would cement that. It's quite the opposite, actually. It has instilled a determination in me to prove to be a better mother than the one I had. It's made me want to have my own family and raise my future kids with so much love and support that they don't doubt their strength for even a second. In the midst of all of this negativity and toxicity, I stumbled upon a sense of self-worth. I began to value myself in a way I never had before. For so long, I felt obligated to accept my situation because it's what I had. Society put this importance on the idea of "family," and I had just accepted that I needed to deal with the manipulation and verbal abuse that was quite literally breaking me down. In reality, just because somebody brought you into this world and their DNA runs through your veins, it does not mean they are your family. You can choose your own family. Family isn't genetics or heredity or the result of a broken condom. Family is love. Mutual, respectful love. It could be the last name you have, the couple who made you, or the people who took you in just because they wanted to. That is family.

you're not special

I don't want to sugarcoat this and tie it up with a nice bow, because I can't. Healing from trauma takes years. I spend two hours a week unlearning behaviors and coping mechanisms that no longer serve me. I'm constantly discovering ways that my toxic upbringing has seeped into my adult life and relationships. Some days I feel like I've made incredible strides; other days I feel like a broken little kid. There is one thing that remains an undeniable fact: I did what I needed to do. There is not one second that I've ever regretted cutting my mother out of my life. To this day, it is the single greatest act of self-love I have ever demonstrated.

finding love
and
being happy

I AM A BIG FAN OF ATTENTION.

chapter 22

obligatory chapter about finding love and being happy

As you've probably noticed, the vast majority of the contents of this book have skewed toward shining a less-than-flattering light on myself. That's not to say that my life isn't great or that I'm unhappy with my situation at all; really, that couldn't be further from the truth. When I decided that I wanted to write a book, I wanted to write a book that I wish I could have read in my teenage years. I wanted it to be like a best friend and a big sister rolled into one. I wanted it to be all the shit I wish somebody had told me. If at fifteen I could have read about somebody else's awkward moments and all the crap they'd gone through, I sure as hell would have felt a whole lot less crazy in my own life.

You know those people who bounce from relationship to relationship, whose last single days were in the time when AOL email addresses ruled? Those people who've managed to live their years as a series of romantic novels come to life? I hate those people. The prescription-free, perpetually happy, in love, and over-the-fucking-moon-about-their-lives kind of people. Now, I have nothing against relationships at all, or people being happy in them. What I do hate is that those blissfully happy people tend to forget that not every other person in the world cares to hear about every last detail.

These friends always seem to pop up at the worst times, gushing on and on about their significant others while I stuff my face with pop-corn and baby carrots and calculate how many months it's been since I kissed somebody without being paid. And as I'd sit across from them, multiplying the weeks and carrying the 1, I promised myself that I would never become one of them. Even in the (unlikely) chance my icy Grinch heart would thaw and my cynicism would subside, I pledged that I would never be that hair-twirling, gabbing, giggling creature. Who the fuck wants to watch somebody drone on and on about how AWESOME their love life is? Answer: nobody.

And yet, I think the message of this section would fall flat without this part. I divulged terrible dates, earth-shattering heartbreaks, and every embarrassing instance in between. I set out to be somebody you could relate to, to make this book be that comforting reassurance that somebody else survived it all too. If I just stop there, then every self-deprecating story I've shared doesn't mean shit. I guess what I'm trying to say without sounding like an inspirational poster is that it gets better. Despite my lifetime of skepticism, I can honestly and per-sonally say that it actually does all work out in the end. It's pretty fucking cool.

The first time I ever met my (now) boyfriend Mats, I thought he was gay. I had no actual basis for my theory on his sexuality other than that I thought he was cute and with my luck and previous track record, he'd be batting for the other team. That, and every cute guy you see in Hollywood is pretty much guaranteed to be gay. Also, he was wearing one of those Britney-at-the-VMAs microphone headpiece things. That didn't help.

We were in the lobby of my (now) manager's office. He extended his hand to shake mine, zero irony or acknowledgment of the 2001-style headphones he was sporting. If it was any other person, I'm sure I would have been squirming in secondhand embarrassment, yet even with only four words exchanged between us he still managed to make me feel like a freshman at a senior frat party. He likened his name to the applesauce brand for the sake of my own memory and offered a genuine smile at my laughter, as if this weren't the hundredth time he cracked that joke this week. He introduced himself as my manager's new assistant and I felt my cheeks flush. Why couldn't their assistant be a flamboyant gay guy named, like, Fabio or something? Or a petite nerdy girl with glasses? Which is all a long way of saying that he was really cute. Cute enough that a part of me hoped he was gay because otherwise I wasn't sure if I was ever going to be able to look him in the eye. Which of course made me about ten thousand times more nervous. We engaged in surface-level small talk for the duration of the thirty steps it took to get to the conference room, and that was it.

The next time I saw Mats, he told me that he and his girlfriend broke up. I had my answer to my question about his orientation.

Fuck.

The first record I have of my feelings toward Mats was less than two months after we met, when I tweeted this from my (long since inactive) private account:

I have a crush on my managers assistant

I know, so elegant. Classy.

I should be more ashamed to admit it, but I will totally own the fact that I am a big fan of attention. If I could, I would live every single day like it was my birthday (and my birthday was Christmas). This love of attention directly translates into my generally flirtatious nature. Even as a chubby-cheeked ten-year-old I'd twirl my white-blond ringlets around my sparkly blue fingernails and compliment my crush on his new pair of Etnies. I love flirting and batting my eyelashes and having someone to text and that flush on my cheeks. I crush it at crushing. I just have zero to none on follow-through. Intentionally, I may add. Flirting and crushing is safe; the banter and the back-and-forth is innocent and endless. This being said, I also wouldn't call myself a tease, mostly because, like "friendzoning," it's a term created by straight men who feel that women owe them something. I don't make it seem like I'm pursuing something greater or leading somebody on into thinking we're headed toward something serious. Or at least I've learned how to avoid that awkward moment. It's all in the selection process. Subconsciously, I tend to develop crushes on guys classified as so untouchable, it surpasses inconvenient and lands closer to nearly impossible. I crush on the guys I can't have. Not like friends' boyfriends, or married men or anything of that nature. I mean, guys who live in different states, or someone I'm on set with for six months, or somebody I work really closely with. The inconvenience of these crushes ranges from things as simple as distance to complex things such as an established professional tie between us. Inconvenience that is so apparent to both parties that neither of us would ever even consider each other as a candidate for anything long term. For some, this habit would grow frustrating, as the results are unfruitful, but for me this situation is ideal. If I crush on somebody I cannot or should not have, I never actually have to act on my flirtations. It's an endless cycle that leaves me in total control yet totally alone.

Now, this should be the paragraph where I talk about how my cynical outlook on love and relationships stems from the one my parents lived out in front of me, or how I never fully recovered from the first time I let my guard down and got hurt, or whatever explanation justifies my unwavering phobia of commitment. For a while I preached that outlook and succumbed to that belief—the notion that the effects of the relationships of my past were not only lasting but permanent. I was under the impression that my need to self-sabotage every relationship resulted from my deep-rooted belief that love and happiness were a facade and that I was better off alone.

Four months into nearly every relationship I was ever in, a switch flipped in my head. Every romantic or sweet sentiment I had toward the guy I was dating disappeared completely. I wanted what I didn't have and then, when I got it, I didn't want it anymore. It was an endless spiraling black hole and there was absolutely no light in sight. That childhood dream of white picket fences and backyards for kids and golden retrievers named Bandit seemed a greater fairy tale than the ones with glass slippers. I grew up with the story that true love was just a given in life. Something standard-issue that would just "happen" like every tale assures us it will. As time went by, birthdays provoked more empathy than excitement. The fault I pinned on the variables dwindled. I was hit with the harsh reality that *I* was the common denominator in this cycle of failure. *I* was the constant. I was going to end up alone and there was nobody to blame but myself. My inability to maintain feelings for somebody was not caused by the parties in question. I had no one to blame for my shortcomings but myself. My parents' terrible marriage was not to blame for my outlook. That guy who took advantage of me my senior year of high school did not build those impenetrable walls around me. My douchebag addict of an ex was not at fault for my relationships years down the road. They all played a factor, yes, but I couldn't commit because I hadn't met the person who made me want to. It only takes one person. It only has to work out once. That's all.

I'd be lying if I said that I knew right away that Mats would be that person. Yes, that story would be far more romantic but far less star-crossed and millennial than the truth. Before I can get into how it all happened, I first have to explain the professional circumstances in which our friendship arose. As my manager's assistant, Mats was not only privy to every work obligation on my calendar and every project in the pipeline. He wasn't just cc'd on every email and connecting me to every phone call. He wasn't just my point of contact on set, a messenger for PR packages, and an active participant in our group chat. He was the first person I talked to every morning and the last person I talked to every night. Looking back on this, it's blatantly obvious to me that this kind of treatment was reserved for me alone, as he claims his crush started early into our meeting. In this industry, your work is your life and the people you work with become your family. Hell, you probably see them more than your actual family.

I could not have picked a safer crush than Mats. We were in constant communication, and our professional relationship was so central to our daily lives that I never read too much into our flirtatious interactions. I knew how off-limits he was, how many boundaries that a romantic relationship would cross, and the consequences if we ever did do anything. Also, let it be stated that I was pretty certain my innocent schoolgirl crush was totally one-sided. I think when you file somebody away as a "non-possibility," you let your guard down. There is no body language to read into or texts to analyze, because you've already written them off. Any sort of flirtation that occurs is completely not registered because it is such a non-thing. That situation is where Mats and I lived. Or at least that's how I saw it. I was also under the impression that he was a total player who probably texted heart-eyed emojis to every female client. Either way, my guard was down, a friendship formed, and my crush on Mats continued harmlessly.

I hate feelings. I am aware this sounds psychotic and alarming, but let me explain. I love the feeling of freshly washed sheets. And the feeling you get when you're at a restaurant and they're walking toward you with your food. I thrive in the feeling you get during the holidays when everything is covered with twinkling lights and synthetic snow. I revel in what it feels like to be surrounded by your best friends when your karaoke song comes on. I love those kinds of feelings. I understand and recognize them as I feel them. What I hate are those feelings that live inside you and are nameless, mysterious, and unfamiliar.

I'm decisive in my choices, I'm rarely surprised, and I swear I get a high from planning things in advance. I'm not a know-it-all, but I do like to know it all. I had no idea how I felt about Mats. I knew I had feelings, but I had no idea what they were or what they meant. So I did what I do with any delicate situation that requires me to tap into my emotions: I ignored it. I ignored the feeling I got when my phone vibrated with a non-work-related text. I ignored what I felt when he went out of his way to compliment my character traits. I ignored the glances of our mutual acquaintances, and I ignored the air of sexual tension between us. I had gotten so used to shutting my feelings in a box far, far away that I almost started to believe they never existed in the first place.

That spring our friendship reached a whole new level. No, we did not have sex. We did something much dirtier. Something much more intimate. Some may even classify this experience as "life changing." We went to Coachella together. Now, everything you see and hear about Coachella from Vanessa Hudgens's Snapchat is true. It's this otherworldly, trippy, fringed haze of a mirage past Morongo Casino. It's insane. It's like limbo. It's far enough from the 405 that you forget you're within government jurisdiction and your morals are looser than your culturally inappropriate crocheted caftan. Coachella is where sexually shy twentysomethings engage in fivesomes with Justin Bobby look-alikes who keep their beanies on past foreplay. Coachella is the backdrop and music score of fever-dream love affairs between acid-dropping nine-to-fivers. There are no limits; there are no inhibitions. At Coachella anything can happen. Or, in my case, absolutely nothing can happen. For three days Mats slept on the floor of my hotel room, brought me coffee in the morning, and carried my backpack.

He introduced me to his friends and relayed that one of them thought I was hot. He'd be happy to set it up, he added. I'm sure if I had let myself feel something, it would have felt pretty terrible. But instead I felt nothing.

I'd be lying if I said that when I invited Mats to Coachella, there wasn't a little part of me that considered that something might happen between us. I don't know if I actually wanted him to make a move, or if I just wanted some sort of confirmation that this air of sexual tension between us wasn't just coming from me. Maybe I wanted to gauge my feelings toward him in an unprofessional and somewhat remote setting—to see if this crush I had developed stemmed from a convenience and close proximity, or if in fact it remained past the comfortable confines of the corporate world. I just needed an answer. He liked me or he liked me not. I liked him or I liked him not. Or a cocktail of the two. As the desert got smaller and smaller in the rearview mirror and the familiar smoggy skyline came into view, I realized I never got my answer. I returned to the city more confused and conflicted than I had left it. Great.

If this story had been a movie, this next part would have been done in a hyper-speed time lapse. The seasons changed, but we remained exactly the same. Our texts still read like confiscated middle school notes. Our in-person interactions still sparked endless insinuations and assumptions that we had embarked on an illicit fling. I went out with other guys, he went out with other girls, and we gave no thought to the fact that nothing ever panned out. We had spent the past ten months entangled in this "thing" with no end in sight. It seemed as if we could live in this gray area forever. Until we couldn't.

By August, I decided that enough was enough. I had spent nearly a year invested in and consumed by a non-relationship relationship. It was in fact hindering the rest of my dating life. I was dating haphazardly, one foot always already out the door. Mats was like my work husband but also a friend and also just a what-if presence in my life.

I think that motivation to put yourself out there and date comes from loneliness and desire for companionship. But when that spot in your life is halfway filled, you don't have that same fire under your ass. I was turning twenty-two and I was nowhere near where I thought I'd be romantically. So as the planning of my twenty-second birthday commenced, I saw it as an opportune moment to figure my shit out. Four of my best friends and I would be spending the weekend in Vegas. In that time I pledged not to speak to or speak of Mats. Instead, I would speak to and do *ahem* other stuff with any other guys. My goal was to figure out how I really felt. With Mats out of sight and mind, and a bunch of other eligible bachelors at the ready, what were my true feelings? With another guy's tongue down my throat, would I still be thinking about Mats? Or would that kind of male attention result in feelings similar to those I had toward him? I had three days to find out.

It may take you by surprise, but I love Las Vegas. Since I'm normally somebody who's a self-proclaimed grandma and avid member of the #LetsStayHome squad, Vegas doesn't seem to fit that bill. For one weekend a year, that persona drops and I tap into my eighteen-year-old dancing-on-tables self. I wear teeny-tiny dresses and heels that come with altitude warnings, I down shots out of frozen glasses, and I dance like I'm expecting a downpour of singles. There's a reason why they say "What happens in Vegas stays in Vegas." We spent our first day in Vegas in our own cabana at the Marquee Dayclub at the Cosmopolitan. The only thing low about me was my inhibitions. Our cabana was conveniently placed between a bachelor party and a group of twentysomething LA agents. My best friend Sydney bartered with the best man for the homemade T-shirts their group was sporting (she decided the perfect souvenir for the weekend was their iron-on Tinder T-shirts with the groom's face). I chatted it up with two brothers from the agency cabana. Less than ten minutes into our conversation they asked me if I knew Mats. I laughed, telling them I did and ruling them out as prospects for the weekend. When the sun began to set, Sydney gave up on her T-shirt conquest (settling instead for a lifetime supply of Jimmy Johns, courtesy of the best man, who turned out to be a stakeholder). I deemed every eligible (and ineligible) poolside bachelor as too Ed Hardy, and we retired to our suite to rest up for the evening. By "rest up," I mean attempt to sober up with french fries and overpriced minibar nuts, all of which I'd throw up mere minutes later. While my friends took cold showers and power naps, I took up residency in the bathroom, vomiting vodka sodas, mimosas, and tequila shots while feeling the comedown of the knockoff ecstasy I had taken that morning. Don't do drugs, kids.

When I had nothing left in my stomach to heave, and the thought of alcohol was no longer nauseating, I joined my friends in getting ready for the night. We bopped along to Calvin Harris, caking on our makeup to conceal how crappy we actually felt. I popped a few more pills. I think they were called moon rocks? I have no idea. And for serious, don't do drugs. And if you do drugs, don't be dumb about it. Don't get drugs from somebody you don't know, don't take something if you don't know what it is, don't mix drugs together, don't take them when you're alone, and only take them in safe situations with people you trust. Or better yet, just don't do drugs. Good talk!

You know those annoying girls who sit at a table at the nightclub just bobbing their heads to the music and sipping on "skinny" cocktails and giggling among themselves? That was us. But then we proceeded to get plastered. We scream-sang a Diplo remix, enjoying that point where you're inebriated enough to think you look like Kendall Jenner but sober enough to keep your heels and underwear on. It was in that peak moment where the music swelled, and I raised my arms above my head, rocking my body along to the music, mouthing the words as if we were starring in our own music video, that it happened. For the first time all weekend, the name that lit up my phone was Mats. I smiled smugly as I showed it off to my friends. I had won the unspoken contest: he had caved first. As I reveled in the praise of my friends, I placed my thumb on the home button, unlocking it. I was sure he had conjured up some work-related excuse or some other fabricated reason I would see right through. Instead, I was met with a screenshot of the out-of-character bikini Instagram I had posted earlier that day (I blame the drugs) along with the following three words:

Mats

you

Mats

look

Mats

incredible

I dropped my phone. Literally, as if I no longer had opposable thumbs. My face must have been a dead giveaway of my surprise. My friends scrambled to retrieve my phone from the sticky ground. Their eyes darted across the screen, scanning the conversation as their expressions mimicked my own. We traded shouts of "What the fuck?" "Are you fucking kidding?" "What are you going to say?" "Stop, let me read it again!" "Wait! Stop! Check to see when he screenshotted it!" "STOP!" "No way!" If any onlookers had been observing our previous behavior and thought we couldn't fit the basic bitch stereotype any more, our high-pitched squeals and Cher Horowitz–like mannerisms surpassed their expectations. I'm sure we were the object of countless annoyed glares, but I wasn't thinking about that. I wasn't even thinking about the letters my thumbs were tapping, or my lack of hesitation in pressing the "send" button, or my disinterest in making him sweat out my responses. I don't remember the conversation verbatim, but it went something like this:

He told me I looked hot.

I compared myself to a hot potato.

He told me I was not a potato.

I said I was a tater tot because I was tan and bloated.

He said I was not a tater tot.

I said I was a french fry.

He said I was not a french fry.

He said I was sexy.

I asked him why he was being so nice to me.

He told me it was because he liked me.

I told him that he was paid to like me.

He told me he wasn't paid to like me the way he does.

I told him that I didn't think he was allowed to like me.

He told me he wasn't allowed to like me.

He asked me if I liked him.

I told him I didn't think I was allowed to like him.

He told me I wasn't allowed to like him.

I asked him if he was sober.

He didn't respond.

I asked him again.

He didn't respond.

I asked him again.

He didn't respond.

I didn't hear from Mats until four p.m. the next day. Halfway through the excruciating drive back to LA in Lily's un-air-conditioned car, we had stopped at a gas station in Buttfuck Nowhere, and as I handed Lily my card for gas money, my phone vibrated. After fourteen hours of radio silence, he resurfaced with "I was a little drunk." I contemplated throwing my phone out the window, but I was pretty sure I didn't have insurance on it.

You may have noticed my lack of excitement at this pivotal moment. Maybe you're reading this with frustration at my reaction, since it seems as if this was the outcome I had desired. I mean, even my friends questioned my hostility toward the night's events. Let me break it down for you in a far more coherent (and sober) explanation than I gave them. While Mats initially caught my eye in a purely superficial manner, my crush on him developed over nearly a year of friendship. It grew from innocent late-night talks on the office floor and the delirious banter post-twelve-hour-shoot days until I wound up where I was. I pushed those thoughts and feelings aside because of the value our friendship had to me. The stakes were far too high to risk losing what we had established between us on the chance of a half-baked idea. Which was why I had set aside this weekend to flesh out my feelings and finally determine what the next course of action was. There was so much careful thought and consideration behind my process. Mats's text message delivered the harsh reality that I was the only one with that mindset. His seeming recklessness and impulsiveness implied that he had no hesitation toward jeopardizing our friendship for anything more than sex, proving that any of his sentiments that I had taken for true feelings were just lust in disguise. I guess all it took for me to figure out my feelings was to figure out that he didn't feel the same way.

I had a pretty terrible comedown the following week. Mats's version of a white flag came in the form of a Chipotle salad. I was too groggy and out of it to refuse, so I accepted. After about a week of random sobbing spells and daily naps in the double digits, I slowly (like really fucking slowly) started to feel like myself again. (Don't do drugs.) My text messages with Mats that week were sparse and surface-level. We were both tiptoeing around the Vegas incident, unsure of how to carry on our friendship as normal. I had gone out of my way to avoid running into him, asking for meetings to be scheduled at coffee shops near my home as opposed to the conference room we usually frequented. I was annoyed and frustrated at our situation. More than that, I was just hurt. My fear that acting on anything romantic between us would put our friendship at risk was becoming a reality, but I hadn't had any say in that possibility. The outcome I had once dreaded was coming to fruition, and I didn't even have any part in it. I was pissed. I was pissed that Mats had made this choice for us, and I was pissed that I was pissed. It meant I liked him. I was also pissed because I knew that actions spoke louder than words, but both his actions and his words fucking sucked.

Out of the blue, Mats quit his job a week later. He called me into the office to tell me. He had been offered another job at a tech start-up, and he was going to take it. He had already put his two weeks' notice in and was in the process of interviewing people to fill his position. He told me that he would always be there for me professionally, with business advice and support, and that none of that would change. He then told me he'd like for things to change between us personally. I think I tried to say something witty, but I really don't remember. He then took a call, excusing himself back to work. He left me alone in the conference room, speechless and dumbfounded at the incidents of the past few weeks. The saying "When it rains, it pours" seems fitting for this moment, but it felt less like that scene from *A Cinderella Story* and more like a wipeout from *Johnny Tsunami*.

Mats's final two weeks as an assistant were the weirdest fourteen days of my young adult life. They were rivaled only by the time I spent two weeks during senior year attempting to function as a normal human, high off my ass on Percocet as the result of the post-op complications of my wisdom tooth surgery. With the anticipation of his imminent departure, our conversations were no longer tainted with awkwardness. Instead we skipped past our normal flirtations and went straight to blush-inducing territory. Wait, does that sound like it was sexual? It wasn't. It was like an "Awwww"-inducing, gag me (in a PG way), hit-you-right-in-the-feels kind of thing. We were in uncharted waters, and I won't lie—I was kind of freaking out. By "kind of freaking out," I mean, like, *really* freaking out. And by "really freaking out," I mean I was balls-to-the-wall, hold-my-hoops freaking out. Or something like that.

Mats's last day also happened to coincide with a party my agency was throwing. I RSVP'd to attend with one of my agent's assistants, Annie. Serendipitously, she had invited Mats to tag along, even though the occurrences of the past few weeks were unknown to her. He and Annie met me at my apartment and we drove to the party together. I attempted to downplay my excitement so as not to draw Annie's attention. I really didn't need to worry, though, because she was clueless. In fact, she remained pretty clueless all night. They rented out some seen-and-be-seen chichi bar in West Hollywood for the party, and Annie abandoned us upon arrival to make the rounds with her colleagues. Mats and I made our way to the bar. We had our work event routine down to a science, but for some reason this felt different. For the first time since he and I had become friends, I was not his designated wingwoman. I didn't strike up conversations with the girls he pointed out at the bar, introducing him as my brother to increase his odds. He didn't introduce me to any of his friends with the not-so-subtle air of a setup. Instead he bought me drinks and asked me to dance, and his eyes never left mine.

He asked me to go out with him no less than one hundred times that night. He insisted that he accompany me on my Uber ride home, and when the car pulled up, he confidently invited himself in for a nightcap. We sat in silence on opposite sides of the room, untouched glasses in our hands, just staring at each other. We stayed like that for a while. The things we left unspoken rang out far louder than anything we could say aloud. He called an Uber for himself and asked me to walk him out. I obliged, hoping he couldn't hear how alarmingly loud my heartbeat had just become. We reached my front gate and the silence between us lingered. I twirled the rings on my left hand, avoiding eye contact. The impatient driver behind the wheel of the Prius with a "U" sticker honked, and Mats tilted my chin up with his finger. He asked if he could kiss me. I said no. He nodded, dropping his hand as he leaned in to kiss my forehead. "It's okay. I'm patient," he said. Then he got into the Uber and rode away.

Turns out he didn't have to be that patient. Somehow, I ended up agreeing to go out on a date with him the following evening. He had conjured up tickets to a Dodgers playoff game, knowing I was a fan of baseball. He also knew I'd look like a real bitch if I turned it down. Though let the record state, I did not make it easy. The series of texts in which he attempted to convince me read more like he was talking me off a ledge, with lots of soothing words and reassurance. He told me that I'd never lose him as a friend. He said it was just one date. I didn't have to commit to anything more than that. He also reminded me that I did really love baseball games. Plus he had texted my closest friends about his plan, and they all offered to ignore me that day so I couldn't even claim I had prior plans. He had thought of everything. I couldn't run away from my very real feelings. I was backed into a corner with no graceful exit in sight. So I sent my reply before I could talk myself out of it: "I'm in." Then I texted Lily: "911 come over. Bring vodka."

I was already three shots in when he picked me up. He walked through the front door without even a knock and caught me with Smirnoff in hand, jokingly asking Lily if she had planned to escape through the window. Somehow the sight of this did not deter his feelings. Minutes later we were buckled up in the car on our way to Dodger Stadium. To this day I cannot recall another car ride that was as painfully awkward as the one we had to downtown LA. You'd think with three shots in me the liquid courage would at least begin to rear its head. Nope. Nada. My palms were sweating, I was pretty sure I was only breathing through my mouth, and I don't think I had finished a complete sentence since we got on the highway. In typical form he seemed unfazed by it all, or maybe it was just that, in contrast to my contorted body in the passenger seat, any sort of awkwardness he was feeling paled in comparison.

I don't remember who won the game. I could google it, but I think that defeats my point. My point is that I had a really good time. We drank overpriced cocktails and split french fries, and the closest thing he made to a move was closing the gap between our knees until they just barely touched. He didn't fake yawn to drape his arm around my shoulders or pretend to be cold to warrant holding hands. He laughed at my jokes and took the long way home. I was too busy being smitten to make a snide remark about it. He walked me to my front door. For the second night in a row, he asked if he could kiss me. This time I said yes.

In a perfect world, now would be the time for puppy love and making up for lost time. Instead, this is the beginning of what we now (not so) fondly refer to as the "Meghan Is a Fuck Boy Era." If you're unfamiliar with the term "fuck boy," let me break it down for you, or better yet, let's give Urban Dictionary the honor:

fuck boy

He will lead girls on just for hookups, says hes [*sic*] really into you but doesn't want to deal with all the "relationship bullshit" just to mess with you. He thinks about himself and only himself all the time, but pretends to be really nice. He always walks with his squad never alone. He will say hi to you once then won't talk to you for the rest of the day. YOU HAVE TO TEXT THEM FIRST BECAUSE THEY "FORGET" He's [*sic*] seems quiet but in reality he [*sic*] just a fuck boy

Lisa: *look at that fuck boy*
Bob: *Yeah he's such a fuck boy*

In my defense, their definition is far more terrible and extreme than I'd ever classify anything I did, but I won't deny my actions were in that vein. Before I get into it, let me first clarify that I'm not proud of my behavior in the following month. There is no excuse other than that I'm pretty sure I was Pauly D in a past life and those tendencies can creep up on me. In all actuality I'm not even really all that sure what I did. In the moment I had justified all my actions, so—to get a clearer and more colorful perspective—I've enlisted Mats to recount this part. Take it away, babe.

* * *

Thanks, Meghan! And hello to you, reader. It's me again, Mats, the aforementioned boyfriend.

After I dropped Meghan off at her apartment, I was riding a pretty strong high. Like anyone, I've been on great dates, mediocre dates, and unmitigated disasters, and I knew this was the first. I hadn't overplayed my hand or come on too strong. I was even more assured when the next day, as we exchanged a flurry of text messages, she asked me to come over to the apartment. We watched a movie and made out a little, and she even snuggled a little bit, which was something she'd professed hating when we were just friends. I walked back to my car supremely confident that this was the beginning of something.

And then I started getting the runaround.

Mats

Hey, what r u doing on Wednesday night?

(Wednesday night passes)

Meghan

Hey! Haha just saw this—sorry been suuuuuper busy

I knew what "been suuuuuper busy" really meant. But I tried not to let myself get perturbed. I had said that I was persistent. While Meghan and I were friends, we'd been pretty open about our personal lives with each other. I knew she didn't really feel like getting into a relationship. There had been one guy she'd liked, whom she always seemed to be circling back to. I remember she'd been really excited that they were finally getting dinner, and like a gentleman her date had paid. Unlike a gentleman he'd Venmo'd her for half the check a few days later, and that had made her more leery of feelings than ever.

All I could do was keep trying, not become annoying, and not expect anything. I could hope for the best, but, alas, as much as it sucks, you cannot force someone to like you if it's just not there. But I knew that the first date and the day after weren't her fronting. So I kept trying.

Mats

I know, I used to manage your life lol 😊

Mats

All good, let's plan on something this weekend.

Meghan

Ahhhh, don't hate me buuuuuut

Meghan

I have a thing on Saturday & Sunday is a little up in the air.

Mats

Okay, maybe next week?

Meghan

For sure!!

Meghan

I mean think I should be good? Idk I'll double-check

This went on for many days. Finally, on a Thursday, she said I should come over. It wasn't until I was on my way there that she told me that three of her friends would be over too.

Now, I know what you must be thinking: *Give it a break, man, you tried and she's not really into you.* I was thinking it, too, and I really didn't like getting blown off. I also felt like I was too old for moves right out of the middle school playbook. But I was almost to the apartment. At the very least, if it went bad, I could stew for a few minutes to get my point across before leaving.

You know that feeling when you walk into a room full of people who were just talking about you? When I walked through the door, her friends all turned toward me with an exaggerated grin. For twenty minutes the conversation was a little stilted, and I did my best to listen and be casual. I remember one of the friends had injured her eye and was wearing a white patch, which helped draw some of the attention away from the awkwardness. (Lindsay, I'm sorry and I'm forever grateful.) Gradually, everyone relaxed and I could tell that I was making the right impression. Toward the end of the evening I looked at Meghan and laughed at her expression: a barely suppressed smile that she was trying to hide by scrunching her nose. Once again I thought I was out of the woods.

Wrong. One thing both of us had forgotten since I'd quit my job at her management was that we shared a calendar. The idea had been that I'd be able to keep easier track of her personal conflicts, and we'd both used it for approximately four days before we forgot about it. Occasionally she'd put something in and I'd ask a clarifying question, but we used it so little that the day I quit I forgot to unlink my account from it.

So when I was sitting at my new job and got a calendar alert that read "Tucker's Formal," I was a little taken aback. Meghan must have been taken aback, too, because she promptly deleted it. I deleted the calendar, and I knew it would be presumptuous to ask about it. It really wasn't any of my business. But I could ask her what she was doing that Friday night and see what she said.

Mats

Hey! What ru doing Friday?

(a few hours later)

Meghan

Hiiiiiiiiiii

(text bubble appears and then disappears fourteen times)

Meghan

I promised I would go to something . . .

I thought about it for a minute and then typed:

Mats

Okay, no worries. What're you getting into?

(text bubble appears and then disappears fourteen times)

Meghan

Tucker's formal

Now, I was a little shocked she was being that frank. I was also a little surprised she was going on another date with a guy who had picked up the check and then changed his mind after the fact. I had thought that this was going to be the last straw, but her honesty surprised me enough to probe a little more.

Mats

Really?

Meghan

Yeah, promised I would go

(text bubble appears and disappears fourteen times)

We kept talking, and she decided that she would come over before she headed out to the formal. I said okay, and she did. We made out and we laughed at all of each other's jokes. My roommate came home and he cooked us some food. When it came time for her to leave, I walked her to the door and she told me she didn't want to leave.

I'll let Meghan pick up the story again, but I will say that after that night she's been the type of girlfriend you hope you get: funny, smart, kind, and beautiful. She's great; it just took her a little while to get there.

*   *   *

I wish I could say Mats's version of the story has been exaggerated for the sake of your entertainment, but, sadly, it's not. If anything, he's being a little nicer to me than he should, probably because I'm cooking him dinner right now and he doesn't want me to spit in his food. He (sweetly) neglected to divulge that even three months into dating I still insisted we were not exclusive and reiterated to him that he was more than welcome to see other girls. As I've mentioned, I have a strong aversion to feelings. I refused to let him say anything sweet or sentimental to me. To honor my wishes yet still get his point across, he decided that the eyeballs emoji would stand for those feelings.

Anytime he wanted to tell me how he felt about me, he'd text me that emoji. Or several of those emojis. The idea of PDA of any sort gave me the visceral reaction of utter disgust, and I think I visibly dry heaved the first time he drunkenly referred to me as his girlfriend. Honestly, what eventually sparked my acceptance of that label was the first night he tried to tell me that he loved me. We were lying on my bed, he had just come from a bar crawl with his friends, and he was a little tipsy. I had just finished an episode of *Parenthood*, and as the end credits were rolling, Mats asked me if he could tell me something.

I told him that it depended on what it was.

He told me that he thought I knew what it was.

I did.

I told him he couldn't tell me.

I didn't look at him as I said this. Ultimately I knew I was being an insensitive asshole, but I still said this. I cut him off with "If you still want to define us or put a label on it, I don't hate it as much as I did." Mats sighed, nodded, smiled, and told me that he did still want that. I knew he wanted to say it, but he waited until I was ready. Except when he was really tired, then sometimes he accidentally said it.

Just so you know, I am completely aware of how terrible this makes me come across. Because I *was* terrible. There is no way to sugarcoat it: I was really, really, really shitty. Which probably seems unwarranted and completely out of left field considering how much I anticipated us getting together. And I wish there were some sort of explanation other than that I sucked at dating. The concept of commitment is smothering, and anything that could be classified as romantic results in me visibly cringing. I'd lose interest out of the blue, and ultimately the monotony of relationships bored me—not to mention that my track record in that area wasn't spotless. I'm pretty sure every guy I dated before Mats had a criminal record. I really hope this doesn't come across as a "cool girl likes the bad boys" kind of thing, because it's not cool. It's self-destructive. Seeking affection and attention from the people I sought out could probably be classified as some form of self-sabotage. I hated that, as much as I promised myself I would not let the home I grew up in and the example my parents set for me affect who I was in a relationship with, I *did* let it. If I kept those walls up and never let anybody in, they'd either grow frustrated and we'd part ways, or they'd accept it as our truth and whatever we became was so surface-level that I couldn't be bothered to maintain it. Mats was different. I was standing firmly behind those walls I had built, and Mats sat there patiently waiting for me. On a particularly cold night in February, those walls came down.

We were lying on the bed of our Manhattan hotel room, staring out at the skyline framed by our nineteenth-story view, when Mats said I love you. This time I didn't stop him. This time I said it back.

There was no one moment that I fell in love with him. There was no instant when the wave of feelings came over me. There was no lightbulb that went off in my head or flashing neon sign sprawling across the sky. There was nothing he said or did that sent me falling head over heels. To be frank, there was nothing romantic about it in the slightest. But in a way I kind of think that's the most romantic thing of all. Falling in love with him felt so natural, I didn't notice it had happened. I don't even know if I'd call it falling.

They say when you know, you know. When you meet the person you're supposed to spend the rest of your life with, your vision is clouded with fireworks and an overwhelming awareness of it all happening right in front of you. I, on the other hand, had no idea. I had no intention of falling in love with Mats. The first time I met him, I sure as hell had no idea that would be the outcome. Even in our early stages of dating, I wondered how long we'd last. When things got more serious, I *still* didn't know. I took us for what we were and I thought about nothing but the present. We carried on with our lives. Somewhere along the way, with no fuss or flares, we realized that when we weren't paying attention, we had somehow managed, in a sea of billions, to find our one.

So that was my chapter about falling in love. I don't have the words to express it, and saying that I love him more than I thought humanly possible doesn't even cover half of it. But that doesn't mean that that love comes without struggles. Relationships are hard work. I truly thought that if you were with "the one" it would just be a breeze. But life isn't a breeze. Life is fucking hard. Shit happens, and you're not always prepared for what's coming next. Just like friendships go through phases, relationships do too. We're ever-changing beings and with every decision and choice we make in life, we shape who we are as people and what partner we look for. We're all flawed; it's not about finding someone who you think is perfect. It's about finding out whose flaws you want to deal with. Who you want to fight with. Who you want to spend the shit times with. Who you want to go to therapy with. (Side note: Every couple should go to therapy. It's life changing. Shout-out to our therapist.) For me, that person is Mats. Hopefully it will be for a long time.

As I write this, we've been together for more than four years. Now, I won't lie: I've taken those rose-colored glasses off, and so has he. This is both the longest and most serious relationship either of us has been in. We *unofficially* moved in together less than a year in, and *officially* just a month after that mark. In hindsight I don't recommend moving in together that soon. Living with a partner is a lot. It escalates a "serious" relationship and gives it much higher stakes. It also makes it more serious—which might seem obvious, but I think I was surprised at how quickly it made us talk about the future and our plans. It makes some things way easier, like having someone to grocery shop with or someone to take out the trash. Someone to fall asleep next to and wake up beside. But it also makes some things harder: the trivial things like watching your show without the other, or realizing that your ideas of quality time differ completely. Sometimes you go to bed mad and you wake up mad. When you live with someone, you can't just leave them on read. You can't run away from your problems if you live with the person you're having problems with. It's hard. I won't say it's not. And maybe there was a part of me that didn't expect relationships to be hard. Maybe that was the tiny hopeless romantic hiding inside my jaded mind, telling me that when you love someone, everything is easy. But I think it's exactly the opposite. When you love someone, it makes it hard. (Yes, yes, yes, penis joke. We get it.) I don't necessarily mean that in a bad way. I think anything worth having won't come easy. I once asked a friend if she thought the couples in wedding videos were lying when they said their partner was "the best person they've ever known." I asked her if her boyfriend was the best guy *she* had ever known. She laughed and said, "Fuck no." We cracked up in the line at Old Navy, making up our own versions of more realistic vows. Things like "I'm so excited to marry this man who I find to be incredibly annoying only a few days a week" or "I couldn't be more in love with this man who does some super-stupid shit sometimes." If Mats told me I was the best woman he's ever known, I'd say something along the lines of "Well, you haven't met Michelle Obama." I knew to be cautious of the expectations fairy tales and movies put on "true love," but I forgot to look for those unrealistic stories in everyday people, in celebrity couples, #instagramgoals, or even in my own friends' relationships. It wasn't until that moment in Old Navy that it finally clicked. Nobody's relationship was easy, people were putting in work behind the scenes, but nobody wanted anyone to know it was anything less than perfect. So I'm here to set the record straight. Relationships are hard. There are amazing and fantastic things that come along with dating your best friend, but it doesn't come without hardship. I don't think it's about finding a relationship without any hurdles; I think it's about finding someone you want to tackle them with. The first time Mats and I went to our couples therapist, she asked us if we were married. We said no. She asked us if we were engaged. No. Did we have a kid? No. She looked at us and said, "Well, you two must really love each other." She said that she wished more people like us went to therapy—that the biggest act of love is throwing pride to the wind and admitting when you need help. We saw her on and off for three or four months, stopping every time things "got good"—a fucking rookie therapy mistake. We eventually started going weekly. There's something to be said about going to an unbiased third party to discuss your relationship when things are going *well*. That's when you're receptive, when you're not speaking or acting out of hurt. It's when you think that everything is all fine and good that you learn the most. I used to think if we needed a therapist, it meant that this wasn't "it"—that it was some sign that we weren't meant to be. And of course there are some incidents and relationships where that's the case. I'm not telling you to stay with something that's hurting you; I'm saying that some days we love with ease, and other days we love despite our better judgment. Don't trust anyone who says their relationship is perfect. What we project out into the world about our lives says much more about what we're struggling with than what we have. If you love someone, put the work in, and if they love you, they will too.

acknowledgments

The Oscars speech I always wanted to write!

First of all, thank you for reading this book. To everyone who supported my content and followed me over the years, you're the reason why this book is here. Thank you for letting me be me.

There was a time when I wasn't sure this book would happen. After spending the better part of a year butting heads with my old publisher, I did what everyone told me not to do: I gave my book advance back, took my manuscript and walked away. I was told that I would now be deemed "difficult to work with," and that the book I had poured so much of myself into would never see the light of day. A few weeks later we heard from Jeremie Ruby-Strauss at Gallery Books. They had read my manuscript, and they wanted to publish my book. Jeremie, I can't thank you enough—from our first phone call when you told me you saw yourself in my writing ("even though I'm a bald man"), to your patience with me while I took my time editing. Your whole team at Simon & Schuster not only made me feel seen, but heard. You never made me kill my darlings. You took my darlings and made them better. This book is truly an extension of me, and without you, Jeremie, and the whole team at Gallery Books/Simon & Schuster, this book wouldn't exist.

To my manager, Kendall Rhodes, thank you for believing in me when I don't believe in myself. You're at the receiving end of all my late-night text rants or blubbering meltdowns, and you have an answer for everything. Thank you for taking care of me.

Thank you to Frank Jung, Cait Hoyt, and the rest of my CAA team for your endless motivation and guidance. I'm not sure what you saw in that girl so many years ago, but I'm forever grateful.

To my attorney, Hannah Mulderink, thank you for being a constant reminder that women are the superior species. You're a fucking badass.

To my friends, thank you for loving me through the transition lenses. I couldn't have gotten through all this shit without you. Sydney and Jerri, you two will never understand how much you mean to me. Nobody in the world understands me like you two do, and I'm not sure how I got so lucky to have you both in my life. And to their parents, thank you for making sure that I always had a place to call home. Sierra, there's nobody else I'd rather have as a "sister." Well, maybe Oprah, but you're a close second. To Mats, thank you for loving me. Sometimes it's messy, but there's nobody I'd rather do life with.

To my parents, I'll send you my therapy bills. Kidding (sort of). But seriously, Dad, thanks for being my cheerleader. I hope this book doesn't make you hate me.

Finally, to my demons, both tangible and hiding in my brain. I am who I am today because of you. Despite your best efforts, I'm still here. Thank you for showing me how strong I really am. But don't take that the wrong way—I still hope you burn in hell.

> *"Suck on that."*
> —Janis Ian, *Mean Girls*